The
NIAGARA

BOOKS IN THE
RIVERS OF AMERICA SERIES

Rivers of America
Edited by Carl Carmer
As planned and started by
Constance Lindsay Skinner

Associate Editor Jean Crawford

Donald Braider

The

NIAGARA

Holt, Rinehart and Winston

New York   Chicago   San Francisco

Grateful acknowledgment is made to the Power Authority of the state
of New York for permission to use illustrations on pp. 48-49, 272, and
to the Buffalo and Erie County Historical Society for the frontispiece
and illustrations on pp. 7, 15, 35, 78, 120, 126, 134, 135, 136, 153, 155,
170, 175, 181, 182, 193, 197, 215, 218, 250

For Agnes and Louis Jones,
with much affection and gratitude

Contents

Introduction

The creation of the earth, it is generally agreed by geologists, generated tremendous heat. In the ages that followed this event occurred a very long epoch of cooling with a consequent condensation of atmospheric vapors. This condensation eventually produced millions of centuries of continuous ice formation. The self-perpetuating freeze resulted in a gradual accumulation of a glacier system that ultimately covered most of what are now the seas and territories of North America and Northern Eurasia. As this period of constant frost approached its term, layers of glacial ice attained an average thickness of ten thousand feet above what was then the level of the unfrozen equatorial seas.

During this era, so protracted that it is scarcely imaginable to man, a terrible stillness enveloped all the northern third of the earth, a silence broken only by the hollow wailing of even more terrible winds which whipped the superficial snows into mammoth drifts. The drifts thus formed were given relative permanence by the falls of subsequent snows, by subsequent winds and drifting.

Above the area of the Niagara's modest little flow today, where Lake Erie empties into Lake Ontario, these mountainous drifts stood as much as four thousand feet above the general level of the already massive and dense glacier. It must have been a scene to inspire awe—except, of course, that it was beyond awe; for there was no living creature on hand to be awed by it.

A comparatively brief period of equilibrium followed the termination of glacial aggrandizement; the temperature of the still-cooling earth was in approximate balance with that of the atmosphere. The long, seemingly inexorable advance of the ice southward in all directions from the North Pole was slowed, then completely arrested. The onset of a great and prolonged series of thaws was at hand.

The heat of the sun began to melt the southernmost edges of the immense, thick blanket of compressed ice that cloaked the top of the world. The vast cap of ice dissolved much more rapidly than it had formed. As it melted, and as huge blocks of the glacier broke away at the receding southerly fringes, the waters coursed with increasing volume and speed and frequency downward to the levels of the oceans. These ever-growing torrents tended to follow paths of least geophysical resistance as they gouged mercilessly at the more tender surfaces of the denuded earthscape. They were turned successfully aside only by formations of rock that refused to yield to the formidable pressures of water flows that were choked with mud and the extremely abrasive fragments of softer stone.

In this manner were created the mountain and valley chains of North America. So too were created the five freshwater seas that are the Great Lakes. So was dug the channel between Lake Erie and Lake Ontario which we call the Niagara River. The Niagara is thought to be a product of the fourth and final era of melting, the Wisconsin Thaw; it commenced forty or even fifty thousand years ago and has continued into our own century, though its rate has been steadily diminishing.

Although no book purporting to devote itself to the story of an inland waterway can fail to come to grips with the problems of ecology (or, in this instance, limnology), I don't propose to divert the reader into the even larger and more tortuously hypothetical questions that are now being raised about the possible effects of contemporary air and water pollution on the atmosphere of the present and future. Whether the ultimate result be a "hothouse" or a "new ice age," we may all with good reason accept the wisdom of the adage: "Whether the jug hit the stone or the stone hit the jug, it was bad for the jug." The air and water of the Niagara region today are in a very bad way, as we shall have occasion to note several times in these pages.

It was the final thaw, the Wisconsin, that carved out the major waterways of North America east of the Rockies—the Mississippi-Missouri valleys, the Ohio, the valleys of the Appalachian and Allegheny chains, and the lesser vales and dales that still drain off the receding polar ice from northern Canada and the Arctic into the hollowed-out basins of the five Great Lakes.

Geologically, the table levels of the four Upper Lakes do not differ very markedly from one another. The surface of Lake Superior is normally six hundred two feet above sea level. Its waters descend only twenty-two feet through the Strait of Sault Sainte Marie to the twin lakes of Huron and Michigan. The waters of these lakes, in their turn, have a fall of a mere eight feet through the Saint Clair River, past Detroit, to reach the level of Lake Erie. Thus, there is a total drop of only thirty feet from the highest of the Upper Lakes to the lowest, a feat the water manages over a distance of about a thousand miles. This makes for a comparatively gentle, almost imperceptible current.

The volume of water that moves so majestically downward in the direction of Lake Ontario and the Saint Lawrence is, for all its tranquility, very great indeed. Moreover, *all* of the Upper Lakes water, which covers an area of something like eighty-seven thousand square miles, follows this single course

toward Lake Ontario. However, at the eastern extremity of
Lake Erie, the calm is very abruptly terminated.

For the difference in level between Lakes Erie and Ontario
is about three hundred twenty-five feet, a descent that is accomplished as the water passes through the thirty-five-mile
stretch of the Niagara River. Even if this drop were achieved
at an absolutely equal angle of decline over the river's entire
distance, the rate of descent would be nearly ten feet per
mile—a fall that would make for an extremely rapid and
powerful flow. The eccentricities of the geological formations
here, through which as much as two hundred fifty thousand
cubic feet of water must pass in any given second, have decreed very dramatically otherwise.

Like a very long Russian novel, things begin slowly for the
Niagara, where the waters of Lake Erie gradually contract to
enter the channel. The rate of flow is very dignified—six or
seven miles per hour—until it reaches the first of several
splendid climaxes, the Upper Rapids. There the pace acceler-
ates briskly as the level makes a steeply graduated descent of
about sixty feet past the edges of Goat Island, a distance of
approximately one mile. Then, with unwonted brusqueness, the
waters arrive at the twin cataracts of Niagara's justly celebrated
falls.

Just how high the falls actually are remains a matter of
dispute—even in this age of scientific exactitude. It depends,
for one thing, on the volume of water passing over the two
precipices. This, in turn, depends on seasonal factors and on
the demands of the two electricity plants that divert a great
portion of the river's flow (from points above the falls) in the
interest, literally, of human enlightenment.

The height of the falls depends as well on the imagination
of the teller. The guides, who instruct the patrons of the two
vessels (both called *Maid of the Mist*) as they ply their
hazardous-seeming passage along the spumy and vaporous
fringes of the waterfalls, are inclined to exaggerate. Consciously
or not, they are following a noble tradition: Father Louis

Hennepin, as we shall observe, overestimated the heights of the cascades in both of his first written descriptions of them. The reader must, therefore, take any stipulated figure on faith.

According to the U.S. Army Corps of Engineers, the mean drop of the American (Rainbow) Falls is one hundred sixty-seven feet; that of the Canadian (Horseshoe) Falls is one hundred fifty-eight feet. By any measurement, the falls are vast, generating a stupendous amount of energy which is not greatly tamed while the course makes two subsequent descents—the first of about fifty feet as it passes through the Whirlpool Rapids, three and a half miles downstream from the falls, and the second of forty-seven feet down the Lower Rapids, about three miles beyond. At the Whirlpool Rapids, the water attains the rather spectacular velocity of twenty-seven miles per hour (some say thirty). Only after traversing the Lower Rapids, by which time it has nearly attained the level of Lake Ontario, does the Niagara resume its initial aspect of a proper and easily navigable stream.

A zeal for as much descriptive accuracy as possible compels one to remark that what we call the Niagara River isn't a river at all. It is rather a gorge or channel or strait that joins the Upper Lakes with Lake Ontario. It is endowed with several very modest tributaries which add but insignificantly to the already enormous volume of water it accommodates.

Perhaps, to carry this line of utterly scientific reasoning to its logical conclusion, one should add that the mighty Saint Lawrence, which carries all the water accumulated by all five of the Great Lakes to the Atlantic, isn't properly speaking a river either, but merely the last link in what should more suitably be termed the most important and longest, single, navigable, inland water system on the earth's surface.

But there is nothing mere about any of it—least of all about the Niagara. This waterway's brief course is, mile for mile, the most magnificent and most treacherous run of "white water" in the world. Although even today it fairly beggars the usually egregious superlatives lavished upon it, geologists are of the common opinion that some ten thousand years ago or so, the Niagara's twin cascades were probably a single waterfall and were certainly a great deal higher and more impressive than they are as we behold them now. They believe that at the time when the definitive pathway for the channel's flow was determined, the location of the falls may well have been at or near the Ontario end of the Lower Rapids, which would mean that they were about a hundred feet higher than they are today.

This theory is predicated on the rate at which the Canadian Falls have receded upstream since the time when they were first seen and recorded by French missionary explorers three centuries ago. This recession speed has been calculated at about five hundred feet per century, or roughly one mile per millennium.

Whether or not this estimate is approximately exact, certain it is that since 1678, when Father Louis Hennepin viewed the falls for the first time, the crust of Silurian dolomite that covers the river bottom on the Canadian side has been eroded away at precisely such a rate; certain too that the great Niagara gorge below the falls was created by the wearing away of the soft, flaky shale that underlies the harder material of dolomite that only thinly protects it.

This epic phenomenon of glacial geology—the rapids, the falls, and the gorge—has been a source of wonder, a cause of war and frequently the site of battles, an object of pillage and human rapacity. It has also been one of the earliest battlegrounds for the type of conservation movement that is at long last becoming a common, if belated, North American crusade. But the preservation of the river and falls from the total catastrophes of man's depredations has failed to prevent the Niagara from becoming, during the past century, the world's most spectacular open sewer.

For the story of the Niagara is linked inextricably with the stories of the Erie and Welland canals, the Saint Lawrence Seaway, the Great Lakes in general and Lake Erie in particular. It is the waters accruing to Lake Erie that the Niagara conveys so conscientiously toward the sea. And Lake Erie, as every reader *ought* by now to know, has become the Dead Sea of North America. One limnologist states categorically that it is no longer a lake at all, but instead a wide, sluggish, lifeless stream.

The Niagara's story consists, unfortunately, more often of accounts of greed than of gallantry, of bad temper than of goodwill, of betrayal than of honor, of cupidity than generosity, of stupidity than of foresight. It is, I mean, a tale of mankind's curious and frustrating race against himself—one which discloses him at his occasional best and far too frequent worst. The Niagara story embodies, too, many of the great and little lies that have for so long comprised the myth that we have chosen and have, until all too recently, accepted as "American history." For possession and management of the Niagara have contributed some important chapters to the generally appalling narrative of the European white man's rape of the Western Hemisphere. It shares with the Rio Grande the distinction of being one of our two most "political" rivers.

The
NIAGARA

LAKE SUPERIOR

Sault Ste. Marie

QUEBEC

LAKE NIPISSING

INTERNATIONAL
BOUNDARY
TO LAKE MICHIGAN

ONTARIO

GEORGIAN
BAY

LAKE HURON

LAKE SIMCOE

INTERNATIONAL BOUNDARY

Toronto

INTERNATIONAL
BOUNDARY

MICHIGAN

NIAGARA
RIVER

Hamilton

WELLAND CANAL

Niagara
Falls

LAKE
ST. CLAIR

Fort Erie   Buffalo

Detroit

NEW YORK

LAKE ERIE

Erie

Toledo

INTERNATIONAL
BOUNDARY

PENNSYLVANIA

Cleveland

ALLEGHENY R.

N

OHIO

Pittsburgh

0   Miles   100   map by palacios

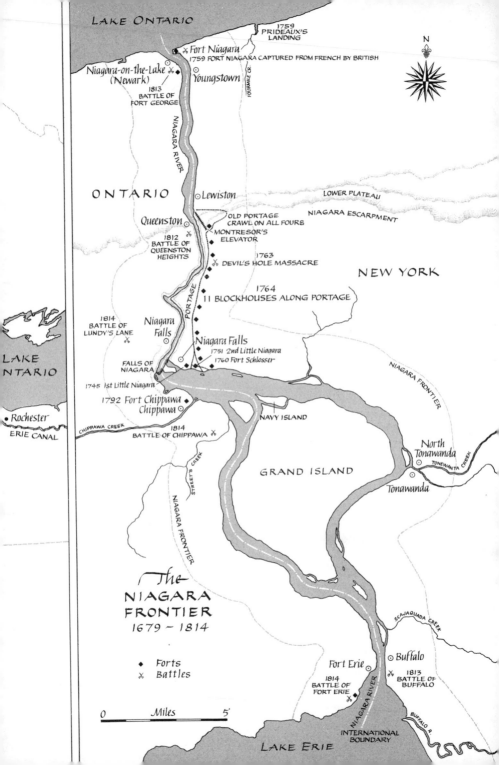

LAKE ONTARIO

1759 PRIDEAUX'S LANDING

N

Fort Niagara
1759 FORT NIAGARA CAPTURED FROM FRENCH BY BRITISH

Niagara-on-the-Lake (Newark)
Youngstown
1813 BATTLE OF FORT GEORGE

FOURMILE CR.

NIAGARA RIVER

ONTARIO

Lewiston
LOWER PLATEAU

Queenston
OLD PORTAGE CRAWL ON ALL FOURS
NIAGARA ESCARPMENT

1812 BATTLE OF QUEENSTON HEIGHTS

MONTRESOR'S ELEVATOR

1763 DEVIL'S HOLE MASSACRE

NEW YORK

1764
11 BLOCKHOUSES ALONG PORTAGE

PORTAGE

1814 BATTLE OF LUNDY'S LANE

Niagara Falls

Niagara Falls
1751 2nd Little Niagara
1760 Fort Schlosser

FALLS OF NIAGARA

LAKE ONTARIO

1745 1st Little Niagara

NIAGARA FRONTIER

Rochester

ERIE CANAL

1792 Fort Chippawa
Chippawa

NAVY ISLAND

CHIPPAWA CREEK

1814 BATTLE OF CHIPPAWA

STREET'S CREEK

NIAGARA FRONTIER

GRAND ISLAND

North Tonawanda
TONEWANTA CREEK

Tonawanda

The
NIAGARA
FRONTIER
1679 – 1814

SCAJAQUADA CREEK

◆ Forts
✕ Battles

Fort Erie
Buffalo

1814 BATTLE OF FORT ERIE

1813 BATTLE OF BUFFALO

BUFFALO R.

0   Miles   5

NIAGARA RIVER

INTERNATIONAL BOUNDARY

LAKE ERIE

1

This Is the NIAGARA Primeval

Had you been alive at approximately the period of Christ's brief stay on this planet, you would perhaps have been able to contemplate the Niagara and the countryside that flanks it in all its primordial splendor. In such a rarefied circumstance, you would doubtless have been a member of that mysterious red-man family called the Mound Builders, a tribe that is believed to have settled in the Niagara region at about this time —though archaeologists remain uncertain about the duration of the Mound Builders' occupation of the territory.

As one of these natives, you would very likely have subscribed to the belief that the falls had attributes a lot less prosaic than those which inspire the mild wonder evinced by visitors here in the twentieth century. For the cascades *must* have become a religious shrine for the pagan red man. We are told that the falls represented a deity of vast and terrible authority—a god, some think, of war, whose thundering voice issued imprecations that were softened only by the gigantic freeze which set in from late December and continued through the end of March in this heartland of the Great Lakes snow belt. Since the Mound Builders were mainly hunters and fishermen, they surely moved south with the game in the autumn, before the onset of the cruel winter. Thus they would not have known that this imperious god of Niagara could be silenced and intimidated by the frightful chill, even as were they themselves.

Let us attempt, by means of a conceit, to take ourselves back to those chartless years of North American protohistory. Let us make the conceit even more extravagant by imagining that we are equipped with an anachronistic helicopter (there are several that hover above the falls and the gorge during today's high tourist season). Better still, since we are already on the point of entering the realm of purest fantasy (over which, nonetheless, we retain absolute mastery), let us imagine that we have the use of a free but completely manageable balloon, a perfectly silent means of aerial transport. From its basketwork undercarriage we may view the prairies and woodlands and the waterway that lie between Lakes Erie and Ontario— the region which, with the advent of the white Europeans, came to be known as the Niagara Frontier, a territory comprehending the extremities of each immense lake and the thirty-odd-mile stretch of land that separates them.

The day we have chosen for our imaginary flight is a hot, dry, clear, sunny afternoon in July. What we take in at first panoramic glance from a high altitude is the general outline of the Frontier's terrain. The land that borders Lake Erie rises not much more than twenty-five feet above the water's surface. Only in the remotest northern distance, and only on so crystal a day as this one, can we detect a trace of significantly higher ground in any direction. This comparatively level plateau extends generally northward from the end of Lake Erie for about two-thirds of the Niagara River's short passageway.

Although it isn't easy to discern from the air in this primeval epoch when few trees have been felled, there is at roughly this line, twenty miles or so down the river's serpentine course, an exceptionally abrupt escarpment that runs at right angles to the river's general course of flow. This east-west bluff drops sharply, some three hundred feet, at the northerly edge of the plateau. Below it, spreading much farther in all directions than the naked eye can perceive on the clearest afternoon, is the Ontario basin and the flatlands surrounding it.

This escarpment denotes the northern end of the deep Niagara gorge. Long before the afternoon of our languorous aerial journey, the great falls probably cascaded just here, where the line of the bluff separates the basins of the Upper Lakes from that of Lake Ontario. As we contemplate the falls in this early Christian year, they are situated about two miles downriver from the site they will occupy in the twentieth century. They tumble much nearer the head of the Whirlpool Rapids.

From the air, the impression created by the cataract does not invite very great astonishment; for it is at eye level or below that the cataract has the capacity to seem overwhelming. What we remark from our present altitude is a great cloud of vapor that punctuates the Niagara's winding passage. On a day so still as this one, the mist rises more than two hundred feet above the crest of the churning waters—hence, more than three hundred and fifty feet from the pool into which they crash with thunderous force. If we can direct our craft to hover just downstream from the base of the falls, we shall for a certainty discern the rainbow refraction of the sun's light against the molecules of vapor that are hurled incessantly skyward from the reckless turbulence of the pool. This prismatic effect, like the falls' great sound, was undoubtedly worshiped— thought to be endowed with some kind of supernatural powers during pagan times. It would be pleasant, but absolutely speculative, to imagine the rainbow a sign of hope.

Although we may best view the falls from ground level, our lofty exploration of the rest of the river's tortuous run is instructive. It is difficult to state at precisely what point Lake Erie ends and the Niagara River begins. Topographers and geographers are not in total accord (in the same way that they are unable to agree about the height of the falls); hence one reason for the difference in length ascribed to the stream by various authorities. Most select as the starting point the site now occupied by the Peace Bridge that connects Buffalo, New York, with Fort Erie, Ontario. There the river is a bit more than six hundred yards wide. As it proceeds downward, the course widens rapidly after it passes the first of numerous islands and islets that brave the flood of the Upper Niagara. This one, Squaw Island, hugs the east bank, protecting the mouth of Scajaquada Creek, and is barely separated from the mainland by a pair of narrow, sluggish channels.

A mile and a half farther downstream is another significant island, Strawberry Island. It stands approximately in the center of the river which, by this point, has broadened to a width of somewhat more than a mile. A little beyond, the Niagara divides into two streams (averaging some four thousand feet in width) that embrace Grand Island in their casual meanders. Grand Island, by far the largest of the river, has a form that rather resembles that of a distorted pear. Its length and breadth at the greatest are about seven miles. Like much of the surrounding landscape in this first Christian century, Grand Island is entirely forested—mainly with bass and white oak and conifers of various kinds and a generous but lesser mixture of birch and ash and locust.

Though both of the channels that flank Grand Island are navigable, the earliest boatmen (and the majority of their more knowledgeable successors) utilized the left one because it is shorter than its alternative by three miles. More important than the matter of distance—indeed, crucial—it affords a natural impediment to a most perilous further descent at the island's northern extremity, a venture that would lead any vessel either toward a collision with Goat Island or, even worse, an ineluctable journey down the rock-strewn Upper Rapids and a decidedly undesirable descent over the falls. This natural impediment is Navy Island, the second largest of the Niagara. It stands directly opposite the mouth of Ussher's Creek, one of the many minor waterways that empty into the mainstream from the Canadian side. The most important of these tributaries is Chippawa Creek (also called the Welland River), a stream whose spelling is officially thus in Canada—though often *Chip-*

pewa to Americans, and sometimes even *Chippeway* to writers who are, in any event, transliterating. Just below Navy Island the two Niagara channels reconverge.

The fifteen-mile eastern course of the river around Grand Island is nourished by several tributaries, of which two merit attention. The first is Tonawanda Creek, about seven miles downriver from the head of the island. The other is Cayuga Creek, six miles farther along. Like Scajaquada Creek, the mouths of these two brooks are sheltered from the river's powerful current by islands. In the earliest days of the white man's permanent establishment on the Niagara, the banks of Cayuga Creek would serve as the construction site for the first sailing vessel to travel over the waters of the Upper Lakes—and of many ships thereafter.

Immediately below Navy Island the Niagara attains its greatest breadth—almost two miles. From this point of confluence of the two streams, where the river makes a sharp turn to the west-northwest, its pace begins to quicken as the banks draw nearer to each other and as the bottom slopes downward at a much steeper rate over the next three miles until it reaches the head of the Upper Rapids. Here the river is sundered for a second time, by the tenacious upcropping of Goat Island. This is a low, flat, oblong obstruction whose sturdy flanks have successfully resisted the terrible and relentless pressures of the twin rapids that drop as much as sixty feet in less than a mile. In our own day it is at the lower end of Goat Island that the two raging streams come upon the greatly receded upper rim of the Niagara escarpment and make their spectacular fall into the gorge.

In the early years of the Christian era, Goat Island extended about two miles upstream from the falls—a fact we shall overlook, having already thrown hopelessly out of joint all strict notions of time. In our own century the two great cascades make their terrible leaps into the vaporous cauldron just at the lower end of Goat Island. The semicircular falls of the west branch, which one of the first white men will inevitably compare to a horseshoe, covers an edge about twenty-five-hundred

feet long. The line of the falls on the east side is only about a
thousand feet, though its drop is about nine feet higher than
that of its more dramatic counterpart. This curiosity is due to
the steeper decline of the river's bottom at the Upper Rapids
on the Canadian branch. Goat Island is not alone in its stolid
resistance to the assaults of the rapids. On each of its flanks
there are several islets that try to interrupt the water's turbulent
passage toward the two precipices.

A hundred yards beyond the vapor-obscured pool at the base
of the falls, the course of the river makes another major adjust-
ment, to the north-northeast. Its flow seems to have abruptly
slackened, as if the waters have been stunned into tranquility
by the stupendous magnitude of their recent plunge. What has
occurred is that the bottom of the still-narrow Niagara's pathway, now walled in by sheer cliffs whose striations have much
to tell geologists, has leveled off. The gorge attains heights of
more than two hundred feet above the water's gently revolving surface. It continues to flow down the next three miles and
a bit, bending gracefully to the north-northwest to arrive at
the upper end of the Whirlpool Rapids.

Over the ensuing half mile, the water level drops fifty feet,
terminating in an elbow of spinning currents that give the
rapids its name. The treacherous and often inescapable revolutions of the Niagara at this section are occasioned by the haste
of the river's downward flow (many connoisseurs of "white
water" think the Whirlpool Rapids the most stirring of the
river's many marvels), the narrowness of the gorge, and the
ninety-degree turn of the channel's bed. It now follows a bearing once again of north-northeast, a direction it retains for
three further miles before veering due north in its approach
to the Lower Rapids—the ultimate declivity. In one-third of
a mile, the water tumbles and stumbles forty-seven feet to
reach, at the rapids' end, almost the level of Lake Ontario.
There it begins to right itself.

About two miles below the Lower Rapids the walls of the
Niagara gorge suddenly vanish. The river, which has been

The Niagara Primeval

knifing its way through the dolomite and shale of the Lake Erie plateau for thousands of years, has at last crossed the boundary of the Niàgara escarpment. At this point, where the escarpment disappears, the falls in all likelihood had their birth. From here the banks sprawl outward generously to an average width of half a mile for the remainder of the river's journey north to its mouth at Lake Ontario. Its speed is even slower than it was at the headwaters; for in the final seven miles of its course, the level drops merely one foot. Consequently, at neither end does this river afford the innocent voyager the slightest inkling of the dreadful hazards it has in store for him.

So concludes the use of our conceit of a free balloon flight over the Niagara Frontier in the period before it was molested by that most terrible of all natural predators, western European man.

2
The
Long
Red
Twilight

The canoe and the paddle gave the red man access to the sumptuous immensity of the Great Lakes wilderness and, in particular, to the jugular artery of that wilderness, the Niagara spillway. Archaeologists conjecture that this momentous pair of inventions occurred before 2000 B.C.; for by that time the canoe (at first, adzed out of the trunks of trees) was in fairly general use. Craft of bark and frame were of substantially later confection.

The "Indians" of North America were probably all descended from the intrepid hunters of seal and moose and bear, the fishers of salmon and sturgeon, who had migrated across the Bering Isthmus from Siberia in one of the earliest eras of human prehistory. The various tribes evolved and contrived to maintain their individual cultural and economic integrity in very much the same fashion followed by aboriginal peoples elsewhere on the globe. (The black tribes of New Guinea, so movingly described by Peter Matthiessen in *Under the Mountain Wall*, managed to accomplish total isolation and, thus, total integrity until 1938.)

To a critical degree, customs, costumes, utensils, weapons, diets, and creed were shaped and tempered by the climate, the terrain, and the natural abundance of the lands to which each community of red men laid claim—and which it guarded zealously and jealously; the territorial imperative was a primordial absolute for man as well as beast.

Within the generous confines of the huge tracts they occupied and declared to be theirs alone to exploit, the tribes were at first regularly migratory, followers of the fish and game that (in addition to the tree, the reed, the wild fruit and vegetables, and the conveniently configured stone) provided them with the essentials of survival. Once isolated from each other on territories whose every boundary sachems and braves knew with a certainty that would be envied by the most skillful modern surveyor, tribes for centuries saw nothing and heard nothing of their fellow inheritors of the commodious North American continent. Overland transport was impracticable where substantial distances were involved, for there were no pack animals. The horse and the ox were unknown in the Western Hemisphere—though fossilized traces of a remotely ancient ancestor of the horse have been unearthed in western North America. It appears that at some point in the Pleistocene Age, possibly around 10,000 B.C., in the middle of the Wisconsin Thaw, his genus vanished from the region, not to be seen again in what would be called the "New World" until the early sixteenth century, when *equus caballus,* the modern horse, was brought along with cattle and swine and domestic fowl by the first of the Spanish adventurers and plunderers.

With no strong, easily domesticable beasts to assist him, the red man's early exploration and exploitation of the soil were limited and mainly desultory, devoted primarily to a most casual harvesting of the wild-growing comestibles. There are but few meaningful exceptions to this generalization. He did, however, learn to fabricate pemmican, "travel food," a delicacy whose recipe varied somewhat from tribe to tribe, but whose method of preparation appears common to all. It was a concentrate of bison or venison or bear meat, which was air-dried and then pulverized. The powdered viands were flavored to personal taste with wild herbs and berries, then ultimately blended with an equal measure of rendered fat. When compressed into balls or cubes or tablets and stowed in oily rawhide pouches, pemmican would keep almost indefinitely. It provided a remarkably well-balanced regimen—as the hardy French missionaries, the *voyageurs,* and the *coureurs de bois* were to discover; for pemmican comprised the bulk of their diet during a century and a half of travel in the North American wilds. To the contemporary gourmet, pemmican may seem an acquired taste—like the fruit bar in World War II K ration kits, which had its inspiration in pemmican.

For many centuries prior to the advent of the European in North America, the canoe was deployed by the red man with a marked degree of trepidation. Rare indeed was the distant sortie, and that undertaken only in cases of grave emergency— famine or epidemic which would drive an entire village from its setting. So that although individual tribes, and particularly those that inhabited the Great Lakes country, were but loosely rooted in their soil (in the sense that they failed to become conscientious, systematic agrarians), they were very securely restricted to their own lands. They neither cared nor dared to venture very far from the native patch or village.

However, what was *generally* true was not *wholly* true. Trade did begin in the Great Lakes area many centuries before the earliest of the European incursions into North America. How and when it began doesn't figure in the transcribed chronicles of red-man history that were taken down by missionaries (and a few interested white laymen) of the seventeenth and eighteenth centuries. Perhaps, hunting or fishing parties of two tribes came upon each other one day on the frontiers of their respective territories. To demonstrate that neither group meant harm to the other, they exchanged gifts (a ritual that characterized all subsequent intertribal encounters that were not of a warlike nature).

Certainly, these tokens would have been objects that had

caught the fancy of the potential recipient—things the hunter or fisherman had never seen before or materials of which his own tribe suffered a deficiency. It is very likely that in some such offhand way a trickle of commerce began. Evidence has been found, on both banks of the Niagara, of copper tools from Wyoming, war clubs studded with the fangs of bears that were indigenous only to some far northwestern regions, and shell ornaments and wampum belts contrived of materials from the shores of the Gulf of Mexico—objects all believed to antedate the year A.D. 1000.

The Niagara spillway, then, was probably a trading center at least six centuries before the appearance there of the first Europeans. The finds unearthed in the region are persuasive in themselves. The geography of the Great Lakes area is reason for further conviction. The Niagara's particular situation is unique. For anyone wishing to travel over water (and that was the *only* way to travel if one intended to carry quantities of trade goods across a continent that was endowed with no pack animals), there were two paths of eastward egress from the Upper Lakes to the Saint Lawrence and Hudson valleys— the Niagara and the Georgian Bay-Ottawa River routes. The latter, long employed by the Hurons and their French allies, was by far the longer and more hazardous; moreover, it involved many more portages than did the Niagara. Consequently, the dangers and climatic difficulties quite aside, it could remain economical only as long as profit in pelts was sufficiently exorbitant to offset the higher cost in time and labor.

The first Niagara portage was situated along the east bank of the river. It began at a point just above the Upper Rapids and terminated at the site, approximately, of modern Lewiston, New York, downriver from the Lower Rapids. It comprehended about nine miles in overland length—not an excessive distance when compared with the several portages of the alternative route. It had, however, the dubious distinction of being the most difficult single portage of North America. For all goods to be transshipped at Niagara had to be carried up and down

the sheer three-hundred-foot escarpment, ascents and descents
so precipitous that cargo bearers could manage them only by
creeping on hands and feet. Thus did this appalling section
of the portage acquire, from the earliest red men who made
use of it, the name of "Crawl on All Fours."

Who controlled the Niagara, therefore, controlled the great
majority of commerce between the immense areas of the Upper
Lakes and those of the eastern seaboard. Who did, in fact,
control it first? Historians remain uncertain. Archaeologists
have concluded, from detailed studies of the earliest remains
yet discovered (dug up near Lewiston) and from Carbon-17
analyses of cremated human relics found nearby, that the
Mound Builders, who probably came to Niagara from the Ohio
valley, were established here no later than the second Christian
century. Whether or not they were the first settlers of the spillway territory is still problematical.

Since the Mound Builders, as a distinct tribal entity, vanished
both from the northeast and midwest long before the arrival
of the Europeans, and since there is no surviving evidence of
their remarkable seventh-century pyramidal burial mounds in
the vicinity of the Niagara, it seems reasonable to presume
that they were driven off by more powerful warriors sometime
before the middle of the first Christian millennium. The in-
vaders who thus took possession of the Niagara region were in
all probability the direct ancestors of the tribes which, in the
epoch of the white man, would come to be known alternatively
as the Confederacy of the Five Nations (as the British and
Dutch referred to them) or the Iroquois (the French name)—
the Cayugas, Mohawks, Oneidas, Onondagas, and Senecas.

The flanks of the Niagara River represented a property of
great intrinsic value—its strategic position apart. In both the
Erie and Ontario flatlands important villages grew up. These
consisted of bark-and-pole cabins, longhouses of palisaded
construction, with each agglomeration surrounded by deeply
implanted, palisaded walls. These were meant to thwart, or at
least to deter, invasion. But no materials employed by the red

man were proof against the torch. Fire was the most fearful weapon of devastation available to the aboriginal Americans; they used it on occasion with terrible effect, but it remained for the white man to instruct them in the more efficient application of fire.

Just beyond the walls of each red-man hamlet on either side of the Niagara and on the banks of the nearby lakes lay paradise, Eden—almost everything required for the good life. In the hunting seasons of spring and autumn, game abounded. The air and the virgin trees were alive with birds throughout all the warmer months. The grasslands and bushes and creek-sides teemed with wildfowl of most descriptions—none more remarkable than the awkward turkey, whose feathers were both useful and ornamental, whose eggs and flesh provided nourishment.

Primitive man did little to disrupt the ecological balance. He seemed imbued with an intuitive understanding, stemming perhaps from his early appreciation of the natural significance of the circle of the seasons. He grasped, one may rationally suppose, that there was a more important cycle of life and death in nature as a whole that he might tamper with at his peril. For juxtaposed with Eden was Inferno—fires due to natural causes, as lightning struck in drought-stricken forests. When the cycle was disrupted by whatever cause, the red man perceived that he would suffer as a result. In his hunting, he was rarely guilty of overkill; until the coming of the Europeans, North America saw no species made extinct by man's hand.

As with the terrestrial and aerial game, so with that of the lakes and streams. Salmon and sturgeon traveled in the late winter up the ice-free reaches of the lower Saint Lawrence, hurled themselves up the important rapids above the present site of Montreal, and entered Lake Ontario as soon as the spring thaw set in. Some of them swam as far as the mouth of the Niagara to discharge their burdens of eggs and then to die. A pair of skilled red fishermen could, in the early spring, fill a canoe to its wales with salmon and sturgeon in less than half

an hour, making use of an implement no more subtle than a
club. Occasionally, a third hand was required to aid with the
catch, for sometimes the sturgeon were as large as sharks. The
lakes were inhabited the year around with pike, pickerel, and
the legendary muskelunge—not to overlook the eel and trout
and bass, nor the freshwater crustaceans and bivalves.

Gradually settling himself more permanently on his land,
the red man learned by trial and error to cultivate the arable
clearings beyond the village walls. Here he made room for
orchards, berry patches, and vineyards. He dug crude plots
for maize, squash, pumpkin, beans, and herbs. The various
herbs served medicinal and ritualistic purposes as well as being
used for seasoning and preserving foodstuffs, for curing hides,
and for providing the bases for artful color to embellish dress
and utensils. Pigments were derived from earthy substances
too.

Once the aboriginal red man had assured himself and his
tribe of the absolute essentials for survival, he began to
brighten his life with decoration—as did his brothers in every
other corner of the earth. Earliest pre-Columbian art, like that
of almost every primitive culture, seems to have been associated with apprehension about the three aspects of existence
that man was unable to master—the elements, pestilence, and
death.

The settlers of the Niagara territory apparently created for
themselves two principal deities—the Holder of the Sky and
the Great Voice. We can scarcely doubt that while other red
men regarded thunder as the Voice, the inhabitants of the Niagara region looked to the falls as the personification of that god.
It is saddening to have to puncture popular faith in one extremely colorful legend—that of the Indian maidens who were
sent over the falls after the first full moon each spring, their
deaths a sacrifice to the Great Voice (who represented fear
and war and natural disasters) that he might spare their fellow
tribesmen any great catastrophes during the year to follow.

The escarpment and mouth
of the Niagara

Persistent though it be, this tale is a canard—the invention, it must be regretfully asserted, of tourist-orientated guides of the last century at Niagara. It simply does not figure in any reliable surviving documentation of Iroquois practices. Not even in the records of the zealous and scrupulously careful Jesuit missionaries of the sixteenth century is there a single reference to this or any similar ritual.

This is not to suggest, however, that the Great Voice was thought any less baleful for this particular want of propitiation.

To counterbalance this dark spirit, the red men of Niagara conceived the Sky Holder to be the source of all wisdom. He must be consulted, as was the Delphic Oracle by the Greeks, before any major tribal decision was arrived at—a declaration of war, the possible conclusion of a treaty of peace, or removal of a community to a new location. The village medicine man (who served as high priest and entertainer when he wasn't ministering to the sick with effective herbs and symbolic—but ineffective—dances) was the sole interpreter of the Sky Holder's answers to prayer.

Village and tribal political administration demonstrated an ingenious accommodation to the harsh realities of wilderness civilization. The chiefs of each community were men, the sachems—warrior-hunters who had managed to survive the rigorous life of pursuing game, combating the attempts at encroachment by braves from rival tribes, and, the most terrible hazards of all, exposure (in inadequate dress or with inadequate gear) to the violent forces of nature. We cannot be sure of the average life expectancy of the protohistoric brave, but it was probably not much more than thirty years.

Women, on the other hand, although they suffered a truly staggering mortality rate during the childbearing period of their lives, tended to live longer (if they lived at all) than men because they were only rarely subjected to the dangers of life beyond the village limits. Consequently, it was the older women of each community who selected the sachems.

Until the white man discovered a simple method of rigging these elections and of corrupting those who were elected—by intoxicating the electors and/or the sachems—these societies functioned reasonably well, certainly as well as any other social unit and better than most in the "civilized" lands of western Europe. Earliest fair-minded reports by white visitors to the New World suggest that village and tribal life were orderly, moral, and basically (though not entirely) monogamous. There was a system of justice that protected rudimentary human as well as property rights.

One of the most ironically curious criticisms made about aboriginal American customs by the first Europeans to travel here is the complaint that the red men dealt much too harshly with captured enemies, subjecting them to torture and burning at the stake. The long journey across the North Atlantic had evidently caused the voyagers to forget the instruments of torture invented and put to very frequent use in their native lands. That torture in Europe usually served the interests of Christendom (Catholic or Protestant) or individual states in no way alters the essential fact: it was at least as sadistic as any practice evolved by the natives of North America.

So far as I have been able to determine, there was only one local custom that was not better achieved (in terms of exquisite brutality) by the Spanish Torquemada in the fifteenth century and refined in the sixteenth by Pieter Titelman of the Netherlands. This exception was cannibalism, which had by then lost its vogue in Europe. It was, we learn, a taste of certain Mohawks—but one that was considered a distinct social aberration and frowned on by the sachems. The braves who indulged this outlandish practice found every human member delicious except the fingers, which were "stringy." The warriors who partook of human flesh believed that it enhanced the likelihood of a happy life in the Great Beyond. It was a kind of aboriginal soul food.

The Five Nations occupied the area that lies between the eastern end of Lake Erie and the confluence of the Mohawk and Hudson rivers. The territory included the Chautauqua basin, the valley of the Genesee River, the entire Finger Lakes region, and what is today called the Southern Tier—which incorporates the headwaters and upper reaches of Schoharie Creek and the Susquehanna River, and comprehends a portion of Pennsylvania.

The westernmost of these nations was that of the Senecas; then, moving eastward, came the lands of the Cayugas, the Onondagas, the Oneidas, and finally those of the Mohawks. The five tribes got along with one another not one bit better than they absolutely had to. Each coveted some portion of a neighbor's terrain. Each made occasional raids of plunder on another's villages, especially at the time of the harvest. And it was not uncommon for a young brave to carry off a pretty squaw as a part of his private booty. These sporadic and usually impetuous adventures were not regarded by any of the Five Nations as cause enough to conclude anything more rigid than a casually observed agreement to do nothing to one another that was really serious—though they might have been hard put to define such an understanding more precisely, because they had never had any reason to do that.

The genuinely savage raids that were the work of Five Nations tribes were, strictly speaking, beyond the purview of the loose confederation. For the Mohawks, these consisted of sorties which frequently devastated the villages of the Mohicans in the upper Hudson valley. Since the Mohicans were not parties to the confederation, the Mohawk raids were of no significance. The same applied to the activities of the Senecas at Niagara, who had now and then to offer exemplary reprisal for attacks from western tribes, Hurons, Lakes, and Ottawas, which were designed to wrest from them control of the precious portage and the flat, fertile, game-strewn lands on either side of the river.

The Five Nations knew from long experience that they could live beside each other in comparative tranquility, even if, occasionally, some of their members behaved like a pack of unruly urchins. Why go to the trouble of holding an assembly of the Grand Council on the hill of the central tribe, the Onondagas, which could accomplish little or nothing by way of preventing a few annoying but quite impulsive and not very important sibling rivalries and petty skirmishes? In other words, the sachems deemed it useless to enact legislation that they were in no position to enforce; it would serve no purpose but to inspire disrespect for empty authority.

What was of immense significance, however, was that the machinery for collective action in the interest of mutual security did exist long before the arrival of the Europeans. The very fact that the Five Nations had achieved a surprisingly effective and durable *modus vivendi* was evidence of the degree to which they were truly civilized in the centuries before Holy Mother Europe sent her first emissaries.

3

Excursions
and
Alarms

There is no record that tells us precisely when a sachem of the Five Nations first learned of the white man's earliest steps on the continent of North America—nor is it to be discovered *whose* steps were initially reported to him. Of the Spanish invasion of Mexico we may be comparatively sure the red men of the American northeast knew nothing for a very long time.

Since 1500, however, fishing fleets from western Europe's most active maritime countries had found the schools of cod and halibut that favored the Grand Banks. These hardy mariners often beached their fragile little craft on the shores of the prodigiously tidal Bay of Fundy or on the banks of the lower Saint Lawrence to make repairs, to dry and salt their catches, and to take on fresh water.

Huron or Algonquin braves would certainly have studied these odd personages, remarked on their strange vessels that were propelled by the winds, their extraordinary attire, their beards and hairstyles—and perhaps above all, the color of their skin. They could scarcely have failed to pass on the factual but incredible intelligence to their own sachems who, in their turn, would have informed the intertribal traders. These individuals, by the onset of the sixteenth century, constituted a vital element of native American life. The traders were particularly astute and intrepid and trustworthy braves who met to exchange goods and information (most of it doubtless irresponsible gossip) with their counterparts from adjoining peoples. Thus was created an informally organized but essential network for the transmission of great and little bits of news—accurate, false, or half-true.

The alien fisherman first observed near the mouth of the Saint Lawrence seemed to represent no great threat to the American red men. They never traveled great distances inland. But the sachems and braves and wisewomen of the Five Nations may well have inquired of the Sky Holder what lay ahead for them. If that deity was at all attuned to the events that were soon to follow, his augury could only have been a dark and dusty one. Indeed, it must be observed that the European colonization of the Americas that impended was the greatest single, comprehensive act of human depredation ever undertaken. The white conquest of Africa and India cannot be placed in the same category of horror, for in both regions the Europeans constituted a minority of the population and in all but a few instances were compelled to relinquish their control. In the Americas, because their natives were relatively unorganized and without adequate means of transport and communications, there was no impediment to easy and permanent domination. By the time the red men had access to most or all of the white man's war-making facilities, their ranks had been so terribly diminished and their territories so shamelessly narrowed that effective resistance was sporadic and ultimately futile.

In 1513, the Seminoles reported north that Ponce de León had come ashore on the east coast of Florida at the head of a most improbable-looking band of scoundrels. The men wore iron suits. They carried long knives and tubes that exploded with a terrifying roar, hurling missiles which could maim or kill from a distance of a hundred feet or more. These bizarre creatures were borne about over the land on the backs of beasts that were larger and swifter than any ever seen in eastern North America, taller and much more agile than the undomesticable elk or moose or bison.

Such a stirring tale must have gained a good deal of colorful detail and embellishment in the retelling as it was passed up the Atlantic coast. What the sachems of the Five Nations made of it we cannot say. Nine years later, the Seminoles had an ever sorrier account to relate—the arrival on the coast of Florida of a second force of Spaniards. The leader of this expedition made it obvious to the "enemy heathen" that his purpose was not merely one of conquest but of colonization. To make matters more conclusive, he had the power of the horse and the gun to give vigorous effect to his plan. The torpid, amiable Seminoles were in no position to offer serious resistance; it was, moreover, not in their nature to be warlike. They bowed as gracefully as might be in the face of the inevitable, but their meekness disinherited them of the earth they had so long and so peacefully possessed.

How much these descriptions of the Spanish invasion of Florida were altered as they were translated from dialect to dialect on their way up the eastern seaboard, we may only imagine. It is clear that all red men who listened and paid attention to the tales came to more or less the same conclusion: the Spaniards were imbued with a magic not yet accorded by the gods to the natives of North America. They were sure that a very dangerous but supernatural force had been let loose in the land of the Seminoles. The sachems of the Five Nations soon came to the decision that something drastic must be done to prevent this irresponsible phenomenon from reaching their collective domain.

Though there was as yet no indication that a similar assault could soon be anticipated against more northerly coastlines, the Grand Council of the Five Nations must have sensed that the Spanish occupation of Florida was the terrible and frightening first act of a great but squalid tragic drama. But of how long that tragedy would take to play itself out, and that its end would be the confinement of the American red men to penitential "reservations" where they would eventually be objects of obloquy, contumely, curiosity, condescension, contempt, and total human degradation—of *that* they probably never dreamed even in their most horrendous nightmares.

Jacques Cartier's first exploration of the upper Saint Lawrence in 1534, as soon as word of it reached the south shore of Lake Ontario and the Niagara spillway, gave the sachems of the Five Nations an extremely nasty turn. The Frenchman's single, very peculiar craft didn't remain at anchor long enough to occasion more than a fleeting tremor of anxiety among the natives. Parties from his vessel went ashore that summer, armed with unwieldy arquebuses, but they appeared mainly interested in what lay beyond the upriver passages of the Saint Lawrence, not in the vast tracts of virgin timberland that flanked its long and tortuous course.

The next year, however, Cartier returned in the early spring. His commission was the same as the one that had brought him here the previous summer—to find in the name of France a northwest passage to the Far East. His voyage by ship took him to the hill that would be called Montreal. There he moored his little fleet, for native scouts had warned him of a hazardous set of rapids that tumbled just a few miles upstream. Cartier led a small patrol to the point where the Saint Lawrence made its swift and turbulent descent. Huron braves, more intrigued by these European adventurers than frightened by them, agreed to accept their offers of utensils and cloth and brandy. In exchange, they led this party above the portage and sufficiently far up the river to permit Cartier to draw the conclusion which conformed exactly with his dream—that the lake which he beheld, Ontario, was in fact the

Pacific Ocean. He was sure he could accurately report to his
king that he had discovered the long-suspected passage to
China. Consequently, as he traversed the rapids above Montreal on his return journey, he gave them the name of "La
Chine."

Although Jacques Cartier remained true to his promise that
he had come in peace, as an explorer, neither as a despoiler
nor as a conqueror, he was of course speaking only for himself and his own mission. The experience of the Seminoles in
Florida, more than two decades earlier, hardly set an en-
couraging precedent so far as the North American red man
was concerned—nor should it have. The appearance of Cartier's
ships, of their crews and their armaments, was not intended
to foster confidence in the reliability of his sworn word—nor
did it.

His voyages up the Saint Lawrence were followed shortly
by the arrival in the American northeast of exceptionally
gaudy accounts of simultaneous invasions by the Spaniards
de Soto and Coronado. These assaults, which began in 1539,
plundered and sacked the entire southeastern quarter of North
America, from Florida all the way to modern Kansas, during
the ensuing four years. The *conquistadores* gave the red men of
those immense but geographically indefensible areas a very
fearful example of the way that "civilized" Europeans fought
their wars and dealt with captives, whether the latter offered
resistance or not.

After 1550, the sachems of the Five Nations at last began to
appreciate the scope of the impending white menace, and
they decided on countermeasures. A Grand Council, representing all the villages of all five of the nations, congregated on
the Hill of the Onondagas to devise a strategy of mutual defense. Decisions were arrived at by a process that seems at
least as expressive of popular sentiment as that employed for
the selection of candidates for the presidency of the United
States. Each delegation cast a single vote after polling its
sachem constituents. The structure and functions of the Five

Nations Confederacy were to receive the unstinting praise of Benjamin Franklin two centuries later. He believed that these red men were more wisely and less selfishly ruled than were the American colonists of his era.

The decisions reached by this convention of the Grand Council were demonstrated to be ineffectual as soon as one tribe of the Five Nations came into direct and violent contact with the European invader. This occurred at the end of July 1609, when a party of Mohawks (engaged in their favorite summer pastime of raiding in the upper Hudson territories of the Mohicans and Hurons) came suddenly upon a group whose composition alone must have startled them. It would soon cause them the most painful dismay. For they found Europeans and Hurons in plainly happy association with each other, hunting in the country of the Mohicans and pillaging their settlements. The palefaces carried arquebuses whose alarming fire instantly killed a couple of Mohawks and seriously wounded several others.

This historic skirmish (which many historians are pleased to call a "battle," in the same way that street fights become "massacres" in the retelling) took place near Crown Point on the lake that would thereafter bear the name of the French adventurer who led the victorious party, Samuel de Champlain. The Mohawk's braves who survived this initial encounter immediately related their traumatic experience to the sachem of their village. He, after consultation with the chiefs of other Mohawk communities, agreed that something had to be done—but what, the sachems in their collective innocence and ignorance were unable to say. All they could immediately perceive was that the white man was very dangerous and that he had reached some kind of accord with the Hurons—the great nation that controlled the valley of the Saint Lawrence and much of the northern shores of Lakes Ontario and Erie. That was, in a sense, the most ominous aspect of the situation, for it suggested plainly that the natives of the continent had already been divided by the invading whites.

The leaders of the Five Nations soon discovered that the French were not the only Europeans who were beginning to demonstrate an interest in the riches of a region over which the red man had for so many centuries maintained an easy control. Five years after the Mohawk braves met Samuel de Champlain on the lake that was to bear his name, the Protestant Dutch were so securely affiliated with the Mohicans and Shinnecocks of the Hudson and Long Island that they considered it safe and almost certainly profitable to open a trading post on the present site of Albany. Soon afterward, a second Dutch community was established at Schenectady by Arent van Corlaer. This character's gentle dealings, initially with the Mohawks and eventually with all the tribes of the Five Nations, caused his name to enter the red man's language; "Corlaer" meant "Governor" for the next two centuries—and though the title became sullied by degrees as his successors abused the position, its origins were honorable, given the unfortunate context of conquest and colonization in which they were set.

Just beginning to understand what it was that the Dutch and the French were seeking in the New World, the sachems came to the conclusion that they must emulate the Hurons and come to some sort of agreement with one party or the other. They elected to side with the Dutch, principally because of the good impression van Corlaer had made on them as so vividly contrasted with the single unhappy memory they retained of their only meeting with Champlain. The Dutch were only too eager to accommodate them. The red men exchanged pelts, especially beaver, for goods manufactured of iron (mainly pots and pans) and for guns and gunpowder. This new association was mutually satisfactory—or so it seemed; nor was it blemished by the introduction in quantity of the European barter commodity that would win for the paleface the entire continent of North America and destroy the red man's dignity and his very considerable civilization—distilled alcoholic beverages of every variety.

This original and informal accord between the Five Nations and the Dutch was almost immediately made to appear an arrangement of great significance to the red men. In the summer of 1615, barely a year after the opening of the Albany trading post, Champlain and a handful of French *arquebusiers,* together with a much more substantial collection of Hurons, crossed to the south shore of Lake Ontario to the village near Onondaga Hill, principal meeting place and holy ground of the Confederacy tribes. A series of skirmishes and sieges followed.

From the outset of his venture, the French leader had believed that the "enemy" would merely offer token resistance —for in his view the white man was irresistible. When it became evident that the Onondagas' defense was both serious and effective, Champlain dispatched a Huron-speaking comrade, Etienne Brulé, across the Niagara portage to Lake Erie's north shore where he was to rally more Huron braves to come to the assistance of the French. It was suggested, as an inducement possibly even more enticing than trade goods, that the Hurons sack and burn Seneca and Cayuga villages as they made their progress toward the country of the Onondagas—for the Hurons had suffered frequent and humiliating defeats especially at the hands of the Senecas who guarded the Niagara spillway.

To Brulé's chagrin, however, the Hurons of Lake Erie refused to budge. History offers no documentary explanation, though we may plausibly infer that this great nation, no matter how frequently it had been repelled by the Senecas, was not yet so enamored of the extremely one-sided arquebuse wedding with the French that it was willing to help Champlain pull his chestnuts out of the fire.

When it was learned that there would be no assistance from the west, the French abandoned the siege of the Onondagas. The paleface leader of the expedition had received a severe wound which he retreated back across Lake Ontario to lick. This successful defense was salutary, for it was the first evidence, so far as the Five Nations were concerned, of the lengths to which the Europeans were willing to go to satisfy their apparently limitless appetite for furs. The Confederacy sachems immediately made sure of a permanently friendly relationship with the Dutch, for they alone provided a source of weapons that could offer the red men of the immense Niagara-Hudson territory a measure of military parity with the French and their Huron clients.

It is also perfectly clear that the sachems who participated in the meetings of the Grand Councils during the years that immediately followed Champlain's alarming sortie across Lake Ontario, were anxious to avoid further conflict with the whites if that were possible. Their assemblies were devoted primarily to discussions of how best to negotiate treaties with the Europeans and their native allies who retained nominal dominion over the northern shores of the eastern Great Lakes. The arrangements sought were intended to facilitate commerce. It was in this period that the Five Nations issued their first call for "a great peace," and at the beginning of their campaign in its behalf, they believed that their policy could best be implemented by agreement rather than war. Surely, they reasoned, all red men must sympathize with their own appreciation of the situation: effective red power could be achieved only as a result of red solidarity.

But there were complications that the Confederacy leaders knew nothing of. Had their treaty proposals been matters for decision entirely through deliberations of the Huron chiefs, they might very well have been accepted. However, they were not a bit to the liking of the Hurons' powerful French masters, nor—it should be added to keep the record straight—did the Dutch consider the Five Nations' policy with very much favor. For what neither the Confederacy nor the Hurons understood was that the French and the Dutch, Europeans though they both were, white though they both were, spoke neither the same tongue nor worshiped the same deity in the same manner. The Wars of Religion, which had been one of the most calamitous aspects of European life and history for more than a century past, were thus translated to the New World, where they lost not a whit of their mad, zealous fury, nor gained a single morsel of intelligibility.

These early decades of the seventeenth century were the initial phase of the epic adventures of the foreign missionaries in the Americas, South as well as North. Both the French and the Dutch made it transparently plain to their unwitting and unwilling hosts that there could be no possibility of reconciling their respective religious views or their political differences—even in the glorious name of profit. Each alien nation wanted not only a monopoly of the commerce in pelts but also of the faith that would be espoused by all, late or soon, in this corner of what both were pleased to call the New Christendom.

If they were absolutely unable to fathom the niceties of the religious questions, the Five Nations sachems readily grasped the concept and implications of a monopoly of trade. They also saw, during the next quarter of a century, that the pursuit of pelts would very soon denude the land of game, especially the territory east of the Niagara (*their* territory), which could not be expected much longer to provide the beaver skins for which the demand appeared to increase by geometric progression.

This ecological estimate produced in the councils of the Five Nations a realization of importance: if they were to continue their profitable relationship with the Europeans they must expand into new, beaver-bearing lands. This understanding, in its turn, inspired a prolonged campaign of terror and plunder against tribes who inhabited the territories to the west and south of the Confederacy. This brutal warfare continued for nearly a generation.

There is a dreadfully sinister and familiar and almost Hitleresque ring in the words of the "Constitution" of the Five Nations Confederacy as they have come down to us by oral tradition. They relate how the "great peace," which they per-

sisted in maintaining to be their true aim, was to be established. When an alien tribe "refuses that great peace, then by
such refusal they bring upon themselves a declaration of war
by the Five Nations. Then shall the Five Nations seek to
establish the Great Peace by the conquest of the rebellious
nation. War must continue until the contest is won by the
Five Nations." No modern oligarch could improve on the bald
cynicism of that language. The Chosen People (as the Five
Nations occasionally called themselves) planned to impose
their great peace by means of a great war.

Because they had encountered practically no difficulty in
winning over the Hurons (with a few blasts of their cannons
and their arquebuses and the liberal dispensation of brandy),
the French were very scornful when they learned of the Confederacy's declaration of what amounted to a general war. The
Dutch, on the other hand (having been shown at very close
range what the Mohawks had so often done to the Mohicans
and being somewhat more circumspect than the French by
nature), were reasonably confident that their friends the Five
Nations might easily succeed in their scheme to implement
their "great peace."

With this conviction growing as they observed their Confederacy allies at closer hand, the Dutch were generous in their
gifts of arms and ammunition, but were much more niggardly
than were the French about the distributions of spirits. They
would keep the Five Nations tribes sober at least until the
outcome of the war could be determined. It was sound reasoning, and it worked. That the Dutch were soon to lose possession of their American colony to the British was no reflection
at all on their intelligent and usually compassionate treatment
of all the red communities that lay within the lands they had
conquered.

During the twenty years between 1640 and 1660, the Five
Nations gained complete control of the south bank of the
upper Saint Lawrence and of all the areas surrounding the
lakes of Erie and Ontario. Nor was their campaign confined

to the northeast. They ventured as far south as Georgia, encountering little effective resistance anywhere. In the Carolinas, they laid waste to numerous Tuscarora settlements. In the process they so impressed the sachems of that tribe with their disinterested ferocity that, a half century or so later, when the Tuscaroras were attacked and routed by the British, they migrated north to seek the protection of the Confederacy. Eventually the Tuscaroras were incorporated as the sixth nation of the group.

Although the principal objective of the war was territorial control, the Confederacy raiders took possession of much livestock. Whether it was from these sorties that they secured their first horses is not certain. It would, in any event, be some time before they became riders sufficiently skilled to make use of the horse in war. They did indeed obtain supplies of domestic cattle as part of the varied loot they brought back from their adventures. The captured women would help to replenish the supply of warriors who had perished in combat. Young enemy braves who were willing and able to run the traditional and terrifying village gauntlet gained admission as full members of the tribes that had carried them off.

In these southern expeditions, the Five Nations also obtained their first supplies of tobacco and marijuana—the latter a Tuscarora delicacy which could be processed and enjoyed in a number of ways—the result always being mild euphoria. (The hemp that was later to provide the raw materials for rope to be manufactured on the banks of the raging Niagara was first planted in the Genesee valley at this time.) Marijuana had been in regular use by some native North Americans for many centuries without apparently producing ill effects. When this certainty is juxtaposed with the deplorable impact of alcohol on red-man culture and society, one finds it difficult to escape the drawing of a very precise moral.

In the interests of objectivity, it is necessary to observe that the Confederacy warriors didn't deal very gently or kindly with the victims of their raids who could be neither of use nor a source of pleasure to them. As I have already remarked, most of the Indians practiced some form of torture. Accounts of cannibalism during these wars are almost surely exaggerated, but there was probably some evidence of it, particularly among the Mohawks. Long before this "crusade" of the seventeenth century, the Mohicans had given their mortal red enemies the name of Mohawk—"cannibal." It was, however, for the Hurons to ascribe to all of the Five Nations Confederacy the soubriquet of "Iroquois"—"serpent"—because the braves of those tribes liked to attack their enemies without warning. It was the Huron name that the French adopted. There was inhumanity on the part of the Five Nations, and it cannot be pardoned by a reiteration that the hypocritical white Christians could learn nothing about cruelty from the people whom they chose to describe as "savages."

By 1660, the Confederacy had so soundly and so repeatedly defeated and depleted the ranks of the Huron warriors, France's most populous native allies, that they had achieved an almost absolute domination of the fur trade as far west as the distant end of Lake Erie, as far south as the Chesapeake.

Unable to make safe use of the Niagara portage, so sternly guarded by the Senecas, French voyageurs and the Huron hunters and trappers were compelled to utilize the much longer route up the Ottawa River to Georgian Bay and the lakes of Huron and Michigan and Superior, carrying their goods to and from lands that were still outside the control of the Confederacy. This remarkable feat of arms and strategy had been accomplished by a maximum force of twenty-five-hundred warriors—and usually with far smaller numbers. But the Five Nation hegemony was destined not to endure for very long.

4

Downhill
All the
Way

By 1660, by which time the Confederacy Indians had achieved their most widespread territorial control, they were already victims of the two conditions that would induce their steady, inexorable, and utterly tragic decline—an alarming susceptibility to various diseases that the Europeans had brought with them, and an unquenchable thirst for alcohol, a libation to which their physiological tendencies made them very often addicts.

In the early days of the white man's epoch in North America, the ravages of pestilence and those of drink were of approximately equal virulence. Literally thousands of red men perished in epidemics of measles, chicken pox, smallpox, and other minor and major ailments that the Europeans had developed some natural resistance to. Gradually, the natives also acquired a degree of immunity to these illnesses. As they did, their inclination to chronic alcoholism (and to its acute form, at times) assumed an importance in the subsequent history of the New World that it would be difficult, if not impossible, to exaggerate.

Their potation of choice was French brandy, but like all alcoholics, they were willing in a pinch to drink anything that was offered to them. Their need and eagerness for drink, taken in combination with the physical frailty effected by a series of dreadful epidemics, led them at last to seek some sort of understanding with the French—sole purveyors of cognac. Before 1670, the Jesuits were traveling freely among the Confederacy villages, spreading the gospel of the Counter-Reformation and turning their backs discreetly as their white companions, the coureurs de bois who acted as guides and messengers in the great wilderness lands, doled out lashings of cognac with which the red men might wash away all evidences of their disbelief in the missionaries' preachings. Having so brilliantly won the long war, the natives of North America, and especially those of the Five Nations, were gradually losing the peace. Eventually, they would lose everything—their homes, their sacred honor, their very lives.

The friendly new commercial relations with the French were not entirely predicated on an Iroquois predilection for cognac. At the moment of the Five Nations' apogee, the Dutch were engaged in a distracting war with the British for possession of the great colony which bordered and, indeed, seems to have incorporated substantial parcels of the same territories that the Confederacy laid claim to by right of conquest.

In the four years after 1660, the British, who had already established themselves securely in colonial settlements to the north and south of the principal Dutch holding of Nieuw Amsterdam, were exerting increasing pressure on the whites from the United Provinces of the Netherlands. In 1664, the representatives of Westminster assumed "lawful" title to what became, thereupon, the town and colony of New York. The period of instability, while neither the British nor the Dutch could concern themselves with problems outside the immediate, afforded the French an opportunity which they were quick to exploit, for they had no serious rivals to their authority over Canada, which they called *"la Nouvelle France."*

This was an area of such magnitude that no one could even venture a guess as to its dimensions, so little of it had been systematically explored, let alone settled, by citizens of the great nation that claimed ownership of it.

French traders, missionaries, and adventurers swarmed out from Montreal and Quebec over the areas beyond the Niagara spillway—south as well as west. They began the construction and occupation of modest trading centers which would soon become forts and eventually permanent civilian habitations. Certainly, several white men, following the example of Etienne Brulé in 1615, had crossed over the Niagara portage well before this time of transition. However, no one who had actually seen the river and falls had theretofore left a surviving written record of his experience—though there are a few secondhand accounts of but minor historical interest.

This lacuna must appear the more remarkable because, by the last quarter of the seventeenth century, the history of North America had become essentially the history of the Europeans and their rape of a vast continent, in which annals the red man figures as no better than a brutal savage who

Whites and red men below Niagara Falls

should have been and who decidedly *was* savagely brutalized. Written narratives of travel through this sector of the American wilds are confined in the main to the astonishingly extensive and comprehensive *Jesuit Relations* and to less organized accounts of a few other wandering clerics. For the great majority of other white men who observed such wonders as the Niagara were illiterate, and the lettered few who traveled here preferred to act rather than to write about action.

The first white layman to leave a significant mark on the long, disturbed narrative of the Niagara River and the land that flanked it was Robert Cavelier de la Salle, a young Norman from Rouen whose twin motivations were adventure and avarice. He could have remained at home and reasonably satisfied his lust for gold, but only in New France, where his older brother was abbot of a Sulpician monastery at Montreal, could he attain great riches adventurously, audaciously.

Cavelier was twenty-three when he made his appearance in the colony's second city. The year was 1666. He was penniless —but in a gentlemanly sort of way. His father had warmly disapproved of his decision to quit the well-managed family countinghouse and the architectural glories of a fine town on the banks of the Seine. It was one thing for the older brother to follow his religious calling wherever God in his mysterious wisdom saw fit to summon him. Even for a soldier of the king such a journey would have enjoyed a more or less rational justification. But for a young man to abandon the certainty of wealth and position simply because he was restless as well as greedy . . . no. The Abbot Cavelier was equally if more charitably skeptical about his brother's dream of glory. He could offer the gently reared, Jesuit-schooled Robert little hope of gaining great profit and greater fame from the immense Canadian wilderness. All of the most prosperous trading areas so far opened up had become the capital of the merchants of Montreal and Quebec, men who were distinctly uninterested in sharing a mite of their wealth.

The abbot need not have troubled himself. The younger

Cavelier defied all right-thinking prognoses by developing, in the spring after his arrival, a farming and trading village on the banks of the Saint Lawrence, overlooking the Lachine Rapids —property bequeathed to the Montreal Sulpicians which they had never attempted to exploit, because this stretch of the river was a favorite fishing site for the Cayugas, Onondagas, and Senecas during the months of late winter and earliest spring. The monks had no wish to lose their lives as a result of attempting to make use of a modest strip of land that seemed to them, in any case, not particularly promising.

Cavelier reasoned otherwise, and proved himself right. Instead of evincing hostility to this white man's encroachment, the red men who fished the rapids expressed pleasure over the construction of a new community. It was a nearer source than Montreal for brandy and other more essential but less interesting trading commodities. A party of especially bold and curious Senecas even accepted with eagerness the young Frenchman's invitation to winter on the outskirts of Lachine —as he called his settlement. He put this period to good use by beginning to learn the rudiments of Confederacy dialects.

The hamlet was an immediate financial success. Therefore, so far as Robert Cavelier was concerned, it was almost immediately a colossal bore—for it was not small profit that he sought, but rather something truly magnificent, treasure so prodigious that one man couldn't count it. Nevertheless, he persisted admirably in his exploitation of Lachine through the end of his third year in the New World. By then, he felt himself linguistically qualified enough and secure enough financially to embark upon a venture of greater daring.

Exploration of the wilds was a privilege to be dispensed, in theory, only by the ministers of the king in Paris. In practice, however, modest requests could be granted by the royal authorities at Quebec. Cavelier had little difficulty in securing the right to traverse Lake Ontario in his quest, which had its antecedents in Jacques Cartier's expeditions more than a century before, for a riparian route to Mexico and, possibly,

to the Pacific Ocean. He sold his interest in the village of
Lachine back to the delighted Sulpicians. With the proceeds,
he purchased and equipped four large canoes. Late in July
1669, he set forth on the first of a series of journeys that would
situate him firmly in the half truth, half legend that comprise
the account of the opening of North America by the Europeans. In the process, Robert Cavelier became, in the accounts of his career, simply La Salle.

With a small company that included a pair of Sulpician
monks and some of the Senecas who had been tamed by the
domesticity of life and the comforts of drink at Lachine,
La Salle paddled across Lake Ontario to Irondequoit Bay (near
the spot where the modern city of Rochester, New York, is
situated), reaching this inlet on August 10. The intrepid
Frenchman, guided by his red friends, made his way to the
summit of a low hill that stood in the approximate center of
a clearing "nearly two leagues [six miles] in circumference."

Though this meeting place of the Senecas had several names,
it has long been known to white historians as Boughton Hill.
There, La Salle immediately made the acquaintance of Father
Frémin, a Jesuit missionary-in-residence, who vigorously and
resolutely objected to La Salle's proposed journey. His hostility was probably inspired by the presence of Sulpicians in the
young adventurer's party. Father Frémin would do nothing
at all to help persuade the Senecas to allow the group to make
use of the Niagara portage. So great had become the Jesuits'
hold over the Senecas by this early date that Father Frémin's
refusal to intercede was conclusive. The sachems rejected
the request. There was no higher authority to whom the expedition's leader could appeal.

Instead of doing the rational thing—returning to Montreal
in the face of this refusal—La Salle led his party to the far
western end of Lake Ontario where, at a point due north of
the Niagara, there was a Mississauga trading post. The city
of Hamilton, Ontario, stands there now. In late September,
while mulling over his difficulty, he met at this hamlet a

French explorer who was to become hardly less celebrated than La Salle himself—Louis Joliet. The older man was on his way back to Quebec after a long trip through the regions of the upper Michigan peninsula, Wisconsin, and eastern Minnesota, where he had been searching for the source of the copper which the natives of those areas were using to fashion primitive utensils.

A much more orderly and less impulsive creature than La Salle, Joliet had made crude charts of the upper Great Lakes. He showed these to his younger compatriot, whom he also informed of reports he had heard of two great river systems that flowed south and west of the Great Lakes in the general direction of Mexico and, perhaps, the Pacific. Such was the imperfect grasp of continental geography at that time.

Joliet further counseled La Salle at all costs not to dream of disregarding the Senecas' injunction against his use of the Niagara portage. Their protection of this "throatway," as the word Niagara signified in English, was absolute and their methods for securing it were notorious. The only alternative route west from the point where the two Frenchmen now stood was north of Niagara and its falls, over the upper end of the escarpment, then down the Grand River to Lake Erie. This largely overland trail was much longer and more difficult than the Niagara portage, but it offered the considerable advantage of safety, since it was patrolled by the Hurons who had long been domesticated by the Jesuits and debauched by brandy. The two Sulpician friars who had accompanied La Salle heeded Joliet's advice. Their mission during the next eighteen months provided the first detailed description of the shores of Lake Erie.

La Salle himself decided against going with them on this interesting journey, for he remained obsessed by his dream of finding a water route to Mexico—an ambition which had been fired by Joliet's account. However, what he actually did after he and the Sulpicians parted company is not definitely established. The credible but unsubstantiated report has it

that he returned almost at once to Boughton Hill. Father
Frémin, relieved to see that he was no longer in the tow of
members of the rival order, this time prevailed on the Seneca
sachems to provide the young explorer with a guide. In the
spring of 1670, so goes the tale, La Salle and his companion
went over the Chautauqua portage, across the Alleghenies,
down the Ohio valley as far as the site of Louisville, Kentucky,
where that great river falls. Then, still according to the same
uncorroborated account, La Salle moved overland to the lower
end of Lake Michigan, from which point he resumed his
journey by water to the Straits of Mackinac, where he picked
up the well-traveled trade route from Georgian Bay, up the
Ottawa River portages, finally reaching Montreal late in the
autumn of 1670.

The most persuasive surviving evidence in support of the
foregoing description of La Salle's activities in this period is
to be found on Louis Joliet's maps as they were finally deposited in Paris. These give credit to La Salle as the discoverer of the Ohio valley. Moreover, his explorations of more
than a decade later suggest a prior personal knowledge of the
terrain south of the Great Lakes which he could have obtained
only in the course of this apocryphal year—since the rest of
his career in North America is fairly accurately annotated.

When he reached Montreal, La Salle convinced the governor of New France, Count de Frontenac, of the wisdom of an
expansionist policy that called for the French colonization of
the major river valleys leading south through the center of the
continent. The plan appealed to Frontenac for two reasons.
One of them was purely domestic; the other was global.
Great as was the territory already administered in a most
slipshod manner by the *intendants* of New France, it was
rapidly becoming too small to accommodate a civilization and
an economy whose basis was almost entirely parasitic in con-
ception and function—taking from the land without returning
anything to it, a practice the French would never have permitted at home.

Rivalries among the religious orders (as evidenced by the animosity between the Jesuits and Sulpicians which had thwarted La Salle's ambitious project of the year before) were increasingly common and endlessly annoying. And the insatiable demand for pelts was, as the Iroquois had anticipated a generation before, depleting the supply not only of the lands east of Niagara's spillway but westward as well. If the appetite were to be satisfied, new lands must be opened up. Twentieth-century ecologists believe that when the first white man came to these shores, the beaver population numbered approximately forty million. By 1900, the creature was nearly extinct. Even in 1670, however, it was obvious that new hunting and trapping lands must be made safely accessible as rapidly as possible, if only to justify the great expense of maintaining the French presence in the New World.

The international implications of La Salle's project were necessarily less precise, depending as they did on the assumption that the European balance of power would remain more or less forever in its current state. This assumption might appear quaint unless one recalls that *all* foreign policies are, at any given instant of history, founded on that presumption. La Salle and Frontenac conceived of this westward and southward thrust, to link the territories of New France with the Spanish-held regions that bordered the Gulf of Mexico (what would eventually be Louisiana) as a means of frustrating British colonial expansion west of the Appalachians, the natural boundaries of their holdings along the Atlantic coastline. British-French rivalries would continue to be a central feature of North American history for almost another century.

The decision that La Salle's scheme was sound in principle was quickly arrived at. The implementation of the policy that underlay it required an amount of time and effort that could only have exasperated that impatient activist—for he himself was charged with the delicate negotiations that would result in persuading the Iroquois to allow the construction of the first of a series of permanent trading posts that would become the main way stations of the proposed great trade route west and south from Montreal. This original community was to be built where Kingston, Ontario, is now situated—at the spot where the Saint Lawrence rises out of Lake Ontario. It was, naturally enough, to be called Fort Frontenac.

Nearly three years elapsed before La Salle gained the rather grudging assent of the Iroquois to this initial phase of his plan. Nor was this the end of his obligation as a diplomat. Armed with a document bearing the ciphers of the great Five Nations sachems, the explorer had then to proceed to Paris to secure the consent of the king for this venture. Frontenac had been acting thus far entirely on his own initiative. The proposed fort that would bear his name, however, could not be constructed without the advance of funds from the royal treasury. Louis XIV, the Sun King, was more easily persuaded than the Iroquois—though he dearly hated to part with any of his gold, for he had committed himself to expend incredible quantities of it for the erection of his new baroque palace at Versailles and, not at all incidentally, to subvert and corrupt the landed gentry who had dared to question the right of the king to rule as he (and God) saw fit.

The actual building of Fort Frontenac required two years. Its facilities, exceptionally elaborate for a frontier community, included a chapel, a flour mill and bakery, a well-equipped forge, and of course a trading post with living quarters for a large staff of clerks and a modest garrison of troops, and camping sites for the transient red men who came to barter and get drunk. Of all Fort Frontenac's features that were unique to New France, the ones which most impressed the visiting natives were the cut-stone walls that surrounded the entire enclave and the fine bronze cannons mounted atop these massive fortifications.

From the moment of its completion, Fort Frontenac was the object of controversy, domestic as well as international. The British governor of New York claimed that it stood on ground which was legally the domain of Charles II, part of the land transferred by treaty with the Dutch in 1664. This document, he alleged, had made all the members of the Five Nations wards of His Britannic Majesty. French merchants at Montreal, who were very influential with the Jesuits (for sound financial reasons very interesting to both factions), protested that Fort Frontenac constituted a threat to the long-established flow of profitable commerce which made use of the Georgian Bay route over which their control was secure. They feared that La Salle's new trading post, which enjoyed a position offering easier access than Montreal to the western commerce, might cut them out altogether in the long run. This was by no means the last opposition that the adventurer would encounter from this quarter, nor even the most damaging. Astute a politician though he undoubtedly was, had La Salle wished to become a political person rather than an explorer, he might as well have remained in his native France and joined the new *noblesse de robe*.

A year after the operations of Fort Frontenac had been fully under way, La Salle delegated the responsibility for its day-to-day operations (though he understandably retained his title and emoluments as commander) and departed once again for Paris—this time to obtain permission and financing from the king for the second stage of his great scheme to extend French hegemony over North America. His plans involved the construction of a fort at the mouth of the Niagara River and a shipyard above the Upper Rapids, where he would see to the building of vessels that were to sail the waters of the Upper Lakes in aid of exploration and expanded trade, particularly in the rich and virgin Ohio valley.

His previous experiences with the intrigues of the French court in 1674, and his dealings with the Iroquois sachems, had made La Salle a most convincing advocate—though undoubtedly the great commercial success of Fort Frontenac and his own unswerving fervor were comparable assets. In May 1678, Louis XIV gave the Norman explorer a patent authorizing him to investigate the "country through which, to all appearance, a way may be found to Mexico." Although this document accorded La Salle a monopoly of the trade he developed in the areas he was responsible for opening up, it specifically forbade him from poaching in regions already under patents held by the merchants and traders of Montreal—that is, the commerce of the Great Lakes.

In addition to the precious patronage of the king, La Salle obtained through Frontenac the support of the Prince de Condé, hereditary Constable of France, who suggested as an aide for the adventurer one of those swashbuckling figures who turn up in history a lot more often than detractors of historical fiction are willing to concede—Enrico de Tonti, an Italian freelance whose right hand had been severed in combat some years before. As a replacement for the lost member, Tonti wore a prosthetic device of leather and steel that was a great deal more lethal than the mere fist and five fingers, which God had endowed him with at birth. La Salle readily accepted the Neapolitan as his second in command.

By September of the same year, the two men were back at Montreal, where reports of the royal underwriting had done nothing at all to improve La Salle's tarnished image in the eyes of the local merchants and entrepreneurs who were still smarting over what they claimed was the great loss of trade resulting from the success of Fort Frontenac. Before the new expedition was ready to set out, at least two serious attempts were made against La Salle's life. And there was even an abortive effort, peculiarly French in its machinations, to compromise his honor by installing his opulently conformed landlady in his bed. These are convincing and relevant measures of the degree of anxiety and apprehension occasioned among those who thought themselves beleaguered by his earlier venture and who feared that they might be ruined outright by its successor.

In spite of all efforts to dissuade him, La Salle did get his enterprise under way. The first vessel to depart was commanded by a brash young French nobleman, La Motte de Lussière. It left Montreal with a crew of seventeen men, among whose number was Father Louis Hennepin, a Recollect monk who had been chaplain during La Salle's brief tenure as active governor of Fort Frontenac. It is to Hennepin that we owe the only firsthand account of this epic adventure. Moreover, his memoirs incorporate the initial eye-witness description of Niagara.

La Motte's assigned mission was to proceed to Boughton Hill, as La Salle himself had done nine years before, and for the same reason: to secure permission from the Seneca sachems to construct a permanent base at the mouth of the Niagara and a shipyard above the falls. He was then to paddle on to the river, unload the supplies his boat was laden with, and prepare for the arrival of La Salle and the remaining members of the expedition.

In his embassy at Boughton Hill La Motte failed, just as had La Salle on *his* first attempt in 1669, and apparently for the same cause: the Jesuits there opposed it, probably on account of the Recollect Hennepin's presence in the company—though the ostensible explanation for the refusal was that the scheme was a foolish one and that La Salle must be mad to consider it. La Motte departed from Irondequoit Bay at the end of November, bound for the wide mouth of the Niagara, where he planned to await La Salle and give him the bad news.

Only in the middle of December did the leader of the expedition and Tonti finally get away from Montreal. Their leaving had been delayed by difficulties in establishing credit and by calamities befalling their equipment that smacked to them strongly of sabotage. Instead of heading directly for the Niagara, they made for Boughton Hill to pay what La Salle imagined was to be simply a courtesy call on the sachems, to thank them for according La Motte the permission he had requested. On learning that his youthful ambassador had been unsuccessful in his plea, the commander asked for an opportunity to refute the charge that his plan was mad. He was quite as persuasive at Boughton Hill as he had been a few months before in Paris.

By the time La Salle and Tonti reached the Niagara's

mouth, on January 3, 1679, La Motte had been encamped
there for nearly a month. But his ship lay at anchor, still
loaded with its supplies. In view of the Seneca chiefs' refusal
of his petition, he had seen no reason to take off the cargo.
The crew had established a temporary base about seven miles
upstream, just below the Lower Rapids, on the west bank, in
the shelter of the escarpment. The only significant structure
the men had built was a bark-and-pole cabin which served
Father Hennepin as a chapel. Here he had celebrated Mass
for the first time on Christmas Eve.

Despite the bitter cold and the fatigue caused by his swift
journey from Irondequoit Bay, La Salle found himself unable
to sleep. Shortly after midnight, he aroused Tonti and invited
him to join him on a journey over the Niagara portage by the
icy moonlight so that they might locate, as soon as the day
broke, a site upriver suitable for a shipyard. A man more rational than Tonti would have dismissed so foolhardy a proposal,
to cross a wide river and then travel an unfamiliar and dangerous footpath in the semidarkness without a guide. But then, a
more rational man would have stayed in the luxurious en-
tourage of the Prince de Condé.

The Italian agreed, apparently without much hesitation, and
doubtless regretted his rashness as soon as he and his captain
sallied forth; for after traversing the river, it was the first mile
of the portage which was the most demanding, that part
which the Senecas called Crawl on All Fours. Spurred on by
eager xenophilia, the two men reached the falls by sunrise.
In the middle of the morning, they found Cayuga Creek and
its protective island and decided that it was the ideal location
for the construction of a ship to sail the Upper Lakes. What
either of them made of the magnificence that surrounded them,
we have no way of knowing.

La Salle and the steel-handed Tonti were back at the base
camp by afternoon. The leader explained to his men the plan
for the shipyard. The two barques, still riding near the Niagara's mouth, were to be paddled as far upstream as possible

the next morning. The cargo would be transferred to the bank at the foot of the portage and then carried up to Cayuga Creek.

But that very night a severe windstorm blew up, heralding a major Great Lakes blizzard. La Salle's barque was hurled repeatedly against the rocky shore of the river mouth and eventually sank. Fortunately, La Motte's craft was safe—but by the time the snow had stopped falling, Lake Ontario was wholly frozen over, making impossible before the next spring a water journey back to Fort Frontenac for supplies to replace those that had been lost in the sunken hull.

Of the three tasks to be undertaken immediately, the least enviable was assigned to twenty hardy young members of the party (about half the total complement of able-bodied hands). They formed relays to plunge into the icy waters of the Niagara to salvage from the the hold of the foundered barque everything not ruined by immersion—anchor, chains, iron ingots, bolts, and rivets. The carpenter and smith supervised the setting-up of the shipyard at Cayuga Creek. A third crew began to build a fort at the river's mouth, on the east bank, at a site later called Crown Point, which had been most carefully reconnoitered by La Salle and Tonti.

The situation of the proposed fort was so ideally chosen that every fort, including the present Old Fort Niagara, has occupied the identical spur of land. The low bluff on which Fort Condé (as they called it) rose was in itself something of a barrier against attack from the water. Moreover, the point commanded an unobstructed view of almost three hundred degrees. Only the terrain and shoreline due east from the fort, toward Four Mile Creek, could not be easily scanned from the barricades when they were finally completed.

When all that could be retrieved from the sunken vessel had been brought ashore, the salvage crew was divided into two parts, to work at the construction of the fort or at the shipyards, labors that continued without interruption throughout the winter under the watchful eyes of La Motte and Tonti. After having afforded himself the honor of driving the first hot bolt

Father Hennepin
blessing Falls
(*Thomas Hart
Benton*)

into the keel of the vessel that would eventually travel the lakes,
La Salle departed with a single Seneca guide to travel by
snowshoes along the north shore of Lake Ontario all the way
back to Fort Frontenac to arrange for the shipment to Niagara
of replacements for the supplies lost when his barque had
gone down. The journey was well in excess of three hundred
miles.

Of those who remained behind, only Father Hennepin was
free of any obligation to engage in manual labor. When not
occupied with his devotions or his spiritual ministrations to
the venial sinners of the party, he looked about him and probably set down some notes for his memoirs. The first edition of
these was published in Paris in 1683. In this work appears the
following description of the arrival of La Motte's barque at the
mouth of the Niagara and the monk's impressions of what he
saw thereafter:

> On the 6th [December, 1678], St. Nicholas Day, we en-
> tered the beautiful river Niagara, which no bark had ever
> yet entered. . . . Four leagues from Lake Frontenac [On-
> tario] there is an incredible Cataract or Waterfall, which has

no equal. The Niagara river near this place is only an eighth of a mile wide, but it is very deep in places, and so rapid above the great fall, that it hurries down all animals which try to cross it, without a single one being able to withstand its current. They plunge down a height of more than five hundred feet [sic], and its fall is composed of two sheets of water and a cascade, with an island [Goat Island] sloping down. In the middle these waters foam and boil in a fearful manner.

They thunder continually, and when the wind blows in a southerly direction, the noise they make is heard . . . for more than fifteen leagues [i.e., forty-five miles]. Four leagues from this cataract or fall, the Niagara river rushes with extraordinary rapidity especially for two leagues into Lake Frontenac. It is during these two leagues that goods are carried [over the portage]. There is a very fine road, very little wood [!], and almost all prairies mingled with some oaks and firs on both banks of the river, which are of a height that inspires fear when you look down.

Age and forgetfulness (and perhaps a desire to improve on his original account) made the monk's pen grow even fonder

later on. The wholly revised edition of his recollections, issued
fourteen years after the appearance of the first, presents a
considerably embellished and even more awesome picture of
the wonders whose dimensions he had already hugely exaggerated:

> After we had row'd above an hundred and forty Leagues
> upon the Lake *Erie* [on returning from the subsequent
> journey to the west], by reason of the many Windings of
> the Bays and Creeks which we were forc'd to coast, we
> pass'd by the great Fall of *Niagara*, and spent half a Day in
> considering the Wonders of that prodigious Cascade.
>
> I could not conceive how it came to pass, that four great
> Lakes, the least of which is 400 Leagues in compass, should
> empty themselves into one another, and then all centre and
> discharge themselves at the Great Fall, and yet not drown
> [a] good part of *America*. What is yet more surprising, the
> Ground from the Mouth of the Lake *Erie*, down to the
> Great Fall, appears almost level and flat. 'Tis scarce discerni-
> ble that there is the least Rise or Fall for six Leagues to-
> gether: The more than ordinary swiftness of the Stream, is
> the only thing that makes it to be observed. And that which
> makes it yet the stranger is, That for two Leagues together
> below the Fall, towards the Lake *Ontario,* or *Frontenac,*
> the Lands are as level as they are above it towards the Lake
> of *Erie.*
>
> Our surprise was still greater, when we observ'd there
> were no Mountains within two good Leagues of this Cas-
> cade; and yet the vast quantity of water discharg'd by these
> four fresh seas, stops or centres here, and so falls about six
> hundred Foot down into a Gulph, which one cannot look
> upon without Horror. Two other great out-lets, or Falls of
> water, which are on the sides of a small sloping Island,
> which is in the midst, fall gently and without noise, and so
> glide away quietly enough: But when this prodigious quan-
> tity of water, of which I speak, comes to fall, there is such a
> din, and such a noise, that it is more deafning than the loud-
> est Thunder.
>
> The rebounding of these Waters is so great, that a sort of
> Cloud arises from the Foam of it, which are seen hanging

over the Abyss even at Noon-day, when the Sun is at its heighth. In the midst of Summer, when the Weather is hottest, they arise above the tallest Firr Trees, which grow in the sloping Island which make[s] the two Falls of Water that I spoke of.

The second of the foregoing extracts is but a minor fragment of Father Hennepin's dilations upon the wonders of Niagara. Yet the very fact that he deemed it proper to make of the river and falls so much more important a portion of his account in the revision is an indication of the amount of interest and excitement that his earlier and more concise descriptions had generated among the literate of France. Europeans had no doubt that they were reading about a natural phenomenon which was to be ranked only with the most astonishing of man's own handiworks—the pyramids.

Hennepin's depiction of *Griffon,* the ship that was constructed on the banks of Cayuga Creek, varies remarkably as well between the first and second editions of his memoirs. In the original, he described her as a "Vessel of only about 45 tonnes and which we might call an ambulant Fort." The ship gained fifteen tons, deadweight, and an enormous amount of firepower in the retelling. Since Hennepin is the only authority to whom we have recourse, and since his sense of proportion was, as we have already noted from his inflated impressions of the falls and lakes, most imperfect, the true size and armament of *Griffon* will just never be known.

What we *do* know, however, is that she was the first sailing ship ever to embark on the waters of the Upper Lakes and that—given the atrocious weather conditions and the shortage of materials available—she was built in a remarkably short time. *Griffon* was launched in the middle of March 1679. As soon as she was seen to be riding smartly and evenly in the waters of the broad Upper Niagara, the crew which had put her together deserted their camp on the shore and went to live aboard her. For the Senecas, choosing to ignore the admonitions of their sachems at Boughton Hill, had shown the alien whites a rather mixed hospitality. They had supplied them with a whore who doubled as a spy—a ploy probably older than recorded history; but they had declined to furnish foodstuffs, and had killed two of the crew members who ventured in search of game on the ground that they were poaching. As a result of these assassinations and other menaces and harassments endured over the long autumn and winter of 1679, there were more than the required number of volunteers to accompany La Motte to Fort Frontenac where the young officer would inform La Salle that *Griffon* was at anchor and ready to sail.

At the French fort at the opposite end of Lake Ontario, the expedition's leader had encountered further difficulties in obtaining goods on credit—this time the problem so grave that he decided he had to violate the injunction written into his patent from Louis XIV and his solemn promise to the Senecas at Boughton Hill: the first voyage of *Griffon* must be to collect furs on the Great Lakes; she would have to serve in the poaching trade. In no other way could La Salle obtain the cash necessary for the continuation of his grand scheme.

La Motte returned to Niagara in June with this intelligence, and then immediately headed back to Fort Frontenac to tell the commander that Tonti was ready to sail at once for Green Bay, on Lake Michigan, before *Griffon* could be seized by creditors or destroyed by the increasingly angry Senecas (on their own initiative, or at the behest of the British). There was much alarm in Albany over the prospect of a French sailing ship exploring (let alone poaching) on waters that, in the opinion of the governor of the New York colony, were holdings or at least protectorates of the Crown.

Although it was perfectly true that Tonti was more than willing to carry out La Salle's orders, he found himself unable to. Knowing nothing at all about the handling of ships, and able to elicit no constructive advice from a crew reluctant to sail under so hard a master as the Italian had demonstrated himself to be, he had twice nearly succeeded in sending the precious ship over the falls. To avoid such a calamity, which would be worse

than seizure, Tonti had the craft moored in the quiet channel
that separated Grand Island from Navy Island, and at once
sent word of his plight to La Salle at Fort Frontenac. The expedition's commander was still attempting to placate his creditors and enemies. Realizing that much, if not all, would be lost
if the navigable season on the lakes were to end without producing gold, the hard-pressed Cavelier hastened to Niagara,
arriving early in August. On the seventh, he ordered *Griffon*
towed up the river by hand. This method of warping or cordell-
ing was almost certainly familiar to at least some of the members of the crew, for they had seen canalboats in their native
France managed in this way. They had simply been disinclined
to do Tonti any favors.

By September 18, *Griffon* had reached Green Bay. There she
took on an enormously valuable but absolutely forbidden
cargo of pelts and was immediately ready to voyage back to
Niagara, under the command of a pilot whose instructions were
perfectly clear and straightforward: he was to tranquilize, with
bribes of hides or brandy, anyone likely to take exception to or
to try to interfere with this contraband traffic. He understood
very well that the ultimate disposition of the skins would
cleanse La Salle of debt and leave his ship free at last to aid in
the pursuit of the explorer's grandiose plan—a journey south
of the lakes to open the great trade routes from which his profit
would be legitimate.

After she set sail from Green Bay, *Griffon* was never seen
again. The generally accepted explanation for her disappearance has it that she went down with all hands during a severe
thunderstorm on September 19 or 20. Skeptics, unable to believe that every soul would have been lost from a vessel which
was almost certainly following a coastwise course, posit some
alternatives. All of them presuppose the fecklessness of the
pilot and the disgruntlement of the crew—conditions for which
there is ample support in the behavior of the ship's company
at Niagara prior to the departure and, indeed, in the very
nature of the voyage.

According to such theories, *Griffon* may have been scuttled after having been relieved of her illicit cargo. The proceeds from the disposal of the furs were divided among the mutineers, who subsequently defected to the British. Another possibility is that *Griffon* was set upon by red men who were infuriated by La Salle's act of bad faith—for they must have known something of the vessel's unauthorized mission. Whatever the true circumstance, the ship vanished.

La Salle, Tonti, and a group of about twenty men, including Father Hennepin and Moyse Hillaret, a master shipwright, explored the territory south and west of Lake Michigan. They founded two outposts, wholly confident that the sale of *Griffon's* bootlegged cargo had relieved the commander of his most pressing financial woes. La Salle was not disabused of this illusion until the spring of 1680, when he returned, full of hope and excitement, to Niagara.

Nor was this the only bad news that greeted his arrival. He learned as well that in November of the previous year, the small garrison he had left behind to protect Fort Condé had either defected to the British or been driven from the stockade by the Senecas. The fort and all its wooden outbuildings had been looted and razed by fire. The probability of defection meets with greater enthusiasm among historians, who point out that the noncommissioned officer in charge of the garrison, Sergeant La Fleur, later turned up in the service of the British. The conviction is strengthened by the fact that the less important but more vulnerable base at Cayuga Creek was intact at the time of La Salle's return in the spring of 1680, and the men who guarded it had not been forced to leave.

This wasn't the end of the Frenchman's run of bad fortune. He had left Tonti in command of Fort Crèvecoeur, on the Illinois River. In early summer, Moyse Hillaret organized a mutiny against the ironhanded tyranny of the Neapolitan. With fifteen men, the infuriated shipwright made a dash in canoes down the lakes to Cayuga Creek. They seized all the portable stores left there, persuaded the handful of La Salle's men still stationed at the shipyard to join them, and continued their water journey across Lake Ontario to Irondequoit Bay. At nearby Boughton Hill, they recounted to the Seneca sachems the extent of La Salle's treachery—seeing fit to add a gratuitous untruth to substantiable facts which were grave enough: the Frenchman, they alleged, was plotting to monopolize the fur trade of all the Great Lakes. As they moved eastward along the shore of Lake Ontario toward sanctuary with the British, Hillaret's mutineers continued to spread ill will for La Salle— who had no need of it.

The reports destroyed all his hopes for immediate success. His dream of empire appeared to be in ashes, like Fort Condé, the Europeans' first but delible mark on the banks of the Niagara. In 1682, the Count de Frontenac was replaced as governor of New France by the venal Le Febvre de la Barré. The successor was instantly and willingly suborned by the merchants of Montreal, proprietors of the Georgian Bay trade route. Le Febvre dismissed La Salle *in absentia* from his sinecure as governor of Fort Frontenac, choosing his moment with singular but wholly unintended irony—just after the audacious explorer had attained his goal of discovering and investigating the lower reaches of the Mississippi-Missouri valley system, which he had followed all the way to the Gulf of Mexico. La Salle called the vast expanses of wooded and marshy flatlands through which he traveled Louisiana. He hoped that Louis XIV would name him to the governorship of this chartless immensity of land and water.

Robert Cavelier de la Salle succeeded in his failure and failed in his success. He made a third and final return journey to France and obtained the title and perquisites he sought. He was killed by mutinous companions in 1687, after a series of catastrophic misadventures in the very bowels of the territories he had claimed in the name of France. He left a far more lasting and more significant impression on the Niagara than on the Mississippi.

5

The
NIAGARA
Comes
into Focus

La Salle's intention was assuredly not to furnish even the ostensible cause for a war. Nevertheless, it was his treacherous failure to keep his promise not to engage in the fur trade on the Great Lakes that gave the Seneca sachems the excuse they had been seeking (not without much prodding from the British) for open conflict with the French. The problem, over-simply stated, was that the Iroquois tribes as a group were growing cooler in their feelings toward New France as their relations with the Anglo-Dutch traders of New York improved.

The explanation for this gradual but nonetheless dramatic change of outlook probably lay in one of the four touches of genius in the British temperament. The first three are literature, a talent for orderly self-government, and a readiness to laugh at the most sacred of their political and social institutions and the most honored of their personal traits. (A. J. Liebling once observed that if the British were half as modest as they claim to be, they would be the most insufferable people on earth.)

The fourth commendable quality is a wonderful chameleon-like adaptability to conditions abroad as they find them. At base, this talent may be an extension of their capacity to govern themselves sensibly (more often than not). Of all western Europe's colonial powers, only the British have managed as a rule to translate their policies, their religion, and their institutions in a manner that makes them comprehensible and useful to the territories they have chosen to "adopt." Upon their departure, whether forced or voluntary, they have usually left behind them significant traces of their flexible political ingenuity.

If this generalization strikes one as a major heresy, we need look no farther afield than contemporary Canada to find an administrative and representative system that is comparatively efficient without being corrupt, one that is exceptionally sensitive to the vagaries of public opinion—hence, one that is genuinely "democratic." An even more striking and surprising example of this brilliant British legacy is to be discerned in the political organization and judicial structure of the Republic of Ireland. Though the Irish had more than sufficient reason to despise all that their quondam British masters stood for, they had little hesitancy about adopting what amounts to a carbon copy of the parliamentary system of Westminster, and a method of dispensing justice swiftly and fairly, most of the time, that must appeal strongly to Americans who suffer so grievously from the law's delay. If George III had been endowed with an English instead of a German temperament, American history and political development would surely have followed a different course. However, George III could only break; he didn't known how to bend. The British bend almost miraculously well.

In 1664, when Nieuw Amsterdam became New York, Charles II Stuart had sat upon the restored throne of Britain for only four years. To the degree that he had anything as formal as a "colonial" policy (one, that is, that meant more than the chaotic plunder of the land), it was best expressed in the humane pragmatism of his local administrators. When these agents assumed responsibility for the government of the former Dutch colony, they remarked at once that they had had the good fortune to inherit no serious "native problems," at least so far as the Five Nations were concerned. They considered this circumstance intriguing and set about quite unsystematically (as was their normally casual wont) to analyze this curiosity.

What they soon apprehended was that the Dutch had prospered in their dealings with the tribes of the Iroquois by imposing upon them as little as necessary. This is not, of course, to suggest for a moment that the red man hadn't been shamelessly bilked in every trade and property transaction (of which the often-cited transfer of Manhattan Island is but a single and not very spectacular example). It *is* to suggest, however, that the red man was rarely allowed to *feel* that he had been cheated, and was *never* made to think that his person or the physical integrity of his community were in any fashion menaced by the presence of the Dutch in his land.

The principal agent of this successful relationship was the squaw man, sometimes referred to as the white Indian—the European who was adopted as a member of a village, a tribe, or an entire nation. The procedure for becoming a squaw man was, in theory, the same as that of an alien brave being admitted to a new community. One had to run the village gauntlet, to take a blood oath, and to espouse a local maiden. In practice, the more hazardous aspects of the ritual were suspended in the case of the white aspirant because of the precious trade goods to which he had unique access—especially arms, ammunition, and alcohol.

The squaw man's readiness to lie with village maidens and matrons was greeted sympathetically by the whole community. The braves believed that sexual intercourse sapped their vigor, so they abstained completely during the hunting season or in periods of war. The women, under no such compunction, willingly accepted the embraces of the bodies that presented themselves.

Squaw men became the intermediaries between the Indians and the whites, interpreters at council meetings, the best-liked and most trusted traders. Their total indifference to the problems that were created by miscegenation produced a hybrid, two-world culture which would eventually help to undermine the teetering social and economic order of the red men a century or so later, when the whites were ready for the first massive invasion of the west, after the War of 1812.

From a date as early as 1632, there are written records of Dutch, Scotch-Irish, and English squaw men traveling with impunity through regions considered much too dangerous for every other European except the missionaries. When La Salle was treating with the Senecas at Boughton Hill in 1669, their interpreter was a French-speaking squaw man from the Netherlands. And later on, when the discoverer of the Mississippi-Missouri valley was exploring farther north, in the vales of the Ohio and Illinois, he frequently encountered squaw-man traders from the coastal colonies of Britain.

We can only conjecture about why the French were so slow to recognize the immense utility of the squaw man. Perhaps it was a question of religious scruples, inculcated by the Jesuits and other missionary orders, that prevented the voyageurs and coureurs de bois from following the brilliant example set by less-principled Protestant counterparts. Or it may simply be that the squaw man's significance only became apparent after the British had acquired title to the colony of New York in 1664. The preceding period had been empty of serious threat to the French position in New France, and they may consequently have found no need to alter or to mend their ways.

However, after some twenty years of reasonably tranquil association with the British, the Five Nations (who had simultaneously been trading with the French) were growing more and more restive about the difference in treatment and attitude shown them by the two European occupying powers. The *affaire La Salle* merely ignited the fuse of a bomb that had been in the making for at least a full generation.

In the spring and summer of 1683, any French craft that dared to venture into the Niagara from either lake was set upon by the Senecas. Its cargo was confiscated and its crew was slaughtered. In the spring of the following year, some bold and thirsty Senecas infiltrated the walled settlement of Fort Frontenac. They locked up the dozen members of the military garrison, terrorized the civilian residents, then proceeded to get themselves helplessly drunk during a night when there was no white man about to limit their consumption of spirits. The next day, nursing very important hangovers, the raiders began the long paddle across Lake Ontario to Irondequoit Bay. Not a solitary soul at Fort Frontenac had been seriously injured, but of course French pride had suffered a devastating blow.

The governor of New France, Le Febvre, read into this relatively harmless escapade (and in the less tender treatment accorded his compatriots at Niagara) the darkest of adumbrations. Punitive action must be taken without delay. He ordered the creation of two forces with which he proposed to break the Senecas' long-maintained grasp of the Niagara spillway, once and for all time. In June 1684, an army of seven hundred, mainly Huron and Ottawa braves who were led by French voyageurs and coureurs de bois, set out for the Niagara from the north shore of Lake Erie. Le Febvre's own army of a thousand whites was ready at the same moment to begin a drive toward Niagara from Fort Frontenac. The plan was for a simultaneous attack against the portage from both sides of the river—a classic pincers movement which appeared particularly apposite in view of the terrain, since there was no route by which the defending Senecas could escape except in the directions of the lakes at either end of the spillway, egresses that were to be guarded by the assaulting troops.

The western army of New France was in position near Niagara at the designated time. But Le Febvre's forces were conspicuously less fortunate. Misled into the Montezuma swampland by their Huron guides (inadvertently or deliberately, it was never determined which), they extricated themselves from the primeval ooze only after more than half their numbers had succumbed to yellow fever or malaria. The survivors were by that time too demoralized to think of fighting a battle.

Le Febvre summoned a meeting of all the Iroquois sachems to inform them, tactlessly, that New France would no longer tolerate the wanton killing of her subjects or the pillage of their barques and canoes at the Niagara portage or anywhere else. The chiefs' response seems a model of good temper in view of the fact that it was *they*, not the French satrap, who should be mollified. They replied coolly that that had no immediate plans for changing their customs, their method of protecting their property and trading rights, or their way of making war. The Niagara spillway was Seneca domain. That was that.

The season for battle had thus spent itself without the occurrence of a single engagement. Le Febvre ordered the native warriors to return to their villages, and he dispatched the fever-ridden remnants of his own army back to Fort Frontenac. For the two following summers, relations between New France and the Iroquois were pretty much as they had been since the discovery of La Salle's treason—in a state that was neither quite peace nor quite war.

Le Febvre was replaced as governor by Jacques René de Brisay, Marquis de Nonville (whose name has come down to us as "Denonville," the style followed hereafter). His instructions from Versailles were explicit: an angry Louis XIV ordered him to defeat the "rebellious" Iroquois so decisively that they would never again constitute a menace to the French or to their commerce in the New World. Denonville, who had had no previous experience in the American wilderness, anticipated few difficulties in carrying out the king's orders. All he needed was "resolution." In a way, he was right. Irresolution and truly ingenious incompetence on the part of his officers were largely responsible for the fiascos that followed.

Denonville's plan of operations was a replica of Le Febvre's
—coordinated sallies against Niagara from the east and west.
This year, the western forces were gathered under the stern
command of La Salle's erstwhile associate Enrico de Tonti.
Tonti, one would have imagined, possessed resolution enough
for any task. He set out in May 1687 with about five hundred
men. On their way east, his coureurs and native braves came
upon two luckless convoys of British traders which had just
crossed over the Niagara portage with the friendly assistance
of the Senecas. The New Yorkers lost their valuable cargoes
and their lives. At about the same time, Denonville, at the head
of a much larger army of something approaching twenty-five-
hundred men, of whom two thousand were French, reached
Fort Frontenac.

From this first great stone citadel of the Great Lakes, the new
governor issued an invitation to the Iroquois sachems to attend
a council meeting whose purported object was to discover a
way of avoiding the conflict that so clearly impended. Why
the chiefs agreed to meet within the confines of the enemy's
awesome fort, we cannot guess. But agree they did, and for
this folly they paid a price that all of them must surely have
considered much higher than mere torture and execution;
they were humiliated and exiled.

As soon as the sachems had passed through the main gate of
Fort Frontenac, they were arrested, put in irons, transported
down the Saint Lawrence to Montreal, transferred to an ocean-
going vessel, and carried off to France. When they had re-
covered from their mal de mer, the red warrior chiefs were ex-
hibited before the king and lesser members of the most elegant
court the world had ever seen, at Versailles; they were tangible
evidence that Denonville was succeeding where Le Febvre had
failed. Once the Indian sachems had lost their novelty value,
they were auctioned off to noble landowners and served out
the pathetic balance of their lives as slaves.

Denonville's purpose in thus betraying his "sacred" word to
the Iroquois chiefs was not entirely a matter of improving

his image in France. By depriving the Five Nations of their most venerable and most venerated leaders, he hoped to demoralize the tribes, and wasted not a moment in seeking to exploit this presumed advantage. A fleet of more than five hundred shallow-draft bateaux, barques, and canoes ferried his army across Lake Ontario to Irondequoit Bay. The last of his men landed there on July 10, 1687, and were soon joined by Tonti's smaller force from the west. From this beachhead, three thousand men marched in the direction of holy Boughton Hill.

The Baron de la Hontan was in command of one of Denonville's companies. He has left us a vivid account of the encounter that came to be known as the Battle of Victor Swamp and of its inconclusive aftermath:

. . . We had but seven leagues to march in a great wood. . . . The coureurs de bois, with a party of savages, led the van and the rest of the savages brought up the rear, our regular troops and our militia being posted in the middle.

The first day the army marched four leagues, and the advanc'd guards made no discovery. The second day our advanc'd guard marched up to the very fields [of Boughton Hill] without perceiving anything, tho' they passed within pistol shot of five hundred [Senecas] who lay flat upon the ground, and suffered them to pass and re-pass without molestation.

Upon their intelligence, we marched with equal precipitation and confusion, being bouyd [sic] up with apprehension that the Iroquois had fled, and that at least their women, children and superannuated persons would fall into our hands.

When we arrived at the bottom of the hill upon which the ambuscade was placed . . . they began to raise their wonted cry, which was followed by the firing of some muskets. Had you but seen, sir, what disorder our troops and militia were in amidst the thick trees, you would have joined me in thinking that several thousands of Europeans are no

more than a sufficient number to make head against five
hundred barbarians. Our battalions were divided into straggling parties who fell into the right and left, without knowing where they went.

Instead of firing upon the Iroquois, we fired upon one another. 'Twas to no purpose to call in the soldiers of such and
such a battalion, for we could not see 30 paces off: In fine,
we were so disordered that the enemy were going to close
in upon us with their clubs in their hands, when the savages
of our side having rallied, repuls'd the enemy, and pursued
them to their villages with so much fury that they brought
off the heads of eighty, and wounded a great many. In this
action we lost ten savages and a hundred French.

So terminated the only more or less formal battle of the
entire war. The sachems of the Senecas and their allies who
had been defeated (or had they been?) at Victor Swamp
ordered the immediate destruction of all the villages within a
week's forced march of Boughton Hill. This seems to have
been an early exercise of a strategy the Russians would use
against the French in the Napoleonic campaign of 1812, scorch-
ing the earth to afford the enemy as few spoils as possible.

Denonville's army found in its sweeps of the region only
abandoned plantations and livestock which the fleeing Senecas
had been unable to carry off in their haste. The frustrated
"victors" furiously ravaged the crops and slaughtered the cattle,
swine, and fowl. They returned to their boats at Irondequoit
Bay with no prizes worthy of the exertions they had volunteered—not a single scalp. It is perhaps important to note here
that according to Dee Brown, author of *Bury My Heart at
Wounded Knee,* the red men learned about scalping from the
Europeans. No one who would wish to understand not only the
total destruction of the red-man civilization in North America,
but the moral conditions that make the most grotesque atrocities seem "rational acts," can fail to read this beautiful and
deeply troubling book.

Tonti's Hurons and Ottawas were particularly disillusioned.

They had lost an opportunity to effect a bit of vengeance against the Senecas who had so often and so terribly decimated their ranks during the previous forty-odd years. Twice in the past four years had they made the long and difficult journey from Lake Erie's north shore, and twice had they been denied the revenge which had been the principal spur to their endeavor. They promised Denonville, as they prepared to depart, that a third call for assistance from the French would go unheeded.

The new governor of New France, convinced that he had already won the war, was unimpressed by this assertion. He ordered the construction of a new fort at the mouth of the Niagara—a symbol of the Gallic hegemony that would rise on the long-scattered ashes of Fort Condé. He imagined that since the Senecas had fled from Boughton Hill, they had conceded defeat; therefore, the Niagara portage was his, and it must be protected. He reasoned that the intimidated Senecas would respect this new outpost of French authority.

To this apparently simple task he assigned the innocent young Chevalier de Troyes and a force of one hundred twenty regulars. In September, the fort was nearing completion. The little garrison was provisioned by a fleet of bateaux from Fort Frontenac with supplies that were believed sufficient for an eight-month stay. The Chevalier de Troyes must soon have been made aware that his "control" of the Niagara spillway was purest fiction. The Senecas had invested all the land on both sides of the river. He therefore realized that his single objective was to hold the fort until spring, when Denonville planned to use it as a base from which to attack and conclusively break the red man's grip of the lands to the west and south.

It was shortly after the supply fleet had sailed away that the youthful commander of Fort Condé learned that even so limited an objective would be difficult and perhaps impossible, for the simple but chilling reason that most of the stores of food and wine that had been deposited for his garrison were spoiled. To compound the anguish of the prospect of certain mass starvation was the inexplicable fact that de Troyes had been left without a single boat, not even a canoe. He wouldn't be able to send a message by water to Fort Frontenac to describe his plight. And he had every right to believe that any messenger who attempted the journey by land would be ambushed, tortured, questioned, scalped, and put summarily to death.

The Senecas had only to wait. They waited. The French hunting party that made the first sortie in the autumn lost two men and returned without game. By the end of the winter, in 1688, the Chevalier de Troyes and two-thirds of his garrison had perished either from exposure or starvation—or both. In March, the chaplain and three terribly malnourished soldiers managed to elude the Seneca sentries (who had grown less watchful as the garrison's condition worsened day by dreadful day), and walked haltingly to Fort Frontenac. However, it was a full month before a French force arrived by water to relieve Fort Condé. By that time, the survivors numbered less than forty.

The new defenders of the fort, though adequately supplied, found the holding operation not a great deal less trying than had their ill-starred predecessors. The Senecas' siege tactics, during the first two months of the summer, were terrifying. They waited in ambush for every forage party. In the dead of night, they hurled their pitch-fired torches or shot flaming arrows against the wooden palisades of the stockade's walls or onto the bark roofs of the huts within the compound.

In August, Denonville suddenly abandoned his strategy of war, which had in any event been proved a pure disaster. He ordered the garrisons of Forts Condé and Frontenac to stand down and return forthwith to Montreal. This astonishing change of policy had been dictated by the growing uneasiness of the merchants of New France and their financial backers in the mother country, who pointed out with abundant cogency, to the governor and to the king's ministers at Versailles, that any plan which called for maintaining control and security of so immense a land mass by force of arms was bound eventually to fail. For such an ambitious project demanded the constant presence of an army of much greater size than France was prepared to commit for any long period to a campaign which the king and his advisers regarded as peripheral. They were concerned mainly with domination of the continent of Europe, the profits from which, though perhaps only short-run gains, were also more readily appreciable.

Besides, even assuming the efficacy of so great an army in North America, what ultimate purpose would it serve? Could commerce be expected to flourish under siege conditions, under the constant shadow of the cannon? Pacification, the Montreal and Quebec merchants now argued, was the logical and much more desirable alternative, and to verify their conviction they had only to point to the adjacent colony of New York for an example of the success of a policy of "peaceful coexistence." It was, however, only after the military calamities of 1684–1688 that the French began systematically to emulate the British in their dealings with the red men. They had a great deal to learn, and the transformation was less than instantaneous.

By 1700, the British had established with the Five Nations a pact of mutual dependence which had been functioning pretty well for almost thirty years. For the Europeans, this arrangement (which disingenuously acknowledged, in so many words, that the lands of the Great Lakes, including the invaluable Niagara spillway, belonged in perpetuity to the Confederacy tribes) was deliriously profitable in terms of trade. For the Indians, it was gratifying and occasionally exciting. Not only did it furnish them with the white man's goods, especially his arms and his alcohol, but it also afforded them sport and entertainment. The British addiction to ceremony and colorful panoply was once again proved to be communicable to other peoples.

Sachems came to look forward eagerly to semiannual and sometimes quarterly council meetings with the New York governor (to whom they still referred reverently as "Corlaer"). These sessions ordinarily involved about seven glorious days of intoxication, judiciously interspersed (though rarely interrupted) by occasional hours of discussion of practical affairs—from which transactions the British invariably obtained what they sought, yet contrived to give pleasure to the sachems even as they turned out their pockets.

Each council meeting began with the ceremonious presentation of a packtrain which was laden with such necessities of primitive life as gorgeous apparel—de rigueur to those gatherings, for it gave the sachems the illusion that they were dealing with their conquerors as equals. No list of gifts offered on these occasions fails to include iron and ceramic utensils, tobacco, and a very substantial amount of drink. As tribal tastes became more sophisticated, white smiths were dispatched to the larger Confederacy villages to repair and maintain the ironware and muskets that had been furnished to the various nations. Many of these European craftsmen were or became squaw men.

The council meeting of the British authorities and the Confederacy sachems in July 1701 resulted in the transfer to New York of rights to the use of hunting grounds that bounded all shores of Lakes Ontario and Erie—an agreement which the British construed to imply that henceforward, all the Five Nations tribes were *ipso facto* wards of the Crown. It was further their understanding that they could make free use of the Niagara portage route; for in no other way would they be able to gain easy access to the northern shore of Lake Erie without traversing territory which the French claimed to be theirs. In fact, the British had enjoyed unimpaired passage over the Niagara portage for almost two decades.

After the débâcle of 1688 at Fort Condé, Niagara rejoiced in a long period of tranquility. The French acknowledged grudgingly the legitimacy of the Senecas' possession and control of the spillway, in exchange for which recognition the protectors of that invaluable route allowed its employment by the traders of New France—though most voyageurs and coureurs de bois usually elected to follow the longer and more difficult Grand River passage to Lake Erie, understandably questioning the good faith of the Senecas and appreciating that the natives, in their turn, had every right to wonder about the good faith of the masters of New France.

By the onset of the eighteenth century, the Niagara portage was so prosperous an undertaking that a Seneca village had evolved on the site now occupied by Lewiston, just down-river from the Lower Rapids, opposite the point where Father Hennepin had caused his rude chapel to be built in the winter of 1678. Sturdy, stubby packhorses carried cargo from the north end of the portage route to the foot of the escarpment. Since this high bluff was too steep for the beasts, the materials were loaded on the backs of Seneca women and children. They scrambled up Crawl on All Fours. At the top of the plateau, the parcels were again consigned to animals which bore them along a trail that followed the edge of the Niagara gorge for a couple of miles before turning inland, terminating at the shoreline about a mile above Goat Island.

Perhaps the most singular occurrence of these peaceful years at Niagara was the first recorded journey of two European women, both of them French, over the portage in the spring of 1702. These pioneers were Mesdames de la Motte-Cadillac and Alphonse de Tonti, the latter a sister-in-law of the re-doubtable Iron Hand. Both ladies were bound for Detroit, a French community on the Saint Clair River founded the year before by Monsieur de la Motte-Cadillac. Their passage was uneventful, though they expressed suitable ladylike alarm over warnings against the rattlesnakes that were said to lurk in the crevices of the gorge that had been eroded away by the down-river rapids—a section of the portage route which was known as Devil's Hole. They were, in addition, properly awed by the glory and thunder of the falls and by the mists that rose from the pool into which the waters tumbled.

Nevertheless, Niagara was still more than a century from becoming an attraction accessible to and safe for the purpose-less traveler.

6

Jean
Coeur

Louis Thomas de Joncaire, Sieur de Chabert, was a lad of seventeen in 1687 when he arrived in New France to serve his king as a very junior officer in Denonville's ill-fated campaign to reduce the Senecas. A native of the ancient Provençal city of Arles, gentle of birth and education, Joncaire seemed not to possess anything resembling the qualities or rudimentary credentials required of one destined to become a legend in his own time, a figure of frontier mythology, creator of a dynasty that would be known to folklore and history as "Jean Coeur." Yet only one other character in the tormented narrative of the Niagara territory ever came close to rivaling his fame. This was the Irish-born Sir William Johnson, forty years the Frenchman's junior, whose style of operation was so different that the two men can only be compared in terms of their respective accomplishments in the interest of their governments. These were signal, if not always salutary.

Joncaire fell into the hands of the Senecas within months or possibly weeks of his arrival in the New World. It may even be that he and a dozen of his compatriots were among the Frenchmen captured during the uneven course of the Battle of Victor Swamp, for they were eventually brought to the restored village of Boughton Hill for extermination in the traditional fashion, on the torture platform—a ritual of agony which, when judiciously administered, could be prolonged for twenty-four hours if the victim was young and of sound physique. All of Joncaire's companions suffered this excruciating death. When his own time came, the young Louis managed to loosen the cords that bound his arms behind him. He knocked down the braves who were guarding him and furiously assaulted a warrior sachem who stood in the path of his escape. He did not, however, get clean away. Other braves recaptured him and brought him before the chiefs for further judgment. His frenzied courage had evoked exclamations of approval from witnesses who had assembled to observe his execution.

After a brief discussion, the sachems agreed that if Joncaire could survive the running of the Boughton Hill gauntlet, he would be admitted to this most important of Seneca communities as a full-fledged brave. Just how this information was conveyed to a youth who had yet to master the Seneca dialect, we may only guess. There may have been a Jesuit missionary on hand, in spite of the current Iroquois hostility to the French. There very likely was a squaw-man representative of the British who may have had a smattering of French or been able to negotiate eloquently in sign language. In any case, the message was got across to him. Having no more to lose than his life, which was in direst jeopardy anyhow, Joncaire naturally accepted the challenging proposition. And since he lived to tell the tale, we know that he successfully negotiated the heavy-handed gauntlet.

In this way began a squaw-man career for one of the most exceptional frontiersmen of North American history. The daring born of desperation, which he had demonstrated in his attempted escape, was proved to be not at all a sometime thing. His exploits in battle and on the hunt, his quick and complete assimilation of the various Iroquois dialects, and his performances as an absolutely honest broker washed away, over the next decade, almost all the rancor that had been the principal legacy of La Salle's bad faith and Denonville's bad judgment and bad policy. Joncaire's brilliant success was aided not a little by the abrupt shift of New France's attitude —from war against the red man to pacification, the more so since the change coincided almost precisely with the young Frenchman's admission to the community of Boughton Hill.

It wasn't long before Joncaire became the archetypal squaw man. He faithfully represented the Senecas to the administrators of New France without ever wholly overlooking his place of birth, the ties of faith and king that bound him to the mother country as well as to the land of his adoption and his new people. He lived two wholly distinct lives. He took an Indian bride soon after his acceptance by the Senecas, and sired a number of half-breed children of whom there appears no surviving record. And after he had shown himself to be a loyal member of the Seneca nation, he won such confidence from the older women of Boughton Hill that they made him a sachem—the first white man of record to be so honored.

Joncaire's missions of trade and diplomacy took him frequently to Montreal. There, he made the acquaintance of Magdalen de la Guay, whom he married in 1706. She bore him ten children over the next seventeen years, which is evidence of Louis's attention if not his perfect constancy. Two of the Joncaires' four sons, Philippe and Daniel, would follow in their intrepid father's footsteps, embracing frontier life with a fervor comparable to his own. It was in considerable measure their continuation of his endeavors, through the period of the French and Indian Wars, that gave such solidity to the legend of "Jean Coeur" as a single individual, a creature of magic who was endowed with eternal life. For there were, in later years, *three* Joncaires who functioned simultaneously along the borders of New France. The name was ubiquitous; so, therefore, was Jean Coeur himself.

Our main concern with Louis Joncaire centers about his growing interest in the establishment of a trading post at the Niagara portage. Just when the squaw man began to lobby among the Senecas in behalf of this scheme is uncertain, but it was probably a few years after his marriage to Mademoiselle de la Guay. For it was then that his status in the eyes of the government of New France attained its zenith. He was commissioned a captain in the Marines and was, informally at least, high commissioner and ambassador plenipotentiary for Indian affairs, author (or ghost writer) of all major decisions made in Versailles or Montreal in their regard.

Joncaire realized that the British had such a head start over the French in the matter of good relations with the red men, especially the long-buffeted Iroquois, that the only hope of restoring France's position lay in demonstrating that Louis XIV (and, after 1715, Louis XV) were more lavish and more generous rulers than dull Queen Anne (and, after 1714, the wicked first of the Hanoverian Georges). The most practical and readily comprehended way of proving such virtues was to make trades more advantageous to the Iroquois than the now-complacent British saw any immediate necessity of offering, and to present gaudier, richer, and more elaborate gifts to the sachems. In the execution of this eminently successful campaign to woo the Five Nations away from Westminster's aegis, Joncaire enjoyed the complete confidence of New France and the court at Versailles.

Obviously, this openhanded treatment, however unexpected and however suspicious it made them, was nonetheless very popular among the red men. If they didn't yet appreciate that in French terms the higher prices now offered for pelts still left profits that were astronomical (upward of one thousand percent, net, was thought merely satisfactory performance by the avaricious Europeans), they had learned, after a century of disillusioning transactions with the white man, that his apparent generosity was never disinterested. So the negotiations concerning the construction of a French trading post at Niagara were not swiftly concluded. They were complicated by the apprehensions of the British, who rightly feared that a "trading post" might all too easily be rapidly converted into a fort. And they were not a bit reluctant to remind the sachems of the Five Nations that, by treaty, they were under the official protection of the new German king who lived in London.

In spite of all the foot-dragging, Joncaire finally succeeded in obtaining the Senecas' permission, accorded with the stipulation that this new post on the Niagara's east bank would remain "forever" under his personal supervision. *Le Magazin Royal*, the royal store which adjoined the Seneca village at the foot of the escarpment, was ceremoniously opened on May 9, 1721, by the Baron de Longueuil, Lieutenant Governor of New France. After seeing the Fleur de Lys hoisted to the top of the flag standard before the main store building, the baron assured the assembled Iroquois dignitaries that the stockade which enclosed the shop and warehouse and living quarters was not intended to serve any kind of military purpose. He had no need to remind his listeners, in support of this claim, that the wooden construction of Magazin Royal was scarcely proof against the Seneca torch and fire arrow. The fate of Fort Condé, thirty-three summers before, was ample evidence of the vulnerability of wooden buildings to flame. He added that the handful of soldiers in his company was bound for Detroit, to form a little garrison for La Motte-Cadillac's trading post among the Hurons. This too was a fact.

About ten days later, the lieutenant governor made a quite similar address at Onondaga Hill, the Iroquois holy of holies, to sachems who had been unable to attend the dedication at Niagara. Whether or not de Longueuil's speeches or Joncaire's repeated assurances were wholly credited by the red men, they were accorded tacit assent. But every detail of Magazin Royal's construction and operation was reported to Onondaga Hill and to the British governor of New York, William Burnet.

There is no room for doubt about Burnet's views of this development. He had made no secret of his misgivings from the outset. A council meeting was convened in September 1721. The serious conversations were prefaced by the presentation of an inordinately bountiful quantity of gifts; these included some fascinating novelties—Jew's harps, mirrors, and scissors with which the red women might cut the bolts of wool and linen that were included in the packtrain's consignment of goods. The governor tactfully informed his interested audience that His Majesty took a very poor view of the permission given the French to build Magazin Royal.

He may not have put it to them so baldly, but he strongly hinted at the idea that he suspected his listeners of playing a double game. Indeed, he knew this to be the case. The chiefs' reply, which may very well have been formulated by Louis Joncaire who was almost certainly among the sachems who attended this important gathering, was equally diplomatic and a great deal less sincere. They pledged with proffered belts of wampum (symbols of their sworn word) their utter allegiance to the great white father in Westminster, George I, and vowed that "as soon as any Frenchmen come to the Five Nations, we shall tell them to pull down that trading house and not come either to settle or to trade among us any more."

Burnet was not deceived. The Iroquois sachems knew he wasn't deceived. But unless the British governor was prepared to take direct military action there was really nothing he could do just now to erase Magazin Royal. For the Iroquois, in Louis Joncaire's absolute thrall (as it appeared, at any rate, to Burnet and his advisors), would have no part of any violent gesture toward the lavishly generous French. The governor could, however, try to create competition for the commerce that was taking place at Niagara, since its presence menaced with virtual monopoly a trade which the British had shared comfortably for years without great effort.

Governor Burnet proposed at first to set up a rival trading post at Irondequoit Bay, near Boughton Hill. In the winter of 1721, he made an abortive attempt to resettle on that spot some Protestant German refugees who had been starving and/or

freezing to death in squalid communities on the west bank of
the Hudson. The Palatine Germans who scouted the site found
the climate of the Ontario lakeside even less to their liking
than that of the Hudson. They did, however, consent to settle
in the arable lowlands of the Mohawk valley, between Schenectady and the principal trading village of the Mohawks, Canajoharie. Later on, they would expand their homesteading
westward along the river.

In a way that no one at the time appears to have discerned,
this settlement of the Mohawk valley was of far greater and
more lasting significance than the creation of a trading post on
Lake Ontario. For the lands occupied by the Palatine Germans
were cleared and farmed; they were, thereafter, not merely
denuded of game, but permanently separated from the Indians
who, according to the same treaties cited by Burnet, retained
"possession" of them. This gradual infiltration of whites westward from Albany was the most ominous of all European
movements in the New World. It was the beginning of the
end for the American natives everywhere—an end which would
not occur until 1890.

Burnet's initial idea of providing the New York colony with
a trading post on Lake Ontario remained to be realized. In
the meantime, Magazin Royal flourished handsomely under
the able direction of Louis Joncaire. In June 1724, a second
effort was undertaken by Governor Burnet to create a fort and
trading community, this time at the mouth of the Oswego
River, on Lake Ontario. The supplies for the construction of
the settlement, which was to be called Fort Oswego, had to be
hauled over three portages from Albany to reach their destin-
ation. The spot, nevertheless, was ideally situated for its dual
purpose. It had a natural harbor, a sandy beach for a shipyard,
and the high ground behind it commanded views of river and
lake which could hardly be improved on as the site for a fort.

By the spring of 1725, British traders and squaw men were
spreading the word among the Iroquois that the New Yorkers
at Fort Oswego would pay much higher prices for pelts than

the French at Fort Frontenac or at Magazin Royal. Great Britain and France were nominally at peace in Europe as well as in the New World (the Treaty of Utrecht had been signed between them the year before), but military peace was merely the condition necessary for the proper conduct of economic and commercial rivalry—and this conflict was decisively joined on the Great Lakes that summer. From a standing start against what amounted to a French stranglehold on that trade, the British of Fort Oswego made important inroads.

So long, however, as the French maintained Magazin Royal on the Niagara, the British could make no appreciable dent on that portion of the fur commerce emanating from the Upper Lakes. Joncaire immediately perceived the need to enlarge the post and to fortify it. For as a Frenchman schooled in the history of Europe, he must have understood that every major military struggle, regardless of its purported occasion, had money and trade as well as politics for its underlying causes. Besides, there were rumors that the British were building many sizable naval vessels at Fort Oswego. If these reports were even partially true (they were wholly groundless), this could only mean that they were planning attacks against Fort Frontenac and Magazin Royal.

In this same summer of 1725, before Fort Oswego was in full operation, Baron de Longueuil visited with Joncaire and the other sachems of the Onondaga, Cayuga, and Seneca nations at Boughton Hill. He there and then made a request for permission to rebuild Magazin Royal. After four years of hard use, he solemnly explained, the hastily constructed shacks had become leaky and decrepit. They ought to be replaced by permanent buildings worthly of the great commerce they were now handling. He placed great emphasis on the proposed name for this new complex, *La Maison de la Paix*—the House of Peace. He described it as a work of stone, like Fort Frontenac, capable of coping with much larger quantities of pelts and white man's trade goods than were managed in the present facilities. It must have an anchorage that would allow much larger ves-

The House of Peace

sels to come alongside its quays. Though the baron assured
the sachems that the ships he mentioned would never be
vessels of war, his owlish conclusion that the new trading post
must be situated at the site, at the mouth of the Niagara, where
Fort Condé had stood, left little doubt in anyone's mind that
warships might one day call there.

At the urgent prompting of William Burnet, the chiefs of the
Oneida and Mohawk nations, who enjoyed a new prosperity
because of their proximity to Fort Oswego, pleaded with their
western brothers to reject the French proposal. But the final
word was Joncaire's, as was usually the case. In the autumn,
de Longueuil received formal authorization for everything he
had requested. Over the winter, two ships were built at Fort
Frontenac solely to carry the materials, men, and equipment
necessary for the construction of the new House of Peace.

The designer of the structure was Gaspard Chaussegros de
Léry, an architect who had had extensive experience in the
field of military design and construction both at Montreal and
Quebec. After surveying the quarries in the vicinity of the

proposed building, which were mainly of the soft shale which underlies the Niagara River's bottom, Chaussegros decreed that the same granite that had been employed in the construction of Fort Frontenac must also be used for the House of Peace. Consequently, great blocks and slabs of this stone were ferried from one end of Lake Ontario to the other.

Chaussegros used as little wood as possible in his design, well aware of the terrible menace that fire represented in peacetime as well as in war. All of the bearing walls were of stone, as were the floors of every level. Heavy oak beams reinforced the mansard-roofed attic, for this deceptive-appearing loft must support the heavy cannons which were to be smuggled ashore and installed secretly at night. The overhanging windows of this top story were also machicolated—each furnished with a hole in the floor so that the soldiers who manned the artillery could aim musket fire downward against any attackers who attempted to scale the walls of this principal building. Machicolation was a relic of medieval fortress construction; in those earlier days, defenders poured hot oil down on the heads of their hapless adversaries.

The House of Peace, for all the labor and logistics entailed in its building, would have been completed by the autumn of 1726 had not the workers engaged in its construction come down with fever. Not until the spring of the following year were the heavy guns ferried from Fort Frontenac, carefully wrapped in duck to conceal their true nature. Since no special rigging could be deployed to haul them up the two flights of broad stone stairs to the attic level, they had to be manhandled in the dead of night, a travail that could not easily be accomplished without detection—or at least without arousing some suspicion among the watchful Senecas. When all was in readiness, Baron de Longueuil's son Captain Charles Le Moyne was given command of the House of Peace, whose complement of "trading post personnel" numbered one hundred carefully selected troops.

Even presuming that no Seneca scout had observed the curious nocturnal activity of introducing the cannons into the House of Peace, an assumption that appears highly improbable, the presence of so large a company of exceptionally well-disciplined "clerks" and "warehousemen" was an indication no one could easily mistake. Word was immediately passed to the governor of New York. In early September, William Burnet summoned the Five Nations sachems to an emergency council meeting that lasted only forty-eight hours and which was destitute of the festivity common to all earlier sessions of the kind. In the clearest introductory phrase, the governor made some urgent points: the Treaty of Utrecht had acknowledged Britain's authority over the Iroquois. This means, he explained, that the French had no reason to be building a fortress on soil that was under the official protection of the British—even if that fortress were given the name of House of Peace.

With a severity remarkable for one who had had so much experience in treating with the Indians, Burnet then submitted for the sachems' approval a document which would accord the British all proprietary rights to a belt of land sixty miles long that followed the south shore of Lake Ontario and included the entire east bank of the Niagara, thereby including the land occupied by the new House of Peace. In addition, the Five Nations were asked to agree to come to the aid of their British "protectors" in the event that the French should attack Fort Oswego. The sachems were given a little time to mull over these stern demands. Whether they were offered libations before according their assent, or as a reward for affixing their marks to these two agreements, agree they certainly did.

These commitments, however, like all the others they had previously signed, didn't for a moment prevent the Iroquois from planning to continue their most profitable commerce with the French. Like Louis Joncaire, the sachems seemed to lead two lives—as they were known by two names. And if they made no further formal concessions to the French in their guise of "Iroquois," they could see no reason for denouncing earlier understandings that had served them so well. The red men, in any case, attached less importance to "pieces of paper" called treaties than the white man purported to attribute to them. No matter what might be explicitly stipulated by these most recent promises to the British, the House of Peace, which was gradually to become known also as Fort Niagara, was allowed to continue its useful and popular operations—because that seemed to the Iroquois to be in *their* best interest. So long as there was no outbreak of hostilities between the French and the British, there need be no conflict between the confused identities of the "Iroquois" and the "Five Nations." The Confederacy Indians could continue to enjoy the best aspects afforded by both of these alien civilizations.

But it was inevitable that there should eventually be war between France and Britain in the New World. The expansionist policies that both nations were pursuing made the clash certain. Only the moment of its beginning, like that of death, was in doubt. The roles of Louis Joncaire and his sons in setting the stage for this conflict were at once simple and complex. Over the years between 1727 and 1758, they opened up the trails and acted as scouts for commercial and military operations down the Ohio River—a stream which the French call *La Belle Rivière*. Ownership of the territory thus claimed for France had also been staked out for Britain—as a portion of its "protectorate" of the Five Nations. That is the simple part.

What makes their contribution harder to explain is the degree to which their efforts drew into the struggle the Iroquois and allied tribes who were settled in the Ohio valley. Of the three Joncaires whose careers in the New World spanned almost three-quarters of a century, only Daniel, the younger of Louis's pioneer sons, left any kind of written record. This account, however, is so self-serving (composed in the Bastille, after 1761, while he was awaiting trial) that it cannot be accepted without serious reservations. This much seems clear: after their father's death in 1739, Philippe and Daniel Joncaire not only explored and helped to establish settlement in the

Ohio valley, but they also and often stirred up the Iroquois, urging them to lash out fiercely at the British.

Eventually, it was at the virtual command of the younger Joncaires that the Iroquois sided with New France when war with Britain was formally declared. They accomplished these feats by emulating their wily father. That is, they became squaw men. It is therefore not surprising that with the declaration of war, it should have been another squaw man, William Johnson, who reversed the situation and helped the British to prevail against odds that seemed quite improbable at the conflict's onset.

7

NIAGARA
Battleground, Phase One

The dark thunderheads of war were slow to collect during the second quarter of the eighteenth century. With only fragmentary awareness of the longer-range international political implications of their actions, the French and British were entrenching their positions in territories over which they confidently believed their control was absolute, and were sending out frequent scouting parties to determine the receptiveness of the red men in the midwestern hinterlands to the idea of rule either from Versailles or Westminster.

There was more than a choice between Tweedledee and Tweedledum to be made. French and British policies on colonialization had one supreme distinction, one that was not at all confined to their practices in North America. The British emigrated to this continent in far greater numbers than did the French. Or, to put it more accurately, more Europeans emigrated to British colonies than to French.

This imbalance, by 1745, was striking. It is estimated that in the British settlements there were as many as one million resident Europeans. In New France at about the same time, white settlers certainly didn't exceed the number of fifty thousand. The British constituted a majority of the population of their American possessions—particularly if by the term "British" we understand that Scottish, Scotch-Irish, Irish, and Welsh were included with the English.

These immigrants had been eager for practical reasons to quit their native heaths—reluctant for the emotional ones that bind one to that earth. For farm laborers and crofters, the heaths had been blasted by the earliest manifestation of the agricultural revolution that would transfigure rural England's social, economic, and political organization—the Enclosure Movement. For others, the British climate just *had* to be more inclement than any other; it was an ugly March day in the British Isles the year around. Moreover, the Crown offered very tempting inducements to emigration. Even for those who indentured themselves for their passage money to America, there was the promise of a large tract of land "in good heart" at the end of their seven years of servitude. And for the Irish, there was the additional goad of mindless English persecution of their Catholic faith at home. They would find the Church of Rome in not very great favor in the British-operated New World either, but here there was less time and energy for that sort of repression.

In such terms as these, the French had no emigration policy at all. Indeed, there were relatively few *habitants* in New France at any given time. Those who had served the court in *any* remote land dreamed of eventually returning home with their accumulated wealth and honors. France's cultural and climatic conditions seemed a lot more salubrious than the extremes of temperature and the inhospitable, backwater civilization of provincial Montreal or Quebec, the towns where most of the habitants huddled together to reminisce, to sing beautiful songs (some of which they themselves had composed), and to agree that there was no place like home.

New France, therefore, was not immediately developed

agriculturally by the settlers—or not, at any rate, by very many of them; there just weren't very many of them. Old France, for one thing, could harvest all the foodstuffs normally required for her people, whereas Britain could not. For another, the wealth of the New World that did interest France had nothing to do with crops, but had everything to do with nature—which was to be pillaged and abandoned. The thrust of the French down the valley of the Ohio was, on the whole, not at all motivated by a desire to settle and harvest the land but rather to plunder it of hides.

The purpose here is not to make moral judgments regarding the relative virtues of the two policies and their results, but simply to point these differences out—for they are relevant to the attitudes of the respective European nationals, when war did come, to the views of the red men, especially the Senecas, largest and most bellicose of the Iroquois nations, when they were compelled to choose sides in that war.

Because the French were not so much interested in controlling the land as in monopolizing the commerce, the Senecas thought them the lesser of the two evils that confronted them. For there could be no doubt of the British hunger to possess the land itself for purposes of cultivation. A farm is no place for a hunter. The red men remained primarily hunters. The Joncaires certainly played an important role in persuading the Iroquois to side with France, but behind their arguments lay abundant evidence that the French had no intention of seeking physically to displace or dispossess the natives.

The British, to the contrary, made elaborate promises to respect the territorial rights of the Indians, but all too frequently elected to ignore these vows, as immigration from Europe reached epidemic proportions, increasing year by year, like an accelerating plague. These Europeans had to be settled on land that could be farmed. The Indians owned the land. Hence, the Indians must be induced, by whatever means came easiest to hand, to give up their land in the higher interest that was European. It was, from the very beginning of the mass immi-

gration to the New World, as simple and as callous a policy of
genocide as that. It would terminate only with the virtual
extinction of the North American red man, near the end of the
last century. There is a bitter but apposite irony in the fact that
Indian and beaver nearly perished in the same decade.

The French had another, even more persuasive and subtler
instrument that they used in their own behalf—the Catholic
orders of missionaries, and most especially the Jesuits. It is
impossible to offer reliable estimates of the numbers of red
men and women who were actually converted to the faith of
Rome. But unlike representatives of any other Christian religion, these missionaries' primary purpose was *not* to induce
the pagans to espouse the cause of France (though this was
assuredly a natural side effect of their effort which they made
no attempt to curtail in any way), but to espouse the cause of
Christ. The *Jesuit Relations* contain accounts of many missions,
beginning in the sixteenth century, to red tribes in every section of the continent east of the Rockies. White explorers,
imagining themselves to be inexpressibly audacious in their
penetrations of the wilderness, often found Jesuits awaiting
them at the adventurous and hazardous journey's end. Though
many of these emissaries of Christ were brutally martyred, and
though much was made in Europe of their martyrdom (where
it served the purposes of the Catholic Counter-Reformation to
exploit such occurrences), the Jesuits at least did not encourage
the Indians to drink before they signed contracts which
stripped them forever of their control of great stretches of
land. In the light of the Indians' eventual fate, we may com-
passionately wonder if the Jesuits' counsel was all that charit-
able. There was a single colony of Jesuit-converted red men
at Caughnawaga, not far from Lachine, where the influence
of the missionaries in determining the Senecas to take up the
French cause was of some importance—but the central reason
was British territorial greed.

As the two factions slowly formed themselves, patterns of
tribal affiliation became somewhat more distinct. The Senecas

were preponderantly sympathetic with the French. The Onondagas and Cayugas conscientiously endeavored to tread a neutral path, *seeming* to remain faithful to the British (because the British could and did get at them more easily and more often than the French—though they increasingly deplored British methods of snookering them out of immense landholdings). The Oneidas and Mohawks, settled nearest to Albany of the Five Nations, also played on both sides of the fence, nominally honoring their pledge to support the British if it came to war, but simultaneously engaging in a prosperous smuggling trade between Montreal and the Hudson valley, for the British were systematically raising the prices of trade goods. These Europeans seemed less and less interested in commerce, more and more jealous of Indian territory. This appearance was a most accurate measure of British policy. By 1738, when young William Johnson arrived in the New World, it appeared that if war were to break out at that moment, the Senecas would do all they could in aid of the French, and the remaining four nations would do all *they* could to remain aloof from the struggle.

William Johnson might easily have served as the original for the "Wild Colonial Boy" of the Irish folk song. He was born to a luckless father, who had supported the losing Stuart cause during the Williamite wars in Ireland, and to Ann Warren, whose brother Peter had come to New York as a naval officer in the service of George I. Once arrived, Warren had made a most advantageous marriage with Susannah De Lancey. Peter Warren's father-in-law, Chief Justice of New York and fourth-generation patroon, had advised him to purchase land in Manhattan and to acquire, in 1735, a fourteen-thousand-acre tract situated near the point where Schoharie Creek enters the Mohawk River, a purchase that cost him twenty-five cents per acre. This immense parcel Peter Warren decided to name after himself; he called it Warrensburg.

Three years after striking this momentous bargain, Warren wrote to his sister Ann, who was then living with her husband

and nine children on a small tenant farm in the County Meath, north of Dublin. Would she by any chance have a son who might be interested in gathering together ten Irish families who would settle the land of Warrensburg? To Ann Johnson, the brother's suggestion must have seemed heaven-sent. She replied without delay that indeed she had a son, William, who would be delighted to accept his uncle's proposal. She failed to inform her brother that William was more like Tom Jones than Bishop Berkeley—for Henry Fielding hadn't yet written his great novel, and George Berkeley was a little-known Irish divine at the time, one of many amiable clerics comfortably attached to Dublin's Trinity College.

William Johnson had no trouble rounding up ten emigrant families from among his destitute, landless neighbors in the County Meath. He arrived with them in New York during the spring of 1738. The arrangement was straightforward enough, as Peter Warren outlined it to his great, black-haired, ferocious-looking nephew. Each of the Irish families was to be assigned an uncleared section of two hundred acres of Warrensburg. Title to each parcel would be transferred only when the immigrants had raised the price not only of the soil but of their passage from Ireland as well. Johnson himself was to open a trading post where he was to cater to the needs of the newly settled Irish and those of the Palatine German families of the valley—and, too, of the Mohawks still resident in the region.

Peter Warren took up a week of young William's time filling his head with what turned out to be mostly nonsense— how to conduct his affairs with the local red man, with what respect he should treat the great patroon families, and how to comport himself as the poor relation of a man who intended to become an American aristocrat through his connection with the De Lanceys.

Within but a few weeks of his arrival, William Johnson discovered the uselessness or fatuity of practically everything his uncle had told him. An exalted gentleman named van Renssalaer sold him six spavined horses. All the merchandise which

Warren had advised him to stock in his new trading post proved of utility or interest to none of his rustic clientele—red or white. But by the autumn, he had grasped the true situation and prepared himself for it. He had salable products to exchange for the Germans' fine crops and the Mohawks' dwindling offerings of pelts.

His store and tavern became a frontier public house that owed much more to Irish notions of hospitality than to British austerity. He was generous with his tots of whiskey, and provided a free lunch of smoked herring and the nearest equivalent of Stilton and port that one could find in this backwoods area—cheddar mixed with rum and caraway seeds. The preparation made his patrons thirsty as well as contented.

Johnson wasn't long at Warrensburg before he came to the conclusion that if he were to prove a success in this wilderness setting, he must get on better terms with the Palatine Germans and the Mohawks. The former, fortunately, spoke English, so it remained only for him to gain their good Protestant confidence. He chose what would seem at first an intelligent way of going about it. He hired Catherine Weisenbergh, a Palatine girl, to be a clerk in the trading post, and often left her alone during his absences among the Mohawks.

Since Catherine had to live under William Johnson's roof, it wasn't altogether surprising to learn that she was soon sharing his bed, particularly during the long, bitter winter nights. By the autumn of 1739, she was carrying his first child. She and William lived together until her death. She gave him three offspring who survived. But they never married. What impression this illicit arrangement made on the pure-thinking, clean-living German immigrants of the valley I cannot imagine. They didn't lynch Johnson, nor certainly did they take their valuable trade elsewhere, because there was no other handy outlet. The relationship posed an amusing problem of protocol years later, when Johnson was awarded his baronetcy. How was the compiler of Debrett to list Catherine Weisenbergh? The editor of that studbook of the British aristocracy looked the other way. She was dutifully recorded as "Lady Johnson."

The match, such as it was, cannot have been an altogether happy one for Catherine. William Johnson was the most promiscuous frontiersman of record, though admittedly the record isn't very reliable. His reputation as a womanizer ascribes to him the paternity of seven hundred half-breed children. There is, however, more or less official acknowledgment of only three —the progeny of that formidable Mohawk maiden Molly Brant. One of Molly's young by Johnson, Joseph Brant, would later attain a certain and very portentous notoriety.

Johnson's traffic with the Mohawks disclosed his remarkable gift for languages. Under the tutelage of the Mohawk sachem Tiyonaga (known to the British as King Hendrick, himself a distinguished linguist who had been presented at Westminster to Queen Anne), Johnson rapidly mastered the tongue of the tribe with which he principally traded. In 1742, he was not only a squaw man but a Mohawk blood brother. If he never became a sachem, he never needed to. His hold over the Mohawks was comparable to that of Louis Joncaire and his sons over the Senecas—and every bit as important to the British as was the Joncaires' to the French.

Johnson was much more richly rewarded for his services to Britain and to the Mohawks than were the Joncaires for their role in the interest of France and the Senecas. The Indians gave him a piece of land, twelve miles square, in what became Herkimer County. The deed was later ratified and is still referred to by some local historians as "the royal grant." It is one of the few land transfers of that era not effected through the agency of drink. In addition to a title and a tiara, Johnson also received from a grateful king much more land and an important sum of gold.

His role in the history of the Niagara began after 1744, with the outbreak of the War of the Austrian Succession, known in North America as King George's War. By this time, he and his uncle Peter Warren were scarcely speaking to each other, for

Johnson had become much richer than the man who had staked him and was demonstrating his prosperity more conspicuously than Warren thought seemly. He had built a great, ostentatious house, Johnson Castle, at Warrensburg, "to shelter his whores and bastards," and there he presided with gaudy ceremony. The quarrel with his uncle was soon to end, however. As commander of a small British flotilla, Warren won sufficient prize money in battles and blockades off the West Indies, the coast of France, and the mouth of the Saint Lawrence, to gain himself a knighthood, the rank of vice-admiral, a fine house in London, and a seat in Parliament from one of England's many rotten boroughs.

The most significant action of the war in New York occurred in 1745, when Senecas, Onondagas, and Cayugas, inspired by the brothers Joncaire, raided convoys of boats and packtrains that were supplying Fort Oswego. In November of that year, a small army of French and Indians burned the village of Saratoga and appeared to be menacing villages uncomfortably close to the colony's capital at Albany.

By the following spring, it was impossible for Governor George Clinton to find mule skinners for the packtrains or boatmen for the convoys of long, narrow barges to make the perilous but vital journey to Fort Oswego. It was at this juncture that William Johnson stepped in with an offer to furnish crews from the Palatine settlements; for he had secured guarantees of safe passage from his Mohawk friends who controlled the route from Canajoharie west. In this same season of 1746, the governor reported to London that "certain persons will undertake . . . to bring Jean Coeur, a French priest, to Albany who is settled among the Sinnicas [sic]. And they are of the opinion that his removal from the Indians will be [a] very great service to the British interest."

It isn't very difficult to see why the attempt to capture "Jean Coeur" should have failed—if, in fact, the effort to kidnap this mythological figure was ever made. The misinformation alone about the Joncaire brothers doomed the venture from the start.

It appears that the British had not learned of Louis's death seven years before, and there was nothing even remotely priestly about him or either of his sons.

Undismayed by the inability of "certain persons" to take "Jean Coeur" prisoner, the governor decreed, as the result of a great council meeting in July, that "of the new levies [of militiamen] now in this province . . . six or seven hundred, together with two hundred Indians, [will] be employed against the French fort at Oniagara [Niagara] . . ." William Johnson was commissioned a colonel in the militia and named commander of the Six Nations—for by 1746 the Tuscaroras had come north and found protection as members of the Confederacy. Johnson was ordered to lead an attack against the House of Peace.

His opportunity to do this failed to develop, because the governments of the several British colonies were too preoccupied with purely local problems and schemes to recognize the military implications of the seizure of Fort Niagara, not to mention the economic and territorial benefits that its reduction would have opened up to them. The colonies sent no troops. Historians who seek explanations for the mutual suspicions underlying the states' rights issue, which would dominate the political history of the United States for centuries, could do worse than to explore the commercial and territorial rivalries of the British colonies during King George's War—for these were at the root of the apparent torpor that afflicted their will to cooperate with each other in what was plainly in the greater general interest of the Crown and even of themselves.

In this period of danger, the French showed remarkably little concern about the security of the House of Peace. It was never provided with a garrison of more than a hundred troops. The post commander reported evidences of rot in the great oak timbers that supported the cannon-laden attic level, and noted that there was considerable erosion of the low bluff on which the fortress-trading post stood. Its heavy armaments were in disrepair.

Had William Johnson been able to muster three or four pieces of heavy artillery and two hundred competent men, the fort could not very long have withstood a siege. The only concession the French made in these months to the safety of the Niagara portage route was to effect the construction, about a mile and a half above the falls, of a small, temporary fort on the east bank of the river, directly opposite the mouth of Chippawa Creek. For the principal French concern of the hour was the blockade of the estuary of the Saint Lawrence, which was seriously interfering with all commerce to and from the mother country—and making Peter Warren and several other British naval officers very rich.

When the Treaty of Aix-la-Chapelle was signed in 1748, the lackluster performance of the British in North America led more than one Iroquois sachem, hitherto loyal to the king at Westminster, to wonder if it might not be prudent to lay off some of his bets by seeking secret alliances with the French. For there was evidence, in the very next year, that the administration in Quebec was planning to strengthen the Gallic hold on the region of the eastern Great Lakes and the land of the Ohio to the south of them.

Charles de Boische, Marquis de Beauharnais, a bastard of Louis XIV who had been governor of New France for more than twenty years, now proposed to erect a fort at the mouth of the Humber River, where a group of Mississaugas had long occupied a hamlet which they called Toronto. This installation, only forty miles by water from the Ontario end of the Niagara, would not only reinforce French control of the lake, but would also serve to inhibit the flow of trade to Fort Oswego, much of which had to pass down the Humber.

This, however, was the least grandiose of Beauharnais's plans. In view of the joint projects of the Pennsylvania and Virginia colonies of Britain to develop and settle more than a million acres of land on the south bank of the Ohio River (and which would doubtless span that stream if not impeded), the marquis organized an expedition whose primary purpose was to reassert, with the aid of soldiers, engineers, and surveyors, the precise boundaries of that same area which was deemed by treaty and tradition to be the domain of New France. Each major frontier division point was commemorated by the burial of a leaden plaque whose wording was clear enough:

> In the year 1749, during the reign of Louis XV, we . . . sent . . . for the restoration of tranquillity in some villages of these districts, have buried this plaque at ———, this ——— July [place and date were to be filled in appropriately by the armorer of the expedition], near the Ohio river, . . . as a monument of the renewal of possession which we have taken of the said river Ohio and of all those [rivers] that fall therein, and of all lands on both sides as far as the sources of the said rivers, as enjoyed by the preceding Kings of France and by treaties, especially by those of Riswick [sic], of Utrecht, and of Aix-la-Chapelle.

Beauharnais's death in June didn't prevent the little company from leaving Niagara in the middle of the following month, after it had received the solemn benediction of priests and the ardent praise of a group of Seneca sachems gathered at the spillway at the behest of the Joncaire brothers—and after having taken part in a ceremonial orgy of cannon fire and a two-day drunk that much exasperated the expedition's commander.

A second and novel aspect of Beauharnais's scheme to Frenchify the Ohio valley and, indeed, all areas not already securely attached to Quebec, also got under way that summer. A small convoy of canoes and bateaux moved up the Saint Lawrence from Lachine, led by a middle-aged Sulpician monk, Father François Picquet. This missionary had already passed fourteen years in New France, most of them among the Algonquins. He had learned the nuances of many eastern red-man dialects and the niceties of their social customs. With a modest band of Algonquin converts and a few habitant zealots, Father Picquet constructed on the banks of the Saint Lawrence, near modern Ogdensburg, a mission that he called La Présentation.

To the unwary, this new mission seemed merely another enclave for the seclusion of natives converted to the Catholic religion—like the Jesuit reservation at Caughnawaga. But the British soon discovered that this village, which they and the Iroquois named Oswegatchie, had a quite different objective. For Picquet was no Jesuit. As a matter of fact, he was unlike any other cleric yet seen in the New World. He was as close to being a nineteenth-century camp-meeting revivalist as any Catholic since the twelfth-century years when Saint Bernard was preaching the Second Crusade, or perhaps a bit later on, when Savonarola was condemning vice in Florence.

Although Father Picquet's avowed purpose, to win souls for Christ and thereby to save them from perdition, was orthodox enough, his methods were certainly not, and their efficacy was staggering. With a small group of faithful followers, he arrived at the Seneca village, near the decaying remains of the old Magazin Royal, in the summer of 1751. There he regaled the braves and sachems, gathered for trade and intoxication, with the chanting of canticles of his own composition, with sermons which evoked the gospel in a vigorous and uniquely personal fashion that had an electrifying effect on his listeners. Thirty-nine warriors found their way to Picquet's Christ during that visit. They quit their sinful habits and their pagan villages and made their way to La Présentation.

By the end of the following year, Father Picquet had won no fewer than four hundred Iroquois families to the Catholic religion, as he had described it for them. According to some estimates, the consequence in much less spiritual terms was a reduction of the Six Nations' fighting strength by as much as one-third—a loss exclusively to the British, for Picquet would have been the last to prevent his new sheep from defending the culture and faith of New France. There were said to be as many Mohawks, moreover, at the Jesuit Indian reservation of Caughnawaga as there were at Canajoharie, the principal Mohawk settlement. The celebrated "Soldiers of Christ" can scarcely be said to have been inert during this epoch either.

In 1750, Daniel Joncaire was named master of the Niagara portage. His first important act was to establish a permanent fort on the site of the temporary one that had been constructed upriver of the falls in 1745. Because it was not so imposing an edifice as the formidable stone compound of the House of Peace, it was called Little Fort Niagara. The blockhouse, barracks, and a carriage house were completed in 1751. During the eight years that ensued, a small village grew up in the shadows of these palisaded fortifications. On this same bank, just where Lake Erie drains into the Niagara River, Joncaire directed habitants and Seneca women to plant vegetables and fruit bushes and orchards on either side of a broad brook which he called *"La Rivière aux Chevaux,"* Horse River. After 1760, the newly installed British occupants of the Niagara spillway translated Horse River to Buffalo Creek—for reasons that remain an insignificant mystery. It was here that the hamlet of Buffalo began to manifest itself at the end of the French and Indian Wars—which were at hand.

Peace between the French and British had in theory been restored by the Treaty of Aix-la-Chapelle, but there remained an abundance of local enmities in North America, many of them inspired by the French practice of arresting British traders whom they found "poaching" in the Ohio valley. Numbers of these captives were brought to Niagara where they were imprisoned, often for several years, in the dank and extremely uncomfortable bowels of the House of Peace. Governor George Clinton protested this maltreatment of his subjects, claiming that they had been engaged in "lawful" trade. Little shrift was accorded his frequent complaints.

Daniel Joncaire didn't limit his activity to the operation of the Niagara portage. Ange, Marquis du Quesne (Duquesne), became governor of New France in 1751. He instructed the master of Niagara's passageway to do everything necessary to protect the route from possible attack—for it was by then the single indispensable link between old New France and new New France—the Ohio valley. Joncaire believed that only an

attack mounted under the command of William Johnson, because he was the cynosure of the Mohawks, could seriously
jeopardize the Niagara. It was, Joncaire reasoned logically
enough, cheaper to get rid of Johnson than to try to protect the
spillway against him. He therefore placed a bounty of £1,000
on the celebrated squaw man's head—or, rather, on his scalp.
It was an immense price. Indians friendly to Johnson alerted
him to the threat of that winter, but the bold colonial Irishman
wasn't at all intimidated. There appears to have been no
attempt on his person, bounty or not.

Duquesne also ordered his officers to strengthen existing
strong points on the Ohio and to add as many more as were
required to ensure the valley's permanent security against
possible British and/or Indian assault. In the spring of 1753,
large vessels commenced the transportation of important quantities of men and material from Fort Frontenac to Niagara.
They were destined for the building of stockades and trading
posts along the entire route west and south to the Ohio. A
message from the Iroquois Grand Council at Onondaga Hill
informed William Johnson that "an army of twenty thousand
Frenchmen and hordes of Caughnawagas [as domesticated
Indians of the Jesuit colony were scornfully called by their
brother heathens], Ottawas, Lakes, and Miamis are invading
the Ohio." The true numbers were more like two thousand, of
whom perhaps two hundred were French regulars, the rest
being habitants and converted red men.

The logistical problems posed by the need to transport and
store the masses of supplies were the preoccupation at Niagara
of Commandant Jean Péan, a merchant from Quebec, who had
as his correspondent in the New France capital one François
Bigot, local representative of the French Ministry of Finance.
Bigot had selected Péan for the task of supervising the operations at Niagara in order that Péan's wife might become Bigot's
mistress. Though it seemed reason enough, an affection for the
same woman wasn't all the two men had in common. They had
agreed to mulct the state of large sums by a mixture of tricky

bookkeeping and an ill-concealed traffic in goods that were the property of New France.

Bigot and Péan conducted their criminal enterprise with so blatant a disregard for the possibility of detection that much of the merchandise which *they* had stolen originally was subsequently stolen from them. Péan's letters to his master at Quebec are riddled with scandalized complaints about the untrustworthiness of man. The cargo handlers were singled out for Péan's most pious remonstrances. In spite of his lack of personal probity, Péan had the distinction of being the first official of New France to bring some intelligent planning ideas to the transshipment of goods over the Niagara portage. The obligation was thrust upon him by the sheer volume of material involved.

In the summer of 1753, he was ordered to transport more than twelve thousand parcels, each of which weighed about eighty pounds, up over the escarpment to the portage head above Goat Island. The task was managed with exemplary efficiency. However, the government at Versailles didn't believe that this achievement offset the crimes of which he and Bigot (and, it was long believed, Daniel Joncaire as portage master) were palpably guilty. Made prisoners by the British during the war that followed, the three men were exchanged for captives of the French and returned to Paris, where they had to stand trial for their offenses, real or merely alleged.

In the meantime, William Johnson decided that he had better determine the authenticity of the reports about Niagara activities that he had been receiving in impressive volume. Four Mohawk braves volunteered to enlist as porters at the spillway. They eventually returned to Warrensburg with somewhat less exaggerated estimates of the numbers of men and the quantities of supplies being moved westward. But even the true figures were so serious that Johnson, in the autumn of 1753, alerted Governor Clinton to the need for the refurbishing and reinforcement of Fort Oswego, an outpost which was, he told the governor, in a condition of nearly total desuetude.

Clinton passed on a summary of the Johnson memorandum to Governor Dinwiddie of Virginia, who immediately mobilized a company of militiamen under the joint command of frontiersman Christopher Gist and a young Virginia landowner, George Washington, to whom he gave a commission of colonel. This force was to proceed westward over the Appalachian Trail to confront the French soldiery of Captain Paul la Malgue, Sieur de Marin. The mission, which culminated in the skirmish of Fort Necessity, was a fiasco.

As soon as he had lodged his report with Governor Clinton, Johnson and his Mohawk friend King Hendrick hastened to Onondaga Hill to address a meeting of the Six Nations' Grand Council. The Irishman deplored the fact that there were "weeds growing in the path" between the British and the Indians. What he specifically requested was a reply to the question that was in the front of every knowledgeable Briton's mind: Was the French fortification of the Ohio valley undertaken with the consent of the Iroquois or not?

The sachems' answer, which took them two full days to formulate, is the first and one of the most heartrending statements ever uttered of the plight in which the American red man found himself:

> We do not know what you Christians—English and French—intend. We are so hemmed in by both that we have hardly a hunting place left. In a little while, if we find a bear in a tree, there will immediately appear an owner of the land to challenge the property, and hinder us from killing it, which is our livelihood. We are so perplexed between both [English and French] that we hardly know what to say or think.

William Johnson lost no time in relaying this moving response to Governor George Clinton. There is, alas, no evidence to suggest that either Clinton or Johnson was even mildly shamed by its content. North America was about to become, for the first time, a major issue in a war between two great

European powers. This war had nothing to do with the American Indians, though ultimately it would be they who paid by far the highest price for its outcome.

The peoples who had inhabited this enormous continent in comparative tranquility for thousands of years had become, in little more than two centuries, not merely superfluous; they were a serious encumbrance. They were in the white man's way.

8

NIAGARA
Battleground,
Phase Two

At a meeting of Britain's American colonial administrators in June of 1754, Benjamin Franklin, Postmaster General, made the novel and, in the view of some, heretical, suggestion that the white man might do worse than to emulate the political organization of the Iroquois tribes:

> . . . It would be a strange thing if Six Nations of ignorant savages should be capable of forming a scheme for union, and be able to execute it in such a manner that it has subsisted ages and appears indissoluble; and yet that a like union should be impractical for ten or twelve English colonies.

It *was* a strange thing. To Franklin's urgent plea there was an immediate and surprisingly favorable reaction among the colonial delegates. They requested parliamentary authority to establish in their part of the New World a government that would operate along the loosely federal lines adopted centuries before by the Six Nations—at the time when there had been only five of them. The specific proposal set before the English

was not unlike the Articles of Confederation which were subsequently enacted by the colonies that rose in rebellion more
than two decades later.

This interesting petition, however, lacked the support of the
most important members of the American colonial economic
structure—the landowners, the new aristocrats. And the British
themselves, however much they might wish for a more cohesive
and more coherent administration of their colonies in North
America, could see no plausible reason to invest so much administrative power in their subjects over the sea, beyond their
immediate, day-to-day control.

As a result of this rejection by Westminster, the ball was
back in the colonial court—or, to put it more exactly, in the
courts of the individual colonies; for they would each still
have to act separately, however common their collective goal.
When word was received at the end of June 1754 that Christopher Gist and George Washington had been thoroughly
thrashed by the French and Indians at Fort Necessity, the New
York assembly responded with a very reluctant agreement to
undertake the equipment of two militia companies to reinforce
Fort Oswego's pathetically dwindled garrison. Not even the
delegates who had enacted this piece of legislation believed
the gesture to be adequate. Yet the threat wasn't considered
sufficiently imminent to warrant any sterner measure.

The British at Westminister delighted the French at Versailles by engaging in dilatory diplomacy, lodging protests with
Louis XV against alleged violations of the treaties of Utrecht
and Aix-la-Chapelle. Thus did they give their enemies in the
New World time to transport two seasoned regiments, from
Guyenne and Béarn, to Montreal. Battalions of these units could
be dispersed to fill many gaps in the French defenses—including Forts Frontenac and Niagara.

British military strategy was in the puffy hands of George
II's third son, the Duke of Cumberland. He was the hero of
the 1745 Battle of Culloden in the Scottish Highlands, that
bloody encounter which had terminated the young pretension

of Bonnie Prince Charlie Stuart to the British throne. Because of his dubious triumph at Culloden, the English had taken to calling him "Sweet William." But the Scots (and the Irish) called him "Stinking Billy." Cumberland proposed a countermeasure that paralleled the movements of the French—the dispatch of two trained regiments under the command of Colonel (soon Major General) Edward Braddock. These troops were to conduct an expedition to wrest control of the Ohio valley from France, once and for all.

In Cumberland's most ill-informed imagination, this mission was to consist more of a ceremonial showing of the flag than a serious military campaign. He expected that Braddock would be confronted by little or no worthy opposition, certainly not from the French; the "savages" might prove ferociously brave, but they hadn't the white man's know-how. The British want of even approximately accurate topographical data prompted them to order Braddock to journey from his landing point in Virginia to Fort Duquesne (where the Monongahela and Allegheny rivers converge to form the Ohio—modern Pittsburgh). His instructions were to reduce that garrison at once, and then to proceed northeastward, over the Chautauqua portages to capture Fort Niagara—the House of Peace. After this second engagement (deemed an even more trifling matter than the first), Braddock would follow the north shore of Lake Ontario, subduing resistance at the forts of Toronto and Frontenac as he marched. With these easy victories behind him, he would cross the headwaters of the Saint Lawrence, pick up the Mohawk waterway at Fort Stanwyx (Rome, New York), and arrive at Albany. There, Governor Clinton would lay on for him and his officers an appropriate celebration. Nothing, the Duke of Cumberland explained to him, could be simpler.

Clinton sent William Johnson to Williamsburg, Virginia, to greet General Braddock on his landing, and to learn from him what role New York was to play in this madcap military adventure. The foppish Britisher, a regular officer of the posh

Coldstream Guards, must have been somewhat bemused by the appearance before him of the Irish giant, for whom he was carrying very special orders.

Johnson had been designated by George II's ministers to be royal agent to all the red tribes of the northern colonies. He was further commissioned to lead an expedition against the newly constructed French Fort Frederic, on Lake Champlain. When this pioneer squaw man protested that he was better prepared to bring down Fort Niagara, the general replied that this particular aspect of the campaign was thought to be of too great a significance to be entrusted to an untried commander. But he did condescend to explain to Johnson his plan to bring down the fort at the mouth of the Niagara. His strategy was a replica of the two earlier and unsuccessful plans conceived by Le Febvre and Denonville against the Senecas in the previous century. Braddock's troops would approach the House of Peace from the Lake Erie end. Forces led by Governor William Shirley of Massachusetts would converge on it from Fort Oswego—by water (for the land approaches were impassable to artillery and wagons).

Johnson dared to venture the opinion that, while he was unable to fault the thinking that underlay the proposed tactics, he felt that Braddock's estimate of the time and travail involved in his march from Virginia to Fort Duquesne and thence to Niagara was hopelessly optimistic. The Englishman, armed with the intelligence offered him by the redoubtable Cumberland, was disdainful. He was persuaded that it would require no more than three days to reduce the French bastion at Fort Duquesne, and he turned a deaf ear to Johnson's exclamations of astonished alarm.

The French, meanwhile, were not comporting themselves with much greater rationality than their enemies were demonstrating. Appreciating that any British attack could not be undertaken before the spring of 1755, they appeared in no special hurry to prepare their defenses anywhere against it. Duquesne himself, pleading ill health, begged to be replaced as governor of New France. His successor was the first native of North America to hold this high post Pierre Vaudreuil-Cavagnal, a son of the Baron de Longueuil, whilom lieutenant-governor.

Named at the same time to be commander of all French forces in the New World was the German Baron Ludwig August von Dieskau, considered by Louis XV's colonial administrators at Versailles to be more than a match for Braddock. By the early summer of 1755, the French were so well informed of British plans and movements that they saw no reason to man Fort Niagara with a more imposing garrison than a single officer and an incompetent handful of *habitants,* most of them adolescents.

Johnson repeatedly implored Braddock's aides for permission to mount an immediate assault against the crucial House of Peace. He asserted (rightly, no doubt) that two companies of reliable foot soldiers and a couple of working fieldpieces could have "severed New France at the throat." The French army in the Ohio valley, he correctly estimated, would be cut off without supplies or means of easy retreat. It was not, however, in General Braddock's nature to give elastic interpretation to the orders of his superiors in London. An official command was incontestably official. He would follow it to the letter.

Unfortunately for the British cause, Governor Shirley of Massachusetts wouldn't do even that much. First of all a self-styled aristocrat, second a politician, and last (and certainly least) a soldier, he was at Albany in the middle of July arguing with Governor Clinton and William Johnson about overall strategy and military policy. He complained that he hadn't enough men or arms to perform the task assigned to him—the capture of Niagara. Iroquois spies, most of them Christianized squaws from La Présentation, infiltrated the British garrison at Fort Oswego; they drank with the British troops and found other ways of diverting them, then reported to von Dieskau that accounts of a great fleet under construction were not to be credited. No more than four vessels were in process, none of which would be in commission before the beginning of autumn.

Von Dieskau's posture was to be mainly defensive. He was to hold French gains, particularly in the Ohio valley. Nevertheless, he felt it would be helpful to menace the enemy where he least expected it. He would lead a force down Lakes Champlain and George with the object of threatening (or at least seeming to threaten) Albany. If the British under Braddock's command made an unexpectedly early appearance on the western approaches to Niagara, the French could make a forced march across the Adirondacks, capture Fort Oswego from the rear, and ambush the advancing Braddock at will.

The French cherished no illusions at all that the House of Peace was impregnable. At the end of July, Governor Vaudreuil-Cavagnal wrote to Versailles: "In regard to Niagara, it is certain that, should the English attack it, it is theirs. I am informed that the fort is so dilapidated, that it is impossible to put a peg in it without causing it to crumble. Stanchions have been obliged to be set up against [its walls] to support it. Its garrison consists of thirty men without any muskets. The Sieur de Villiers has been detached with about twenty men to form an observation post there."

From the French point of view, the position of Fort Niagara to the contrary notwithstanding wasn't all bad. With more than a little assistance from the Indians, their army in the Ohio valley was giving Braddock a very nasty time of it. Though the news that the Sieur de Villiers received when he arrived at the House of Peace was sketchy, he could readily deduce from the softened attitude of the Senecas whom he met there that, for the time being, the French need not be unduly apprehensive. Not long after he reached the fort, sachems from the Oneidas and Cayugas arrived to present portage-master Daniel Joncaire with wampum belts to signify their eternal friendship for Louis XV. This happy augury was reaffirmed when Philippe Joncaire was summoned to a meeting of the Iroquois Grand Council at Onondaga Hill in October 1755 for the purpose of discussing a general peace between them and the French. Of the six nations, only the Mohawks had elected to side with the British—and they with some skepticism. Their fealty was surely not to George II, but to William Johnson.

The reason why so great a proportion of the Iroquois swore fidelity to France was that they had such confidence in the Joncaire brothers, a feeling surely reinforced by recent French successes on the field of battle—the most signal being the hideous little defeat handed to Braddock at Fort Duquesne. But the fate of the French had not been uniformly fortunate. Von Dieskau's procession toward Albany had been interrupted most rudely by William Johnson on September 9—an encounter that cost the life of that squaw man's greatest Mohawk friend, King Hendrick. It resulted, too, however, in the capture of Von Dieskau and the rout of the French and their mixed group of red-man allies.

The remnants of Braddock's army straggled back over the mountains to New Jersey, and immediately prepared themselves to voyage up the Hudson to secure Albany against the threat of further assault from the French. But that was no longer the name of the game. With Braddock's troops no more a menace to Fort Niagara, at least from the Lake Erie approaches, the masters of New France had only to consider the presence of Governor Shirley's garrison at Fort Oswego. Shirley was merely dithering. With three sound regiments at his disposal there, with supplies that were certainly adequate, if not lavish, and with an armed brig, an armable sloop, and more than two hundred whaleboats, his orders were to ferry six hundred men to Niagara.

As Vaudreuil-Cavagnal had reported to the mother country barely two months earlier, the fort and the portage were his virtually for the asking. Shirley was dissuaded from launching this little adventure, apparently by his own timorousness. The whores from La Présentation spread half-truths about a vast number of newly arrived French troops stationed at Fort Frontenac which would soon, they alleged, reinforce Fort Niagara. They took malicious delight in recounting the horrors

that had followed the defeat of the British at Fort Duquesne—
which were real enough.

William Shirley gathered his officers together on September
27 and for three hours subjected them to a rambling and
scarcely coherent lecture on the folly of attempting to subdue
the strongly protected House of Peace in the autumn. The lake
was particularly dangerous at this season, he said, and he had
it on indisputable authority that the fort was now teeming
with fresh and seasoned troops and a great new supply of
arms.

The governor plainly believed what he chose to believe.
He seems to have submitted the final decision to a vote of
his subordinates. It isn't really very surprising to learn that
the officers supported him in his apprehensions. No one likes
to fight under the command of a general who doesn't care to
lead. Shirley then designated a colonel to take command of
Fort Oswego while he was away at Albany trying to explain
to Governor Clinton and General Braddock what must have
seemed to them inexplicable. Had he taken as seriously as he
took the rumors of the Présentation women the accurate intelligence furnished him by Johnson's Mohawk informants, he
could have won a brilliant victory at little if any cost in life.
For practical purposes, he would have ended the war in the
west.

Barely a week after Shirley's ignominious departure from
Fort Oswego, three French vessels set out from Fort Frontenac,
bound for the House of Peace. They carried five companies
of the Guyenne Regiment, under the command of Captain
François Pouchot. Their mission was to render the Niagara
fort defensible, and high time, too.

These were Pouchot's first observations on arriving at his
new post:

> It was at once necessary to build house for these troops in
> the Canadian manner, that is, huts made of round logs of
> oak notched into each other at the corners. In this wooded
> country houses of the kind are quickly constructed. They

have a chimney in the middle, some windows and a plank roof. The chimney is made by four poles placed in the form of a truncated pyramid, open from the bottom to a height of three feet on the four sides, above which is a basketwork plastered with mud. They take rushes, marsh grass or straw, which they roll in diluted clay and drive in between horizontal logs from top to bottom, and they plaster the whole.

Pouchot accomplished prodigies during the harsh Great Lakes winter. First he saw to the housing of his men, and then he reinforced the fort that was crucial to the entire French position in the Ohio valley. All the fine trees that adorned the landward side of the House of Peace were cut down within a radius of about five hundred yards. The outer walls of the palisades were replaced by thick new oaken posts. He saw to the digging of a deep moat just beyond this outermost fortification, giving a curious medieval effect to the setting of a frontier fortress.

While Pouchot was enjoying complete impunity from harassment as he did his superlative best to make the House of Peace siegeworthy, the British and Americans at Fort Oswego had no such good fortune. Constantly, during this same period of winter and spring, the fort was subjected to attack. Forage parties were ambushed by French and Indian raiders who seemed never to sleep. However, despite these annoyances, the defenders of Fort Oswego also accomplished much to render their post more secure.

Their supply difficulties were enormous. Colonel John Bradstreet reported to William Johnson in July 1756 that he and a group of boatmen, returning from a journey to Fort Oswego, had been savaged by French scouts and their Seneca friends at the Oneida-Woods Creek portage. Fort Oswego, the colonel had no doubt, would soon be more directly menaced. Bradstreet passed this same intelligence on to the new British commander Lord Loudoun, who had just arrived from London to assume responsibility for the ragtag army in what was at last an officially declared war against the French—in Europe as well as in the New World. After nearly a month of ponderous consideration, Loudoun ordered Colonel Daniel Webb to organize a force to relieve Fort Oswego. Webb appeared in no great hurry to act; indeed, he seemed to be patterning his conduct on that of Governor William Shirley the previous autumn.

By now there was a new French commander in chief as well, Louis Joseph, Marquis de Montcalm. He had reached Quebec in July 1756. Unlike the phlegmatic Loudoun and the reluctant Webb, Montcalm lost no time in making his presence felt and his intentions clear to his subordinates. On August 2, the French and their Indian allies were blockading the harbor of Fort Oswego; they sank a pair of old Frontenac schooners in the channel. The complete encirclement of the fort wasn't achieved for another week. On August 16, with no relief in sight and no way of knowing when it might arrive, approximately seventeen hundred besieged soldiers and traders and journeymen at Fort Oswego surrendered, with no great struggle, to a force which was deploying against them many of the cannons captured the year before from the feckless Braddock at Fort Duquesne. The French made off with enough supplies and arms to maintain both Fort Frontenac and the House of Peace for the coming autumn and winter.

The public in America's British colonies was scandalized by the apparent lack of resistance offered in defense of Fort Oswego—an impression that was shared by the local red men and one that had a most deleterious effect on their inclination to cooperate with the British. Even more devasting to the prestige of the British, so far as the Indians were concerned, was Montcalm's ingenious gesture of conciliation, a statement that he ordered Daniel Joncaire to pass on to the Iroquois who were now occupying Fort Oswego: "We do not invade your territory like the English. We give this [land] back to you. Remain quiet on your mats and do not meddle with anything."

The Grand Council at Onondaga Hill took ardent heed of the French general's advice and even more gratified note of

his matching deeds. Their conviction that neutrality was the
wisest policy was much encouraged by a report of the conduct
of Colonel Daniel Webb's troops, bound to relieve Fort
Oswego, when they learned the bastion had already surrendered to the French. They were at the Woods Creek portage, still several days' journey from the fort which Webb's
dalliance had helped enormously to doom. They burned their
supplies on the spot, and in the ensuing retreat toward Albany, they destroyed every strongpoint along the Mohawk
waterway as far east as Canajoharie. Thus, to calamity had
been added utter disgrace.

The defeat at Fort Oswego, coupled with the one of the
previous year at Fort Duquesne and the powerful reinforcement of the Niagara garrison added many theretofore neutral,
if minor, Indian tribes to the ranks of New France's active
allies. All of them were more than willing to plunder British-
American villages and hamlets in Pennsylvania and as far east
in New York as the Hudson valley.

The fighting season of 1757 passed without the occurrence
of a significant pitched battle. So confident were the French of
their safety now that the engineer Pouchot was replaced at
Niagara by Captain Jean Vassan, an artillery officer. Discipline
at the House of Peace became a lot less spartan. The wives of
officers at the post were allowed to join their husbands. Prosti-
tutes, mainly from Caughnawaga and La Présentation, were
permitted to take up residence at Niagara. The fort took on
the appearance of a frontier post in Metropolitan France—
Metz, perhaps, or Sedan. To the degree that garrison life can
ever be characterized as merry in time of war, Fort Niagara
was not an unpleasant assignment in this brief period. The
presence of women was, in itself, a source of happiness as well
as pleasure. One likes to picture decorative linen drying on
lines festooned along the ramparts of the House of Peace, of
dances, of carousing, of the rough joys of the soldiery far from
home. Women were, because of their comparative rarity, trebly
welcome.

The impression of security at Niagara was illusory. For

while the British were doing little to dislodge the French from their positions on the American mainland, at sea they were occasioning very important economic and military disruption by their effective blockade of the trade routes with France, especially of the mouth of the Saint Lawrence. Supplies were everywhere running short. To make matters more trying, the spring of 1758 was marked by terrible weather, making prospects poor for the harvest. There was a tremendous inflation in the prices of the few commodities that *were* available.

More unfortunate from the standpoint of the unquenchably thirsty red man, it seemed to take much more of the increasingly costly cognac to produce the same glow of euphoria which made minor problems—like that of survival—appear of little importance. The French were, of course, diluting their brandy with larger amounts of water than before, and were exchanging the weaker booze and other lesser necessities for larger numbers of beaver pelts.

There was yet another source of unrest, this one peculiar to Niagara. The Senecas who carried goods back and forth over the portage route objected to the increased employment of horsepower and, especially, to the introduction of carts as a means of conveyance above and below Crawl on All Fours. "It robs us of the living we were promised forever here," they protested. One more broken contract here or there couldn't matter less to the white man, French or British. The continent was acquired by the process of reneging on agreements they had signed in all solemnity, whenever it suited them. The signs of malaise at Niagara in 1758 were treated with the same complacency the French now felt about the impregnability of the reinforced military installations from Frontenac to the Ohio valley.

"The earth," wrote Carl Sandburg, "is strewn with the burst bladders of the puffed up." The French balloon was rudely punctured at the end of August 1758 when a raiding party of about twenty-five-hundred men under the leadership of Colonel John Bradstreet attacked Fort Frontenac. They captured its treasure of supplies for Niagara and the Ohio forts and withdrew, without the loss of a single life.

The effect on the *vie douce* at the House of Peace was nearly cataclysmic, for there remained in the storehouses less than a month's rations for the fort's own garrison, and from the bases at Detroit and in the Ohio valley came constant requests for materiel and manpower to help withstand an anticipated winter campaign to be mounted by the British. Captain Vassan sent all the women packing. He reduced the size of his own garrison to forty men, dispatching the remainder to the west. The picture was darkened even further by his certainty that the Senecas, previously so loyal, would be disinclined to aid the French when the moment of the British assault against Fort Niagara arrived. He recognized at last that this attack would come sooner rather than later.

Some of the Seneca defection would be attributed to the inflation, some to the ease with which the British had overcome French resistance at Fort Frontenac. Whereas in the spring of 1758, prior to the Frontenac disaster, the Mohawks had been questioning William Johnson's good faith and wisdom, by the early months of the ensuing year they were hastening to assure him of their deathless devotion to the king at Westminster. As went the Mohawks, so by swift steps went most of the other tribes of the Six Nations. This seemed the propitious moment to change camps. The British blockade, which cut off supplies of cognac, was as decisive an element in this decision as the inflation and the recent French reverses. The British had copious quantities of spirits which they were eager to barter for Iroquois promises of loyalty or—at the very least—Iroquois promises of neutrality.

At the end of March 1759, Captain François Pouchot returned to take command of the House of Peace. He was accompanied by four hundred and fifty men, a third of them French, the rest untrained habitant militiamen. When that brave and industrious officer took leave of the Marquis de Montcalm, he is purported to have observed prophetically,

"It appears . . . that we shall never meet again—unless it be on a British prison ship." As matters proved for Montcalm, Pouchot's oracle was exact, but optimistic. The French general would be dead before the end of summer.

William Johnson, now a baronet as well as a colonel, convened as many of the Six Nations' sachems as would heed his summons to a council meeting at the Mohawk village of Canajoharie. Sir William, stripped of his European habit, began a war dance on the afternoon of April 20 that continued through the night. Before it ended, he was joined in this bizarre ballet by all the chiefs in attendance. The day after this tribal pep rally, he received from the chiefs the assurance that "it is the earnest and unanimous request of all the Nations present that you march as speedily as you can with an army against the Niagara, which is in the country of the Senecas, and which they now give up, to be destroyed or taken by you. The sooner this thing is done the better." Johnson had asked for no more. Just how many of the Senecas were present is not disclosed. Yet it is of the greatest importance to know, for what they allegedly then gave up to the British they were never to recover.

The most recent of British commanders, who seemed to change with the spring, was General Jeffrey Amherst—who would later endear himself to the rebellious Americans of 1776 by his refusal to participate in George III's campaign to put down the Yankees' revolt. Amherst did not, however, cherish at this time a very high regard for the colonial forces and was even more scornful of the Iroquois recruits whom Johnson was so eager to lead into battle. He found them "a pack of lazy, rum-drinking people, and little good." On the basis of their previous record of warfare against the French, the colonials as a populace could not have made a very happy impression on the general, who formed a most imperfect opinion of the entire force of men who were to attack Niagara— a contingent to be led by General Prideaux. In addition to its assembly of disillusioned Indians, it consisted of about twenty-five-hundred whites, perhaps a thousand of them British troops of the line, the remainder American militiamen who were not much better trained than their habitant counterparts.

Of future celebrities in the force there was a good smattering. Two of Sir William Johnson's sons participated, John (who was to succeed to his father's title) and Joseph Brant, who would illegally sell the Iroquois birthright in the Mohawk valley. There were two scions of the Clinton family, one Butler, and Captain Charles Lee—a British officer who had served with the ill-starred Braddock expedition in 1755 and whose incompetence was exceeded only by his ambition and his preening vanity, talents all that were to be more fully exploited when he became an American general during the Revolution.

A force of thirteen hundred men, under the Swiss colonel Friedrich Haldimand, was to remain behind at Fort Oswego. Johnson's ranks of Indian warriors were augmented to the number of eight hundred by the arrival of additional volunteers who desired to be counted on the right side of the war when the smoke of battle had cleared. The plan of attack against the House of Peace hinged in some measure on the element of surprise. With Seneca scouts still loyal to the brothers Joncaire on the prowl everywhere in the vicinity of Fort Oswego, the hope of secrecy seemed to depend more on good fortune than on the routine security procedures followed by Johnson's natives. And for once, good fortune smiled on the British rather than on the French cause. The forces voyaged by whaleboat along the south shore of Lake Ontario. Bad weather prevented two well-armed French vessels from spotting the long line of craft that proceeded slowly westward in the first days of July 1759.

Yet Pouchot was not to be taken completely unaware. Since late in June, when he had received reports of a strong British buildup at Forst Oswego, he had dispatched the schooner *Outaouaise* along the Lake Ontario coast on a scouting mission. Certain that an attack was imminent, he had also sent

messengers down the Ohio valley and to Fort Frontenac re-
questing reinforcements. When *Outaouaise* returned to the
quayside of the House of Peace, her master assured the post
commander that there had been no trace of a hostile expeditionary force on the lake. It is difficult to comprehend how his
lookouts, even taking into account the most atrocious weather
conditions, could have missed so important a flotilla of whaleboats—the more so since the craft were traveling, incredibly
enough, in broad daylight. But they missed every evidence of
Prideaux's armada.

On the evening of July 6, the Anglo-American-Indian party
beached at the one point on the south shore of Lake Ontario
near Niagara's mouth that was not within ready scanning
range of the watchtowers of the House of Peace—Four Mile
Creek. By dawn of the next day, a detachment of Prideaux's
men had crossed overland to a spot on the Niagara River about
two miles upstream from the fort, having manhandled a
dozen whaleboats and the disassembled cannons of the heaviest
variety manageable in the field in that epoch. This five-mile
journey had been accomplished in darkness over a footpath
that approached the river through a ravine (incongruously
called *La Belle Famille*) which ended at a narrow stretch of
gravel beach. Only at daybreak of the seventh was this little
company first sighted by the French. The hardy British and
American soldiers launched the twelve whaleboats and ferried
the cumbersome artillery pieces to the west bank of the
Niagara.

The success of this phase of the plan was of critical importance to the entire operation, for these cannons, once they
were assembled on the opposite shore, would be capable of
subjecting the House of Peace to heavy frontal fire. The safe
crossing of the river was, however, only the first essential of
this scheme. Captain Pouchot knew that he had at least a week
to dislodge the three gun emplacements on the west bank, for
it would require that length of time to construct the founda-
tions and protective earthworks for the cannons and to put

them together and make them operative. For a variety of insufficient reasons, he failed in this enterprise, and this failure cost him all hope of surviving the siege.

The Joncaire brothers, in charge of the garrison at Little Fort Niagara above the falls, were ordered to abandon that position. On their departure, they were to destroy everything that couldn't easily be brought down the portage road to the House of Peace. This evacuation was completed by July 10. The horses and cattle that were stranded above the falls were not slaughtered by the departing French. They were immediately set upon by Senecas, hitherto allies of the Joncaires, and marketed at exorbitant prices to Prideaux's troops who had been existing for more than a week on a regimen of pork and beans. This was the only luxury they were offered before the siege was successfully terminated.

In addition to the establishment of the artillery positions on the west bank of the river, Prideaux depended on Haldimand's force of men and ships at Fort Oswego to prevent any French relief expedition from reaching the House of Peace from the Lake Ontario end of the Niagara. He made the further assumption, which he thought he had reason to consider reliable, that no effective and timely aid for Pouchot should be anticipated from France's forts at Detroit and the Ohio valley. He therefore believed that he had plenty of time to dig himself in, to create a series of breastworks for other cannons on the east bank whose main purpose would be to prevent the defenders from concentrating their more powerful guns on a single British artillery emplacement.

On July 16, ten days after the landing at Four Mile Creek, a British officer wrote laconically in his journal, "The garrison and fort are much stronger than we expected." He recorded that the French had already fired about six thousand rounds of cannon shot and yet had occasioned fewer than twenty-five casualties to the attackers. More happily still could Prideaux note that *his* forces were constantly gaining in numbers. Johnson now had nine hundred Indians under his command. Time, the general plainly thought, was completely his ally.

The most inexplicable aspect of these early days of the siege, aside from Pouchot's incapacity to blast the British off their little beachhead on the western shore, was the apparent indifference of the two French schooners, cruising rather pointlessly back and forth in the vicinity of the Niagara's broad mouth, to the British military traffic constantly plying the waters between Four Mile Creek and Fort Oswego. Dispatches from Prideaux and Haldimand passed in both directions without even an attempt at interception. The Swiss officer had, in the meantime, done as he was supposed to do. A powerful French relief convoy had been turned back toward Fort Frontenac with only minor casualties accruing to the British attackers.

With his siege lines set, and certain that no reinforcements for the French could be rationally expected, General Prideaux observed the chivalric custom. He sent a young officer, under a white flag, to solicit Captain Pouchot's surrender. The Frenchman, perfectly conscious of the medieval precedents, responded with exquisitely traditional courtesy (one of the hallmarks of the lunatic military consciousness) that although he appreciated the general's gesture, he wanted an opportunity to gain his enemy's respect before considering terms of capitulation.

Daniel Joncaire, that creature of the vast North American wilderness, had learned nothing from his father about this sort of behavior; he thought such *politesse* on the part of Pouchot mere recklessness. He was certain, moreover, that relief *would* arrive from one end of the river or the other. He sent an elderly Seneca sachem, who also carried the flag of truce, to the encampment of Sir William Johnson's Indians. The expendable emissary proposed a parley, during which time neither side would open fire. Since the old man mentioned no prohibition against further British entrenchment, Prideaux agreed to talks, and saw to it that his troops improved their positions while they went on. The attackers moved the advanced lines ever closer to the outer works of the House of Peace.

The conference continued bootlessly for two days. Joncaire's aged ambassador reported to Captain Pouchot that no argument would deter Johnson's Iroquois because they had been promised all enemy scalps and the opportunity to plunder the House of Peace after its capture. Still persuaded that relief would arrive in time, Joncaire favored a resumption of the conversations. For different reasons, so did Sir William Johnson. Pouchot, however, believed that on balance, time was at this juncture running against him—since the cease-fire was permitting the British to fortify their lines with impunity. Aid might *not* come, or might not come soon enough—in which event the parleys would have worked against the French interest. Therefore, further talks were out of the question. The siege at last began in earnest.

The cannons installed on the west bank opened fire for the first time on July 17, ten days after they had been transported across the river. Their hot shot of that morning inflicted grave damage to the quay, to the outer palisades, and to the roof of the House of Peace (beneath which, of course, were the big guns that had been carried up the stairs in the dead of night thirty-five years before). These incendiary missiles also fired the wooden barracks and the warehouse. On the nineteenth, the British were entrenched within fifty yards of the outer fortifications. The next day saw virtually no change in the position.

That evening, as General Prideaux surveyed the deepest penetration of the enemy's defenses, his aide Colonel John Johnstone was cut down by French small-arms fire. He died instantly. After helping to remove Johnstone's body, Prideaux returned to a review of his positions. He paused to observe the operation of a newly installed mortar. It exploded on its first firing. The general was mortally wounded.

The question of who was to take command of the entire

Niagara operation in Prideaux's place posed a major puzzle of the sort so fancied by the regimented mind. The ranking officer at the site was Sir William Johnson. But in the official table of organization, Colonel Haldimand, still in charge of Fort Oswego, was second in command of the whole army of the sector.

The dispute that ensued is a matter of more than a little perplexity. Johnson immediately sent a message to Haldimand by water; he informed the colonel of Prideaux's death and of his own assumption of command at Niagara pending the Swiss officer's pleasure in the matter. Shortly after the dispatch bearer was on his way, a Seneca scout alerted Johnson to the sighting of a flotilla of canoes and barques at the headwaters of the Niagara. This could only be a relief force for the French garrison at the House of Peace.

Johnson correctly concluded that that battle would have

Fort Niagara in 1759

reached its decisive stage long before it was possible for Haldimand to take personal command of the Niagara campaign—
if, in fact, such was his intention. He sent a second message
to Haldimand on the morning of the twenty-first, apprising
him of the latest intelligence and suggesting that, given the
critical immediate situation, he should remain at Fort Oswego
to prevent possible French attempts to reinforce the House
of Peace from Fort Frontenac. This duty accomplished, the
huge Irishman issued his first order of the day as commander
of the two thousand white and perhaps a thousand Indians
who were besieging the French fort.

As soon as it was known among the junior officers of the
command that Johnson had taken charge, he was confronted
with a jurisdictional dispute which, in such a circumstance,
was tantamount to mutiny. Some of the British regulars on his
new staff privately offered to disobey any orders that Johnson
uttered. The word "assassination" was bandied among some
of the more recklessly recalcitrant. The Scottish captain Allan
MacLean sent a most illicit message to Haldimand imploring
him to ignore Johnson's counsel and to come at once to lead
the siege himself.

It is hardly to be wondered that the Britons and Scots
should suspect an Irishman; they had been doing just that
(and with reason) for centuries. The real wonder of the incident is that the headstrong Johnson, mistrusted by his junior
officers because he appeared to them no gentleman (though
he was a baronet), should have persuaded them by noon of
that same day, the twenty-first of July, that no matter what
opinion they held of him, the danger that was approaching
from the Upper Niagara must take precedence. The question
of their commander's normal deportment and his lineage could
be resolved after the battle.

The magnitude of the menace rapidly taking shape on the
higher reaches of the river was estimated by Johnson's scouts
to be very great. The force was thought to number a thousand
whites and perhaps twice that number of Indians, under the

joint command of Captains de Lignery and Aubry. On the morning of the twenty-third, the newly arrived French sent a small, unarmed party down the portage route under a white flag. The leader requested Johnson's permission to pass a message to Captain Pouchot. The word for the fort's commander was that he need have no fear, for important relief was at hand. The insurgents planned to force their way through the British lines along the east-bank portage road.

Pouchot thought it a certainty that Johnson or his agents had read the message before allowing the party to pass it on to him. He believed, in any case, that even if the Irish commander was ignorant of the relief party's intentions, the tactic was doomed to failure. On the other hand, his own situation worsened hourly. He had suffered more than a hundred serious casualties. Most of his heavy artillery was out of action. He was now deliberately burning all the wooden structures within the fortress compound to prevent uncontrollable fires from sapping the waning energies of his meager force when the moment arrived for the British to make their final assault against the shattered bastions of the House of Peace. He had less than a hundred muskets in working order. Holes punched in the thick granite walls of the main building were plugged up with sacks of gravel. From any point of view, his position was desperate.

Pouchot sent a terse reply to his friend above the falls. When they launched their attack, he advised them, they were to "follow my suggestions of the 10th." This was evidently a reference to his earlier message of distress in which he had proposed that at least a portion of any relief expedition should cross the Niagara at some safe point above Goat Island and try to capture the British artillery battery on the west bank of the stream; for that was his bête noire. Once taken, those heavy guns could be turned against the enemy who was dug in on the opposite shore. With a little luck, fire from his own cannons might force Johnson's men out of their trenches and would certainly divert them from a pure concentration on the balance of the French rescue party coming down the east side of the Niagara.

There is no surviving record to show that Sir William Johnson intercepted either message. In fact, he had no need to; for the possibilities available to the French were so limited that it required no military genius to understand them. For whatever reasons, the officers in charge of the relief expeditionary force upriver elected to ignore Pouchot's very pertinent counsel. Instead of attempting to capture the British guns on the west bank of the Niagara before attacking the entrenched troops on the east side, an action that might easily have saved the day for the garrison at the House of Peace, they chose to make a direct and wholly suicidal assault against Johnson's well-established strongpoints on the portage road. Their attack began in the earliest hours of the twenty-fourth. The result was a foregone conclusion. The French and their Indian allies were mercilessly butchered.

Within hours of this lunatic catastrophe, Captain François Pouchot ran up the flag of surrender. Three days later, William Johnson wrote in his journal: "I divided among the several [Indian] nations [that had aided me] the prisoners and scalps amounting to 246. . . . The [French] officers I released from them by ransom and good words." Captain de Lignery, principal author of the fiasco on the portage route, died of his wounds. His fellow commander, Aubry, survived. Total French casualties of the entire siege and the final battle were reported at the time to be in the range of two hundred to five hundred. No estimate of the losses inflicted on the Indian friends has been recorded; it was thought at the time to be of no great importance—"no big deal," as an American infantry officer would say two centuries later in a different context but of a similar circumstance.

Sir William Johnson's total casualties for the day of July 24 were no higher than fifty, and for the whole siege in the neighborhood of a hundred. It was a victory whose significance was to be obscured by subsequent French surrenders at Montreal and Quebec. The French were soon deprived of all their holdings in North America, except for Louisiana—a condition made official by the terms of the Treaty of Paris, signed in 1763, which terminated the French and Indians Wars in the New World and the Seven Years' War, as the European part of the conflict has been called.

When Johnson led his so recently rebellious staff officers through the handsome Iroquois Gate, the main entrance to the conquered House of Peace, he was greeted by an exhausted but still gallant Pouchot, who invited the victors to dine with him. As soon as the meal was over, the French officers and the Joncaire brothers were placed under close arrest—for their own security, for Johnson intended to make good his promise to afford the Iroquois their night of pillage at the fort.

Among those who supped at the defeated French commander's table that evening was Captain John Butler. Before very long, his name would redound, famous and infamous, across the hills and streams of New York and Pennsylvania as the organizer and leader of Butler's Rangers. It was a name, as well, that would still later be closely associated with the future of the Niagara Frontier. The captain had only to glance across the broad estuary of the river to see the very spot where a permanent encampment would one day carry his name as, not far off, he might have seen the knoll where his remains would be interred.

9

NIAGARA
Battleground,
Phase Three

Immediately after Sir William Johnson's important triumph over the French at the Niagara, Colonel Friedrich Haldimand arrived from Fort Oswego to assume command of the troops responsible for the victory and to direct the repairs to the military installations above and below the falls. He saw to the complete restoration of the House of Peace, thereafter officially known as Fort Niagara. Upstream, he elected not to make use of the burned-out site occupied by Little Fort Niagara. Instead, he decided on a location a few hundred yards south of Daniel Joncaire's blockhouse. There he ordered the erection of a new fort, whose building was under the supervision of Captain John Joseph Schlosser, a German mercenary. When completed, it naturally took the name of Fort Schlosser. This strongpoint would protect the upper end of the portage route. On Navy Island, Haldimand directed Schlosser to establish a shipyard, whose function gave the island its name.

Until the middle of 1760, when Vaudreuil-Cavagnal surrendered Montreal, the British struggled feverishly to restore

Fort Schlosser

all the important military works on the Niagara and to construct on Navy Island vessels for service on the Upper Lakes, and at Fort Oswego boats to ply the waters of Ontario and the Upper Saint Lawrence. Perhaps the most interesting craft to be produced during this period was the "snow," a remarkably maneuverable, shallow-draft sailing ship which had been designed some years earlier at Fort Oswego but perfected at Navy Island under Captain Schlosser's watchful eye. The snow became the most generally useful of vessels to sail the Great Lakes until the development of the steamboat half a century later.

The French defeat solved one major Anglo-American problem but, as so often occurs with societies everywhere, the solution permitted other difficulties, theretofore in abeyance, to manifest themselves. Hardly was the danger of war past before white traders in substantial numbers started to press westward along the Albany-to-Niagara land and water route. They brought with them goods long denied the Six Nations Indians who had served the British cause so well under Johnson's leadership. These peddlers asked prices of the red men that were just short of being prohibitive, far higher than they had been when the French were offering competition to the British for commerce in pelts and for military alliances.

The consequent irritation with what the Indians considered an abuse of a monopoly situation was augmented by other developments which the Iroquois thought even more insidious, because of their longer-range implications. In the wake of the traders came the settlers. Under the protection of the British and American troops who guarded the waterways and portage roads from the Hudson westward, the migrants began to encroach on territories to which the Six Nations believed their own title was guaranteed by the treaties to which the Crown at Westminster made such frequent reference when it was in the king's interest.

A few ugly skirmishes between pioneer settlers and red men lent credibility to the wildest rumors that were in circulation all around the eastern Great Lakes region. Captain Robert Rogers, whose famous Rangers had accepted the surrender of Detroit in October 1760, reported a widespread Indian conspiracy to massacre every white who attempted to take up residence west of the Mohawk valley. Early in the following year, this allegation reached the ears of Sir William Johnson at his fine house in Warrensburg. He must as well have heard tales of the underhanded practices employed by white settlers and peddlers to deprive the tribes of their land.

In April, he felt the situation to be, at least potentially, so serious that he went to Albany to confer with General Amherst. He extracted from the commander in chief a solemn promise to prevent further white incursions on Iroquois hunting areas, which, as their sachems maintained, were indeed protected in perpetuity by the British monarch. At the end of July 1761, Johnson wrote to Amherst from Fort Niagara that he could as yet notice no improvement in relations between the Indians and the white intruders. In the light of the subsequent occupation of the entire North American continent, Johnson's observations are particularly moving:

. . . I see plainly that there appears an unusual jealousy
amongst every Nation, on account of the hasty steps they
look upon we are taking toward getting possession of their
country, which uneasiness, I am certain, will never subside
whilst we encroach within the limits which, you may recollect, have been put under the protection of the King in the
year 1726, and confirmed to them by him and his successors
ever since, and by orders to the governors not to allow any
of his subjects settling therein.

You promised to prevent any person, whatsoever, from
settling or even hunting therein; but that it should remain
their absolute property. I thought it necessary to remind
your excellency thereof, as the other day on my riding to
the place [Navy Island] where my vessels are building, I
found some carpenters at work, finishing a large house for
one Mr. Stirling near the Falls, and have since heard [that]
others are shortly to be built hereabouts. As this must add
greatly to the Indians' discontent, being on the carrying-
place and within the very limits which, by their own agreement, they are not so much as allowed to dispose of, I
should be glad to know whether I can acquaint them that
those people will be ordered to remove or not; and I hope
from your Excellency's answer to be able to satisfy them. . . .

Johnson's indignant inquiry received no written reply. General Amherst substituted deeds for words, and the deeds were
scarcely for the Irish-American baronet's comfort, nor would
they offer any solace at all to the Indians. Despite the fact that
by this summer of 1761, New France was no longer an effective military threat nor even, really, a coherent political entity
in North America, the various surrenders had not yet been
officially ratified by the court at Versailles. Technically speaking, therefore, Britain and France were still at war.

In this circumstance, since it was preferable to an agreement with Johnson that the British were not complying with
their own contractual arrangements, Amherst chose to believe
that the unrest described by Sir William was caused not by
settlers but by the French, who were thus responding as best

they could to demands from their motherland to upset the enemy in North America in every way possible. And finally, since a state of war did still exist, the general had no qualms about disregarding treaties and promises negotiated years before, when conditions had been altogether different from those obtaining now. The Niagara Frontier, and more particularly the portage route, were essential military installations that had to be protected by the white British.

The deeds which gave a definite if wholly unacceptable answer to Johnson's query were grants of land to two additional white men (the Stirling house was already known to Amherst), both of them on the banks of the Niagara. The more significant was the transfer of considerable acreage to one John Stedman, whom the general had designated Master of the Portage with the responsibility for completely reorganizing the methods of transporting material up and down the river. To a Captain Servos, who had rendered valuable services to His Majesty's cause during the recent unpleasantness, Amherst granted twelve hundred feet of river frontage on the west bank for farming and for the construction of a water-operated gristmill. The Stirling, Stedman, and Servos families were therefore the first whites to take up permanent residence on the shores of the Niagara.

To all the Indians making use of the portage, their presence was a perpetual reminder of a simple fact of life with which, temperamentally, economically, and philosophically, they found it impossible to cope: the white man could not, under any but the most remarkable circumstances, be trusted or believed; his word was absolutely worthless. That single sentence summarizes the reality of the Indians' relations with the invading Europeans from the dawn of the sixteenth century until today. The Indians never could accept the idea that the white man's words were almost invariably lies—and still are. By the end of the Franco-British War in America, the red men had relinquished without much of a struggle the entire eastern seaboard of North America to the Spanish, to the British, to the

Dutch, to the French. In exchange for the aid they had so recently and significantly offered to the British in their war with the French, they were now rewarded with a kick in the head. Something had to be done. The most elemental justice demanded it.

In the autumn of 1762, a delegation of Ottawas made the long voyage down Lake Erie to consult with the Seneca sachems. They brought with them a message from their own great sachem Pontiac, who claimed to have been in recent and intimate conversation with the Master of Life, the exchange interpreted for him by his oracular medicine man. The dream journey to the realm of the Master of Life had resulted in an ultimatum of bitterest reproof against the red man's constant compliance to the will of the white intruder in yielding up land that the god had intended for the Indians alone. The Master of Life deplored the red man's increasing dependence on European luxuries—notably the bottle and the gun. He demanded a holy war, a crusade to drive all the whites now on the continent back to the sea from whence they had come: ". . . they know me not, and are my enemies," said the Master of Life. They are "the enemies of your brothers. Send them back to the lands which I have created for them and let them stay there."

Pontiac's embassy to the Senecas was only partially successful. Some sachems elected to join him in his holy war. Others made use of the Master of Life's pronouncement as a bludgeon with which to belabor the British for white incursions and "improvements" in the Niagara region. As their ancestors had protested the use of horses and carts on the portage, so now did the Seneca porters object to the arrival of the covered Conestoga wagons which were employed above and below Crawl on All Fours to carry cargo, a modification introduced by John Stedman. It was a novelty for which, very soon, he very nearly paid with his life. These new and somewhat more efficient methods of transporting goods were creating among the porters a less welcome innovation—technological unemployment.

To parry Indian protests, Amherst offered the same argument he had advanced the year before, which held just as true: human and humane considerations had to be subordinated to the requirements of war. (The identical defense would be asserted by Franklin D. Roosevelt, two centuries later, for confining Americans of Japanese descent in concentration camps in Utah during World War II.) The Niagara portage was a vital artery through which passed supplies and troop reinforcements for consignment to the Upper Lakes area where they would be deployed against the fanatical attacks of Pontiac's dedicated raiders.

This Indian campaign menaced Britain's control of the lands to the west and south of Niagara that had so recently been won from the French. By the summer of 1763, it was apparent that this Ottawa-led operation was no flash in the pan. Fort Saint Joseph, the westernmost of British outposts on Lake Michigan, had been overrun and sacked. Fort Pitt (the former Fort Duquesne) was under attack as were other military and trading installations on the lakes and riparian portage routes of the northern midwest. Rumors abounded that it was only a question of time before Forts Schlosser and Niagara would themselves come under native siege. If that were to occur, the Senecas who had hitherto merely complained about their maltreatment at the hands of the British would almost certainly enlist in Pontiac's forces in important numbers. The logic of the Ottawa plan of battle was obvious. If they could repossess the Niagara spillway, the entire white establishment to the west of it would be desperately imperiled, and perhaps it would be permanently eradicated.

Of all of Pontiac's operations during the hot months of 1763, the siege of Detroit was the most significant. The British had at all costs to resupply that fort before the lake froze over or certainly lose it with the onset of winter. Logistic and reinforcement missions continued to pass over the Niagara portage through September and October. One major troop movement in this season was led by Robert Rogers, who succeeded in effecting the relief of Detroit. In mid-October, Pontiac abruptly renounced the siege and moved his angry, embittered warriors south for the cold months.

The effort to transport matériel over the Niagara portage route during the summer and autumn months of 1763 was often subjected to Seneca harassment. On September 14, however, there occurred an ambush of far more than usual fury. John Stedman was riding at the head of a large supply convoy which traveled southward along the ledge overhanging the deep Niagara gorge. At a point about four miles downriver from the falls, the portage road led steeply upward, traversing a rock-strewn copse that formed the roof of a cave the Senecas called Devil's Hole. So sharp was the little incline that the wagon drivers eased the burden for their horses by dismounting and leading them. Stedman himself, however, was on horseback.

As he reached the center of the copse, Stedman heard a terrible but now-familiar sound—a Seneca war cry. At the same instant (he later reported and often reiterated to fascinated listeners), he saw an exploding curtain of arrow-borne flame aimed at the fabric canopies of his Conestoga wagons. Without a moment's hesitation, he flattened himself against the neck of his mount and spurred the creature frantically, realizing that there was nothing he could do to assist the crews or to save the wagons. His only thought was to alert the troops at Fort Schlosser to what he credibly imagined was the first attack of an Indian siege against the portage route and its installations. His escape, he explained afterward, was nothing less than a miracle, for he was set upon by two Seneca braves, and he swore that he heard the whistle and felt the breeze of a tomahawk as it spun past his ear. The only other survivor of this massacre was a boy stowaway variously described as a drummer or merely a lad traveling up to Fort Schlosser to visit a friend. He was, in any case, thrown clear as the wagon in which he was riding overturned. He hid in the brush until all was clear.

A relief party set out from the hamlet at the foot of the

escarpment (Lewiston, today), for the Senecas' cries and those of the savaged crews were heard by the soldiers stationed there. The Senecas anticipated such an effort and gleefully ambushed the soldiers who had come to the wagon train's rescue. Not a solitary man escaped death that day.

When a second party, from Fort Schlosser, arrived at the scene, they found only corpses, many of them maimed—and only when he saw that the Indians weren't returning did the lucky lad emerge from hiding to tell his terrible tale. Sharing John Stedman's conviction that this had been but the initial phase of a general assault against the entire Niagara establishment, the Fort Schlosser men did not dally long at the site of the massacre, but returned with dispatch to their garrison. Only a few days later, when there was no sequel to this hideous event, did a Lieutenant Rutherford go back to Devil's Hole for a more thorough investigation. The men of his platoon counted eighty corpses, all of them scalped. In the retelling, however, the Devil's Hole Massacre has been much embellished. An account published as recently as 1949 sets the casualties at three hundred and fifty.

Not long after the event, Seneca sachems solemnly informed Sir William Johnson that the massacre at Devil's Hole had been the work of Farmer's Brother, a hotheaded young warrior, and a band of more zealous braves who sympathized with Pontiac's cause. The great squaw man received this assurance with some skepticism, for he knew better than most whites that warriors rarely if ever acted without the full knowledge and approbation of their elders.

Some historians believe that the ambush was occasioned by Seneca resentment of Stedman's innovations in the transport of goods. A somewhat more plausible explanation is that the Senecas of Niagara as a whole, and not merely Farmer's Brother and his friends, had been inspired by the great Ottawa chief's crusade to rid the land of the whites. There was, in any event, no comparable repetition of this tactic at Niagara after the ferocious Pontiac broke off his siege of Detroit. Moreover,

The eleventh
portage blockhouse

since Stedman continued to make use of wagons on the portage road, the inference seems reasonable that the massacre was part of the effort to cleanse the land of the European intruder.

Both Stedman and Johnson profited from the event. Each was given extensive land grants at Niagara, by way of atonement. Johnson received eighty thousand acres, which he immediately transferred to the Crown. Stedman, on the other hand, held on to his—until it was seized by the new government of New York State. His last years were spent in idle but persistent efforts to establish the legitimacy of his claim to all the islands of the river.

Whatever its actual cause, the Devil's Hole Massacre taught the masters of Niagara a lesson which they hastily heeded. The nine miles of road from one end of the portage road to the other were without any form of protection against such attacks. Captain John Montresor, a young British engineer, was as-

Portage log work

signed to Fort Niagara to undertake the construction of a series of small blockhouses, rather like modern pillboxes, of which there were to be eventually eleven from the upper end of Crawl on All Fours to Fort Schlosser.

Making use of troops under the command of John Bradstreet (now a major general) who were passing through on their way to help suppress Pontiac's now abated efforts to capture Detroit, John Montresor was to leave a very important number of marks on the portage route and an even more important impression on the escarpment. He devised a rope-and-

A portage
blockhouse

pulley, inclined-plane, rampway lift system for Crawl on All Fours which greatly facilitated the transfer of cargo from the lower to the upper level. Whatever bitterness the Senecas may have felt about the use of wagons on the comparatively even ground of the roadway, they can only have been grateful to Montresor for his ingenious elevator.

The apparatus was still functioning forty-five years later when the young De Witt Clinton visited Niagara. His is the first more or less comprehensible description of the British officer's invention. However, Montresor's contribution to the military works along the banks of the river was not confined to the blockhouses and the hoist. He erected the first of the forts to occupy the river's headwaters—Fort Erie, on the western

side of the inlet, near the narrowest point of the stream's flow
out of the lake. Nor was this all he accomplished. He built
wharves and barracks at Fort Erie as well, and designed the
massive stone ramparts and redoubts that surrounded the
newly reconstructed Fort Niagara, at the northern end of the
river; these are the sole surviving elements today of his extraordinary efforts on the Niagara Frontier. The entire task,
astonishingly, was finished in something like four months.

While Captain Montresor was occasioning miracles of haste
and engineering on both sides and at both ends of the Niagara,
Sir William Johnson's red messengers were circulating westward with peace offerings and an invitation to Pontiac's Ottawas and their allies to come to the Niagara spillway for a

Montresor's rampway for Crawl on All Fours

great council meeting where the differences that threatened to nullify British victories against the French might be wholly resolved.

In August 1764, there was convened on the east bank of the river the largest and most widely representative gathering of American Indians ever assembled. Through several interpreters, Johnson read out to his guests the terms of what he hoped would prove a Pax Britannica for North America. Its principal feature was a promise, purportedly from the very hand of George III, that prohibited white colonization of lands "beyond the headwaters of rivers flowing into the Atlantic," a provision that was taken by the red men to mean the Lake Erie end of the Niagara. A second stipulation, which the natives thought even more significant than the first, placed all the Great Lakes territories under the administrative jurisdiction of the new British colony of Canada—a clause that mollified the many Indians who had had a bellyful of the land-grabbing colonists from New York, Pennsylvania, and Virginia.

As far as the Niagara Frontier itself was concerned, only the Senecas were directly involved. In exchange for a purely symbolic pittance (because they had made the egregious error of siding with the Joncaires during the recent war), they ceded to the British a strip of land on either side of the river four miles in width—which became, properly speaking, the Niagara Frontier. They further agreed formally to acknowledge John Stedman's right to operate the portage as he saw fit. Thus was the defeat of the proud Seneca nation made absolute and irreversible.

Another two years would elapse before an inebriated Pontiac was finally induced to inscribe his mark on a highly detailed document delineating the frontiers that separated the lands of the Indians from those of the British colonists. But when all had been said and signed, it appeared that his crusade had availed the red men something. By 1768, however, it was amply evident that rum was thicker than blood. What the whites had ceded by treaty they regained by "legitimate" purchase. William Johnson, "friend" to the red man, and Benjamin Franklin, self-styled "admirer" of his capacity to govern himself, were conspiring to acquire nearly two and a half million acres of territory west of the Alleghenies—a region that would later place Daniel Boone firmly in the folklore of early American expansionism. Johnson's death in 1774 prevented him from seeing the mixed fruits of his various and occasionally devious schemes.

The Niagara region witnessed few important alterations during the decade that followed the "pacification" of Pontiac and his crusaders. Since the British were now in complete control of all of North America, except for Florida, the Louisiana territory, and the Spanish holdings in the southwest, and since the Senecas had apparently been tranquilized by defeat and by the application of a reasonably well-administered trade policy that abused all Indians evenhandedly, the operations at the portage went on without serious interference. Further, because only a handful of whites were permanently settled on the Frontier strip in this period, the tensions that typified political and economic life nearer the Atlantic seaboard were absent along the banks of the roaring white water of the Niagara.

At the end of 1775, however, Fort Niagara was once again required to assume its military aspect. Major John Butler, extremely hostile to the "patriots'" rebel cause, arrived at the Frontier with a company of foot soldiers of an identical political persuasion. Butler's orders were to keep the Indians of the region neutral, at the worst, in the struggle that so clearly impended. When George III proclaimed that his colonies in America were in a state of rebellion, on August 23, 1775, the natives of the Six Nations were as divided in their loyalties as were the white settlers of the territory. The Loyalist cause was successfully opposed in the region only by the Reverend Samuel Kirkland, for nearly ten years past a missionary to the Oneidas and Tuscaroras; he managed to persuade most of them not to join with the Mohawks and Senecas who sided with the British.

Within a year of the outbreak of actual hostilities, the Niagara Frontier had become an important Loyalist stronghold and refuge. In July 1777, Sir John Johnson, the wild Irishman's son, joined his brother-in-law Daniel Claus and his despicable half-brother Joseph Brant at Fort Niagara. There, John Butler was organizing his "Rangers," a contingent of whites and red men that would soon attain a quite fearful notoriety as authors of the massacre of rebellious colonists at Forty Fort, in Pennsylvania, in the summer of the following year, and of a similarly senseless butchery at Cherry Valley, New York, in the late autumn.

Butler's forays from Niagara caused considerable and frustrated consternation to General Washington. He invited General John Sullivan to give some urgent thought to a plan to thwart the Iroquois's alliance with the Loyalists—but the Niagara region was, in the main, so remote from the commander in chief's central problem during these early years of the war that his attention to it was fairly casual and inconstant. No American action was immediately undertaken. While John Butler was raiding more or less at easy random, the Swiss officer Friedrich Haldimand was raised to the rank of general by the British and appointed governor of Canada. The security of the Niagara Frontier was very much in his mind, since it served as a principal escape route for beleaguered Tories. He felt that he must, therefore, assure the region a regular supply of arms and food.

The implementation of such a policy was rendered problematical late in 1779 and in the earliest months of 1780 by a combination of a fitfully effective colonial blockade of the mouth of the Saint Lawrence and the joint expedition of rebel Generals Clinton and Sullivan. The latter, while it failed in fact seriously to menace the British hold on the Niagara Frontier, nevertheless gave both whites and their red friends some ugly apprehensions of possible reprisal (for Butler's atrocities) as they found haven near the falls. A terrible winter and an extraordinarily late spring caused many deaths from hunger and cold.

With the discomforts and hardships of the previous season on the Frontier vividly in his recollection, General Haldimand instructed Colonel Bolton, the Niagara's military commander, to institute a plan that carried the perfectly Germanic name "Niagara Plan of Edible Annex." In the spring of 1780, vegetables and fruits were planted in clearings adjacent to the forts and blockhouses on both banks of the river. As the Joncaires had discovered years before, the land was exceptionally arable. The produce grown there, in combination with the supplies that the British managed to ferry down from Fort Frontenac, supported the Niagara refugees, who counted as many as three thousand Indians in their numbers, through the following winter with many fewer casualties to privation. This final year of active warfare saw yet another series of raids led by Butler, John Johnson, and Joseph Brant into the Southern Tier, where their principal depredations were against precious rebel crops.

The surrender of Cornwallis at Yorktown in 1781 brought an end to organized conflicts between British and American forces in North America. But at Niagara and in the lands contiguous to the Frontier, skirmishes continued even after the conclusion of a formal peace agreement two years later. For at the specific order of George III, Haldimand's British troops persisted in their occupation of Fort Niagara and all the Niagara strongpoints on both sides of the river—this in clear violation of the Treaty of Paris which had ceded to the United States the land on the east bank of the Niagara and all the other holdings in the state of New York. Moreover, the British retained possession of these areas as ransom for claims lodged against the American government by more than forty thousand Loyalists who had fled to Canada or England, leaving behind them property valued at approximately £9,000,000 ($45,000,-000), a sum so enormous that the newly born nation could see no immediate possibility of raising it.

One attempt to evict the British from Fort Oswego by force of arms proved wholly unsuccessful. In the summer of

1783, the Prussian Baron von Steuben accepted an American embassy to Haldimand in Quebec; the object was to persuade the governor to give up the forts his troops were retaining on American soil. Von Steuben's pleas were doubtless eloquent, as one German-speaking officer to another, but they were unavailing.

By the autumn of the same year, however, the handwriting seemed to be on the wall. Although it would be more than a decade before the British grudgingly agreed to evacuate all of the strongpoints they held, such figures as John Butler and his white ranger forces, who had remained at Niagara, recognized that sooner or later they would be displaced from the east side of the river. Butler petitioned Haldimand for permission to homestead the Canadian bank of the stream, for the experiment of the "Edible Annex" and brilliantly demonstrated the hospitality of the soil there.

The governor accorded two-hundred and sixty men of Butler's Rangers and their families parcels of land on the west bank of the Niagara from Butler's Barracks, at the Ontario end, facing Fort Niagara, to Fort Erie on the opposite end. The barracks formed the nucleus for the first permanent settlement on that side of the river. It was called Newark (Niagara-on-the-Lake today). A second village, facing Lewiston, evolved a few years later. This was Queenston.

To the Indian nations which had remained steadfast, even in Britain's defeat, Haldimand made his last major gesture as governor. He deeded a tract of nearly eight hundred thousand acres in the valley of the Grand River, northwest of the Niagara Frontier, as a token of gratitude to the natives who had, only a century before, possessed all the territory of North America east of the Hudson. It was a token, however, they had no choice but to accept.

By the ninth decade of the eighteenth century, the tribal numbers had been drastically depleted by war and pestilence and the red man's incapacity to resist the white man's alcoholic carrot and his explosive stick. Advised by such treacherous counselors as Joseph Brant, Farmer's Brother, and Red Jacket, the Indians must have been relieved to contemplate untroubled seclusion on a reservation where their way of life, debauched though it had surely been by the introduction of new and harmful dependence on European "luxuries," might survive in recognizable forms. The tribes were, needless to say, as totally mistaken in their acceptance of the white man's promise in this case as they had long been in allowing themselves to be seduced by his booze and his fundamentally useless trinkets. It would not be long before the Canadians were nibbling away at the reservation they had sworn to be inviolable. And to make this process of territorial erosion even more painful, they deprived the Indians of alcohol. It had served its purpose.

Haldimand's successor as governor of what was now officially called Canada was Sir Guy Carleton, who adhered to his predecessor's policy of colonizing with Loyalist refugees the north shores of Lakes Ontario and Erie and the west bank of the Niagara. In May 1791, Upper Canada was declared to be a separate province, with Newark as its capital. Approximately fifteen thousand whites were then settled in this territory. Their first governor was John Simcoe, who opened an initial sitting of the provincial parliament in the autumn of the next year. Of legislation enacted during this first sitting, the most fateful, from the standpoint of the Niagara Frontier, was a prohibition against slavery. So far as the entire New World was concerned, the bill was something of a sensation. President George Washington, of the United States, had already set the style for his country by repeatedly rejecting all suggestions, from his fellow countrymen and from foreigners, that he free his own slaves.

By 1796, the provisions of the newly signed Jay Treaty, whose main lasting effect was to settle the Loyalists' reparations claims in exchange for the British evacuation of American positions, were made operative. Governor Simcoe presided over the departure from the east bank of the Niagara and immediately ordered the construction of a duplicate portage route on the Canadian side of the river and the establishment of sturdy fortifications from Lake Erie to Lake Ontario.

So certain was Simcoe that there would be at least one more war between Britain and the United States in America that he directed the removal of Upper Canada's capital from Newark to York—as Toronto was provisionally renamed. His prophecy seems all the more perceptive for the fact that at the time of this transfer, the east bank of the Niagara was, for practical purposes, without white families. The 1790 census of New York state enumerated fewer than twenty-five souls in permanent residence west of the Genesee valley.

This absence of white Americans was in part attributable to the Haldimand-Carleton-Simcoe policy of severely restricting American use of the Niagara portage until after the conclusion of the Jay Treaty. Yankee traders had been actively discouraged from venturing into Frontier country. Further, there had been no great inducement for New Yorkers to attempt to settle in an area where the majority of their white neighbors would be hostile to them for political and nationalistic reasons.

However, with the change of real ownership and actual, physical possession of the Niagara's east bank to the United States, a series of transformations did occur—though their rapidity was less than heady and, as might be expected from a study of history, the concern for ethical procedures thus evidenced left a lot to be desired, especially when Indians and their sacred reservations were at issue.

The first event that would dramatically alter the complexion of the American lands in the proximity of the Niagara was the passage over the east bank's portage, in June of 1796, of Moses Cleaveland, who led a party of forty-nine men and two women on a pioneer venture to the west of the Frontier. As soon as he reached the western extremity of Pennsylvania's official boundary on Lake Erie, where the red man's country began, Cleaveland negotiated the purchase of some sixty-five miles of Erie water frontage, extending from the Pennsylvania border to the estuary of the Cuyahoga River, where the effluent city of Cleveland now sprawls. This transaction brought to the gulled native vendors the princely sum of $500 in baubles, and a hundred gallons of red-eye whiskey. Yet are there those who rightly point out that at least Cleaveland paid *something* for his land. The practice was to become increasingly uncommon.

10
NIAGARA
Between the Wars

In September of 1796, just three months after Moses Cleaveland had led his band of pilgrims over the portage, Isaac Weld, an English draftsman and gentleman traveler, arrived at the Niagara, where he composed the first accurate description of the river, the falls, and the surrounding countryside. Weld's observations are of particular interest because they constitute not only a first hard look but a last one, too—in the sense that within the decade that followed the signing of the Jay Treaty, the complexion of the Niagara Frontier would begin to develop the acne of a real estate speculation which was sponsored, as we shall have occasion to note, by the Holland Land Company.

At the distance of eighteen miles from the town of Niagara or Newark [Niagara-on-the-Lake, Ontario, today], are those remarkable Falls in Niagara River, which may be justly ranked amongst the greatest natural curiosities in the known world. . . .
From the sudden change in the face of the country in the

neighborhood of Queenstown [sic], and the equally sudden change in the river with respect to its breadth, depth, and current, conjectures have been formed, that the great falls of the river must originally have been situated at a spot where the waters are so abruptly contracted between the hills [i.e., at the escarpment]; and indeed it is highly probable that this was the case, for it is a fact well ascertained that the falls have receded very considerably since they were first visited by Europeans, and that they are still receding every year. . . .

It was an early hour of the day that we left . . . Newark . . . in order to visit these stupendous falls. Every step that we advanced toward them, our expectations rose to a higher pitch; our eyes were continually on the look out for the column of white mist which hovers over them; and an hundred times, I believe, did we stop our carriage in hopes of hearing their thundering sound; neither, however, was the mist to be seen, nor the sound to be heard, when we came to the foot of the [escarpment]; nor after having crossed [it], were our eyes and ears more gratified. This occasioned no inconsiderable disappointment, and we could not but express our doubts to each other, that the wondrous accounts we had so frequently heard of the falls were without foundation, and calculated merely to impose on the minds of credulous people that inhabited a distant part of the world. These doubts were nearly confirmed, when we found that, after having approached within half a mile of the place, the mist was just discernible, and that the sound even then was not to be heard; yet it is nevertheless strictly true, that the tremendous noise of the falls may be distinctly heard, at times, at a distance of forty miles; and the cloud formed from the spray may be seen even still farther off; but it is only when the air is very clear, and there is a fine blue sky, which however are very common occurrences in this country, that the cloud can be seen at such a great distance. The hearing of the sound of the falls afar off depends upon the state of the atmosphere; it is observed, that the sound can be heard at the greatest distance, just before a heavy fall of rain, and when the wind is in a favourable point to convey the sound toward the listener; the day on which we first approached the falls was thick and cloudy.

On that part of the road leading to Lake Erie, which draws nearest to the falls, there is a small village, consisting of a half a dozen straggling houses [modern Niagara Falls, Ontario]: here we alighted, and having disposed of our horses, and made a slight repast . . . we crossed over some fields towards a deep hollow place surrounded with large trees, from the bottom of which issued thick volumes of whitish mist, that had much the appearance of smoke rising from large heeps of burning weeds. . . . We descended some distance a steep bank of about fifty yards, and . . . at last came to the Table Rock. . . . This rock is situated a little to the front of the great fall, above the top of which it is elevated above forty feet. The view from it is truly sublime. . . .

. . . For the first few miles from Lake Erie, the breadth of the river is about three hundred yards, and it is deep enough for vessels drawing nine or ten feet [of] water; but the current is so extremely rapid and irregular, and the channel so intricate, on account of the numberless large rocks in different places, that no other vessels than bateaux ever attempt to pass along it. As you proceed downwards the river widens, no rocks are to be seen either along the shores or in the channel, and the waters glide smoothly along, though the current continues very strong. The river runs thus evenly, and is navigable with safety for bateaux as far as Fort Chippeway [sic, opposite Fort Schlosser—Niagara Falls, New York] which is about three miles above the falls; but here the bed of it becomes rocky, and the waters are violently agitated by passing down successive rapids, so much so indeed, that were a boat by any chance to be carried a little way beyond Chippeway, . . . nothing could save it from being dashed to pieces long before it came to the falls. With such astonishing impetuosity do the waves break on the rocks in these rapids, that the mere sight of them from the top of the banks is sufficient to make you shudder. I must in this place, however, observe, that it is only on each side of the river that the waters are so much troubled; in the middle of it, though the current is also there uncommonly swift, yet the breakers are not so dangerous but boats may pass down, if dexterously managed, to an

island [Goat Island] which divides the river at the very
falls. To go down to this island it is necessary to set off at
some distance above Chippeway, where the current is even,
and to keep exactly in the middle of the river the whole way
thither; if the boats were suffered to get out of their course
ever so little, either to the right or left, it would be impossible to stem the current, and bring them again into it; they
would be irresistibly carried towards the falls, and destruction must inevitably follow. In returning from the island
there is still more difficulty than in going to it. Notwithstanding these circumstances, numbers of persons have the
foolhardiness to proceed to this island, merely for the sake
of beholding the falls from the opposite side of it, or for the
sake of having in their power to say that they had been
upon it. . . .

. . . To return now to the Table Rock [long since crashed
into the abyss], situated on the British side of the river, and
on the verge of the Horse-shoe Fall. Here the spectator has
an unobstructed view of the tremendous rapids above the
falls, and of the circumjacent shores, covered with thick
woods; of the Horse-shoe Fall, some yards below him; of
the Fort Schloper [sic] Fall, at a distance to the left; and of
the frightful gulph beneath, into which, if he has but the
courage to approach to the exposed edge of the rock, he
may look down perpendicularly. . . . It is impossible for
the eye to embrace the whole of it at once; it must gradually make itself acquainted, in the first place, with the com-
ponent parts of the scene, each one of which is in itself an
object of wonder; and such a length of time does this operation require, that many of those who have had an opportunity of contemplating the scene at their leisure, for years
together, have thought that every time they have beheld it,
each part has appeared more wonderful and more sublime,
and that it has only been at the time of their last visit that
they have been able to discover all the grandeur of the
cataract. . . .

The next spot from which we surveyed the falls, was from
the part of the cliff nearly opposite to that end of the Fort
Schloper Fall, which lies next to [Goat Island]. You stand

there on the edge of the cliff, behind some bushes, the tops
of which have been cut down to open the view. From hence
you have a better prospect of the whole cataract, and are
enabled to form a correct idea of the position of the precipice, than from any other place. The prospect from hence
is more beautiful, but I think less grand than from any other
spot. . . .

Having left this place, we returned once more through the
woods bordering upon the precepice to the open fields and
then directed our course by a circuitous path, about one
mile in length, to a part of the cliff where it is possible to
descend to the bottom of the cataract. The river, for many
miles below the precipice, is bounded on each side by steep,
and in most part perpendicular, cliffs, formed by earth and
rocks, and it is impossible to descend to the bottom of them,
except at two places, where large masses of earth and rocks
have crumbled down, and ladders have been placed from
one break to another, for the accommodation of passengers.
The first of these places which you come to in walking along
the river, from the Horse-shoe Fall downwards, is called the
"Indian Ladder," the ladders having been constructed there
by the Indians. These ladders . . . consist simply of long
pine trees, with notches cut in their sides, for the passenger
to rest his feet on. The trees, even when first placed there,
would vibrate as you stepped upon them, owing to their
being so long and slender; age has rendered them still less
firm, and they now certainly cannot be deemed safe, though
many persons are still in the habit of descending by their
means. We did not attempt to get to the bottom of the cliff
by this route, but proceeded to the other place, which is
lower down the river, called Mrs. Simcoe's Ladder, the
ladders having been originally placed there for the accommodation of the lady of the late governor. This route is much
more frequented than the other; the ladders, properly so
called, are strong, and firmly placed, and none of them,
owing to the frequent breaks in the cliff, are required to be
of such great length but what even a lady might pass up or
down them without fear of danger. To descend over the
rugged rocks, however, the whole way down to the bottom

of the cliff, is certainly no trifling undertaking, and few
ladies, I believe, could be found of sufficient strength of
body to encounter the fatigue of such an operation.

On arriving at the bottom of the cliff, you find yourself
in the midst of huge piles of misshapen rocks, with great
masses of earth and rocks projecting from the side of the
cliff, and overgrown with pines and cedars hanging over
your head, apparently ready to crumble and crush you to
atoms. Many of the large trees grow with their heads downwards, being suspended by their roots, which had taken
such a firm hold in the ground at the top of the cliff, that
when part of it gave way the trees did not fall altogether. . . .

Having reached the margin of the river, we proceeded
towards the Great Fall, along the strand, which for a considerable part of the way thither consists of horizontal beds
of limestone rock, covered with gravel, except, indeed, where
great piles of stones have fallen from the sides of the cliff.
These horizontal beds of rock, in some places, extend very
far into the river, forming points which break the force of
the current, and occasion strong eddies along particular
parts of the shore. Hence great numbers of the bodies of
fishes, squirrels, foxes, and various other animals, that, unable to stem the current above the falls, have been carried
down them, and consequently killed, are washed up. The
shore is likewise found strewed with trees, and large pieces
of timber, that have been swept away from the saw mills
above the falls, and carried down the precipice. The timber
is generally terribly shattered, and the carcases of all the
large animals, particularly of the large fishes, are found very
much bruised. A dreadful stench arises from the quantity of
putrid matter lying on the shore, and the numberless birds
of prey, attracted by it, are always seen hovering about the
place. . . .

. . . From the foot of Simcoe's Ladder you may walk along
the strand for some distance without inconvenience; but as
you approach the Horse-shoe Fall, the way becomes more
and more rugged. In some places, where the cliff has crumbled down, huge mounds of earth, rocks and trees, reaching

to the water's edge, oppose your course; it seems impossible to pass them; and, indeed, without a guide, a stranger would never find his way to the opposite end; for to get there it is necessary to mount nearly to the top, and then crawl on your hands and knees through long dark holes, where passages are left open between the torn-up rocks and trees. After passing these mounds, you have to climb from rock to rock close under the cliff and the river, and these rocks are so slippery, owing to the continual moisture from the spray, which descends very heavily, that without the utmost precaution it is scarcely possible to escape a fall. At the distance of a quarter of a mile we were as wet, owing to the spray, as if each of us had been thrown into the river.

There is nothing whatsoever to prevent you from passing to the very foot of the Great Fall; and you might even proceed behind the prodigious sheet of water that comes pouring down from the top of the precipice, for the water comes from the edge of a projecting rock; and moreover, caverns of a very considerable size [the Cavern of the Winds] have been hollowed out of the rocks at the bottom of the precipice, owing to the violent ebullition of the water, which extend some way underneath the bed of the upper part of the river. I advanced within about six yards of the edge of the vast sheet of water, just far enough to peep into the caverns behind it; but here my breath was nearly taken away by the violent whirlwind that always rages at the bottom of the cataract, occasioned by the concussion of such a vast body of water against the rocks. I confess I had no inclination at the time to go farther; nor, indeed, did any of us afterwards attempt to explore the dreary confines of these caverns, where death seems to wait him that should be daring enough to enter their threatening jaws. . . .

. . . It has been conjectured . . . that the Falls of Niagara were originally situated at Queenstown; and indeed the more pains you take to examine the course of the river from the present falls downward, the more reason is there to imagine that such a conjecture is well founded. From the precipice nearly down to Queenstown, the bed of the river is strewed with large rocks, and the banks are broken and rugged; circumstances which plainly denote that some great disruption has taken place along this part of the river; and we need be at no loss to account for it, as there are evident marks of the action of the water upon the sides of the banks, and considerably above their current bases. Now the river has never been known to rise above these marks during the greatest flood; it is plain, therefore, that its bed must have been one much more elevated than it is at present. Below Queenstown, however, there are no traces on the banks to lead us to imagine that the level of the water was ever much higher than it is now. The sudden increase of the depth of the river just below the hills at Queenstown, and its sudden expansion there at the same time, seem to indicate that the waters must for a great length of time have fallen from the top of the hills [the escarpment], and thus have formed that extensive deep basin below the village [of Queenston]. In the river, a mile or two above Queenstown, there is a tremendous whirlpool, owing to a deep hole in the bed; this hole was probably also formed by the waters falling for a great length of time at the same spot, in consequence of the rocks which composed the then precipice having remained firmer than those at any other place did. Tradition tells us, that the great fall, instead of having been in the form of a horse shoe, once projected in the middle. For a century past, however, it has remained nearly in its present form; and as the ebullition of the water at the bottom is so much greater at the center than in any other part, and as the water consequently acts with more force there in undermining the precipice than at any other part, it is not unlikely that it may remain in the same form for ages to come.

At the bottom of the Horse-shoe Fall is found a kind of white concrete substance [calcite], by the people of the country called spray. Some persons have supposed that it is formed from the earthy particles of the water, which descending, owing to their greater specific gravity, quicker than the other particles, adhere to the rocks, and are there formed into a mass. This concrete substance has precisely the appearance of petrified froth; and it is remarkable, that it is found adhering to those rocks against which the greatest quantities of the froth, that floats upon the water, is washed by the eddies.

We may take certain gentle exceptions to Isaac Weld's idiosyncratic eighteenth-century notions of punctuation, and even to his occasionally rather groping syntax, but we cannot take from him his keen powers of observation and the genuine excitement his description evokes as he tells us, at first hand, about the wonders of the Niagara and its falls. Nor can we fail to respect his astute surmises about the river's geological evolution.

Weld viewed the awesome Niagara's rapids and cascades at the beginning of the river's new phase as a national boundary line between a British colony and the United States, political entities whose interests were not always in harmony as the nineteenth century got under way. These years before the War of 1812 were ones of gradual but steady population growth on the American side. The Canadians had already developed

The Whirlpool

four distinct communities on the west bank of the river—
Newark, Queenston, Clifton (Niagara Falls), and Fort Erie.
It is easy to infer from Weld's description that there was some
development a bit above the falls. This was Fort Chippawa.
The fact that there were guides even suggests a tourist industry
aborning.

On the east bank, however, there was little of permanence,
save for the former House of Peace at the river's mouth, and
the modest hamlets of Lewiston, Manchester (Niagara Falls,
New York), Black Rock, and the insignificant collection of
cabins on the north side of Buffalo Creek—opposite which was
an Indian Reservation. Now that the portage route of the New
York side was readily accessible to Americans, pioneers—many
of them escaping the overcrowded and not very arable land
of New England—began to arrive; some to stay within eyeshot
or earshot of the falls, others to penetrate westward, to take up
residence near Moses Cleaveland's slowly growing community.

Services were necessary to cope with the increasing number
of wagon-train convoys bound west with trade goods and
settlers, with boats and barges reaching the lower end of the
portage from Fort Oswego to pick up pelts and eventually cash
crops. The falls, long celebrated but so far viewed mainly by
visitors whose purpose in coming here had rarely been inspired merely by the casual tourist's curiosity, were on the
brink of becoming objects of surpassing importance as attractions to the same sort of voyager who was earlier devoted to
the Grand Tour of Europe. The scene, as Isaac Weld truly
noted, was "amongst the greatest natural curiosities in the
known world."

But it was far from a simple matter, in 1800, to reach the
Niagara. That was, perhaps, an important aspect of the original
attraction in making the journey. Pilgrimages, whether oriented
to faith or to pleasure, are valued in direct ratio to the danger
and/or the difficulty they involve. It was at least as hard to get
to Niagara early in the last century as it is today to visit Angel

Queenston

Falls or reach the summit of Mount Everest. The usual route for the traveler coming from Montreal or New York was over water. The visitor who approached the Niagara Frontier by way of the Saint Lawrence had much the easier time of it, for General Haldimand had seen to the construction of a six-mile canal which bypassed the Lachine Rapids; this was the first such man-made waterway in North America. The person arriving from New York, on the other hand, had to traverse a number of portages, the most trying of them the three uncomfortable and once-hazardous passages by land from the Mohawk to Fort Oswego. Travelers who came from Philadelphia made the trip by land, over roads that were often just passable, through country that was mainly wilderness, with few inns or other sources of repose.

There was one significant difference in travel now, however. The eastern Indians no longer constituted a danger. If they fail to disappear completely from this narrative, by 1800 they had surely lost their power to cause a tremor even in the most timid heart; what survived was a legend of ferocity that no longer obtained—indeed, it really never had. Their putative exploits of previous centuries could still inspire the imagination, mostly of indifferent writers and mediocre poets. But the red men who remained in the Niagara Frontier region became one of the principal tourist attractions—rather comparable to the celebrated bears of Yellowstone, though less unpredictable in their behavior. They were merely oddities who piqued the jaded interest of sightseers who were thereby reminded of what the red man had once represented in a land to which they could no longer name a claim; *they* were the strangers. As a direct consequence of this new role, the Senecas and Tuscaroras of Niagara subsided into a tragic torpor of desperate degradation which they are only now beginning to shake off—too late, one fears, to achieve anything but cause for bitterness and remorse.

Of many surviving visitors' accounts, the English John Maude's description of a stay here in 1800 records a charming exchange with aging John Stedman, "hero" of the Devil's Hole massacre, who was hoping to regain from the state of New York the very questionable landgrant that had been made to him by the Senecas after his "miraculous" escape from the ambush of 1763. His suit failed; the New York courts were more difficult to intimidate than a hapless tribe of red men. But of all of John Maude's observations, the most delightful for its perversity is ascribed to a New York lawyer who "was this summer induced to visit, [and] who, to have a better view of the Falls, would not deign to dismount [from his horse], but at first sight, exclaimed, 'Is that all?' and rode on!"

The next year, another visitor, George Heriot, came to the interesting conclusion that the congealed "spray" which had been described by Isaac Weld was in fact produced by the interaction of sulfur spring water, vitriolic acid, and limestone rock which in combination made plaster of Paris. Contemporary riparian anglers may grow faint over Heriot's description of spearfishing at the foot of Simcoe's Ladder: "The spear in use is a fork with two or three prongs, with moving barbs, and fixed to a long handle. The fisherman takes possession of a prominent rock, from whence he watches for his prey, and when it approaches within his reach, he pierces it with his instrument, *with an almost inevitable certainty.* [The emphasis is added]." The only fish that regularly survives in the milky, putrid waters of the lower Niagara is the carp, and even *he* is inedible because of the high mercury content of the stream in which he lives.

With ever-increasing numbers of tourists managing to reach Niagara, it was not surprising that a poet should finally put in an appearance. The first of record, and assuredly one of the very best, was the lyrical Irishman Thomas Moore, who wrote in utter ecstasy to his mother from Niagara in 1804:

I have seen the Falls and am all rapture and amazement. . . . Never shall I forget the impression I felt at the first glimpse of them which we got as the carriage passed over the hill that overlooks them. We were not near enough to be agitated by the terrific effects of the scene; but saw through the trees this mightly flow of waters descending with calm magnificence, and received enough of its grandeur to set imagination on the wing; imagination which, even at Niagara, can outrun reality. I felt as if approaching the very residence of the Deity; the tears started into my eyes; and I remained, for moment after we had lost sight of the scene, in that delicious absorption which pious enthusiasm alone can produce. We arrived at the New Ladder [doubtless Simcoe's Ladder] and descended to the bottom. Here all its awful sublimities rushed full upon me. But the former exquisite sensation was gone. I now saw all. The string that had been touched by the first impulse, and which *fancy* would have kept for ever in vibration, now rested in *reality*. Yet, though there was no more to imagine, there was much to feel. My whole heart ascended towards the Divinity in a swell of devout admiration, which I never before experienced. Oh! bring the atheist here, and he cannot return an atheist! I pity the man who can coldly sit down and write a description of these ineffable wonders; much more do I pity him who can submit them to the admeasurement of gallons and yards. It is impossible by pen or pencil to convey even a faint idea of their magnificence. Painting is lifeless; and the most burning words of poetry have all been lavished upon inferior and ordinary subjects. We must have new combinations of language to describe the Falls of Niagara.

Moore's pity for the calculators of "gallons and yards" was certainly well enough placed. Hardly a description, including (alas) one appearing earlier in this very volume, fails to offer dimensions and volumes intended to invite some degree of awe. Yet in the absence of "new combinations of language," writers and poets continued to struggle with the old ones of their day in an effort to come to grips with the staggering impact that the Niagara scene made upon the senses and the passions. The number of actual religious conversions effected by visits to the falls is, however, a statistic I have not so far discovered. Moore's the pity. But it is somehow consoling to think that a foxhole and the road to Damascus are perhaps not the only earthly sources of revealed religion.

By 1805, the American side of the Niagara was beginning to show signs of the kind of activity that makes real estate people rub their hands together merrily. Nevertheless, the Canadian bank still remained by far the more prosperous and more populous. Even as today, such visitors as were essentially tourists preferred to see the falls from the Canadian shore— because the views are vastly superior. A census of that year disclosed fewer than two thousand souls, including slaves (who were presumably enumerated at the rate of three-fifths of a person per capita, as so grotesquely prescribed by the Constitution of the United States), were settled in that portion of New York State west of the Genesee. However, there were increasing quantities of visitors, among them at about this time James Fenimore Cooper, who sailed on *Oneida*, a Great Lakes vessel constructed at Fort Oswego the year before. His recollections of the falls, of Lewiston and Youngstown—the

hamlet that had evolved on the river, not far from Fort Niagara
—and of Fort Oswego are to be found in *The Pathfinder*.

After having dutifully made a tour of all the points from
which the falls and rapids could be seen to excellent advantage,
and providing the first surviving mention of the Porter-Barton
gristmill, about a quarter of a mile upriver from the American
falls, one Christian Schultz, who came to the Frontier in 1807,
noted deficiencies that others must also have suffered from,
but they in more respectful silence:

> I am much surprised that a place so celebrated as the
> Falls of Niagara, which is visited by so many travellers,
> amongst whom are no inconsiderable number of ladies,
> should not yet have induced some enterprising person to
> erect a convenient house on this [American] side of the river
> for their accommodation, as likewise a proper stairs for de-
> scending to the bottom of the falls. Twenty-five dollars
> would defray the expense of a convenient stair-ladder with
> hand-rails; and surely no person, after travelling two hun-
> dred to one thousand miles to view the falls, would hesitate
> to pay one, or even five dollars, for a safe and easy convey-
> ance to the bottom.

As we have already observed, the Canadian side of the
river was the more popular one with tourists, and it was by
far the more populous one. Yet Schultz's complaint soon became so familiar that a good woman with the improbable and
no doubt apposite name of Hustler did open an inn and tavern
in the village of Lewiston not long before 1810. Mrs. Thomas
Hustler is charged with having contributed the word "cock-
tail" to the world's lexicon as a synonym for a primordial old-
fashioned which was to be stirred, one presumes, with the
quill of a rooster. Contemporary records of Mrs. Hustler's
hospitality are not very abundant, but it seems likely that her
establishment prospered mainly from its roughneck clientele
of mule skinners and boatmen—the "posher" visitors opting to
remain on the Canadian shore, where the accommodations
were more civilized and the views more varied and interesting.

In the summer of 1810, De Witt Clinton arrived at Manchester as a member of the party delegated to survey a possible route for a navigable waterway that would extend from the Hudson to Lake Erie. This enormously ambitious project was to require fifteen years to complete. It would, quite naturally, alter the civilization of western New York in general and, in particular, drastically reorder the economy of the Niagara Frontier—for it would render obsolete, literally overnight, the American portage and would have a sharply deleterious effect on the Canadian one as well. The pulling and hauling—political, financial, and geographic—that attended the construction of the Erie Canal are part of the Niagara story mainly to the extent that its ultimate realization affected the life on the river and the life *of* the river. It is to the siting of the canal that Buffalo owes its original impetus.

Clinton visited and described the village of Fort Schlosser, which eventually merged with Manchester to compose the present city of Niagara Falls, New York. There wasn't much to see besides the fortifications and the Porter-Barton mill. As the first significant pollutant of the Niagara River, this enterprise and the community in which it was situated deserve a little attention. Clinton called the site "the best place in the world for hydraulic works." How right he was. Yet it would be some decades before industry fully appreciated its virtues in this respect—when "civilization" caught up with the river's powerful and almost relentless flow. The future governor of New York and Vice President of the United States had a sharp eye, and a head for figures:

> Here is a carding-machine, grist-mill, saw-mill, ropewalk, bark-mill, tannery, Post Office, tavern, and a few houses. An acre-lot sells for 50 dollars [a fortune for land in a remote New York State hamlet—a couple of miles away, farmland was being offered by the Holland Land Company for $3.00 per acre]. The ropewalk is 60 fathoms [360 feet] long, the only establishment of its kind in the western country, and already supplies all the [rope for] lake navigation. The

hemp used . . . is raised on . . . [the] Genesee Flats, and costs there 280 to 300 [dollars] per ton, and when brought here it amounts to 380. Tar [for rope making] is procured from New York [City], there being no pitch pine in this country, and the price there and transportion [to Niagara] bring it in cost to 9 dollars [per ton]. It constitutes in price a 25th part of the rope. . . .

The reader, who may recall that the Senecas had brought the first hemp seeds north from the Carolinas a century and a half before De Witt Clinton visited this area, may well wonder what happened to the by-product of this exceptionally profitable and indomitably hardy crop that was flourishing in the Genesee valley. Except for the portion that was harvested by the few Indians permitted to remain in the district, a number impossible to estimate today, it appears that the marijuana leaves and blossoms were simply discarded by the white farmers. Time was certainly out of joint.

Commerce wasn't the sole concern of those residing on or near the banks of the Niagara, American and Canadian, during the earliest decade of the century—though commerce was in part responsible for the war that impended between the United States and Britain, the conflict that John Simcoe had foreseen twenty years earlier. Because of that governor's clairvoyance, which he must have been able to articulate to his superiors at Montreal with considerable persuasiveness, he had obtained permission to reinforce existing fortifications on the west bank of the river and to add some important new ones. Fort George now rose close to Butler Barracks, facing Fort Niagara on the opposite side of the river's mouth. Fort Chippawa, near the outlet of that creek, confronted Fort Schlosser on the American side. Fort Erie, opposing unfortified Buffalo Creek, was entirely rebuilt.

The Canadian portage route, another of John Simcoe's achievements, enjoyed a natural protection from possible enemy fire that was not shared by the blockhouse-studded road on the east bank—for the latter was exposed to Canadian artillery barrages at many points. The Canadians cherished another advantage over the potential enemy in having developed a dependable highway system that followed the shore of Lake Ontario from Fort Frontenac all the way to the Niagara's inlet, so that the transportation of men and supplies was not confined to shipping. Land approaches to the American bank of the Niagara were frequently impassable to wagons—almost always in winter and spring. Most cargo had to be brought in by water from Fort Oswego. (This, after all, was one of the principal rationales for the eventual construction of the Erie Canal.)

Consequently, from an American military point of view, naval power would have to be regarded as an extremely important factor should war come. It is all the more to be wondered at, then, that there should be no shipyard on the east side of the river above the falls. Navy Island was the possession of Canada. Nor was there any facility of the sort on Lake Erie. Fort Oswego was unique in the region, and it was not very productive. As we shall see, the American officials who were most loudly demanding war were giving no serious thought to the ways of winning it.

Simcoe's apprehensions had led him not only to undertake substantial military and highway construction, but also to create a kind of paramilitary organization which he called the Queen's Rangers, established in 1792, the year of his assumption of the role of governor of Upper Canada. The first recruits for this force were primarily veterans of Butler's Rangers, and in later years it would be their sons who helped to fill the ranks. This volunteer group served a dual purpose. Mostly farmers, they worked in the summer and winter months at the various construction tasks the governor had conceived and which his successors were farsighted enough to complete. In the remaining seasons, they sowed and harvested their own fields.

While the causes of the War of 1812 lie in the main beyond the scope of this book, it is relevant to observe here that one of its most outspoken proponents was Congressman Peter O.

Porter, younger brother and partner of Augustus Porter, co-
founder of the Porter-Barton enterprise at Fort Schlosser, one of
the Niagara's most highly regarded citizens. A member of the
House of Representatives since the election of 1808, Porter's
assignment to the Foreign Relations Committee in 1811 suited
him perfectly. Since their arrival at Niagara in 1804, the Porters had struggled vainly to secure a monopoly of the portage
trade. In spite of their efforts, which were chiefly of the price-
war kind that would be a feature of most venture capitalism
of the American nineteenth century, the Canadian transport
route was at least as prosperous as its United States counterpart.

What might not be accomplished through the operation of
cutthroat laissez-faire economics might possibly be obtained
by war. Other advocates of armed conflict with Britain who
served on the House Foreign Relations Committee included
Felix Grundy, Henry Clay, and John C. Calhoun. Like Porter,
these "great Americans" were strangely persuaded that with
but the most gentle of shoves, the Canadians could be induced
to ally themselves with the Unitred States against the rule of
perfidious Albion. Didn't *everyone* at least secretly want to be
an American? When this notion was proved to be chimerical,
American "war hawks"—and so they were called—persisted in
imagining that the most undemanding phase of the war they
were shrieking for would be the complete military conquest
of Canada. On paper, the figures to which they pointed seemed
very convincing. The difference in population between the
two countries was enormous, and the difference in material
wealth was even more striking. Moreover, said the bellicose of
the House and Senate (and even President Madison himself),
a good proportion of the settlers of Upper Canada had emigrated from the United States—also a fact. They felt certain
that Canada would fall with but a whimper, and not a very
loud one at that.

The War of 1812 was the first of a series of shameful conflicts, declared and undeclared, inspired by greed for land and

treasured minerals that would, in a few decades, acquire the dignified name of "Manifest Destiny." This passion to possess more and more territory was not, of course, unique to the United States. At the same time, Bonaparte and George IV (in 1812, still Britain's Regent) gave the name of "imperialism" to their expansionist policies. Later on, the Prussian Wilhelm II spoke of a "Drive to the East." Hitler referred darkly to Germany's need for "Lebensraum."

Samuel Eliot Morison has described the War of 1812 as the most unpopular war ever waged by the people of the United States—not excepting the war in Vietnam. Its proponents were mainly representatives of the frontier regions, though they carefully masked their lust for land with a cry of outrage against Britain's impressment of American citizens to serve in her navy and of British interference with United States shipping bound for ports controlled by Bonaparte.

Nevertheless, there was sufficient demand for war to permit its declaration in June 1812. To the degree that it was popular (and *most* wars are popular when they begin), the residents of the American side of Niagara had few illusions about its purely local implications. Many political enemies of the congressman called it "Peter Porter's War" and thought it a practical expression of his scheme to gain possession of the west bank portage facilities. But Porter's was a relatively small role in the creation of the hysteria that stampeded a majority of both houses of Congress to vote for a declaration of hostilities. Many, if not most, of the war's more strident advocates stood to gain personally from the pain and death and economic disruption that it would occasion. Nor was his avarice more marked than most. That the Porter family and all other greedy politicians should ultimately have failed to profit appreciably from the outcome of a war which they supported so vigorously seems a most exceptional violation of the law which states that well-organized crime almost always pays.

11

NIAGARA
Battleground,
Phase Four

Whether one chooses to think America's official apology for the War of 1812 justifiable or despicable, the ambitious military adventure failed even remotely to go according to the plan—not least because the plan was shoddy and ill conceived and the execution utterly deplorable. The Canadians evinced no interest whatever in shifting their allegiance from Great Britain to the United States. More embarrassing than that, they refused to conduct the war in a way that conformed to the pattern their more populous and more powerful enemy had so wishfully predicted. In fact, the Canadian aspect of the thirty months of warfare was, from the American standpoint, a categorical disaster from beginning to end. Only Commodore Oliver Hazard Perry's much-inflated skirmish on Lake Erie and some inconclusive but very bloody battles were to relieve an otherwise gloomy scene. Yet this was not without significance; for a major portion of the war's encounters occurred along the U.S.-Canadian frontier, within easy range of the Niagara—and of these, most were to take place on the river itself.

Under the leadership of General Isaac Brock, who had come to Canada from the Channel Island of Guernsey as a lieutenant colonel in 1802, a force of approximately fifteen hundred whites and perhaps half that number of domesticated Indians managed, between early August and mid-October of the war's first year, to defeat two much more important United States contingents, taking as prisoners almost twice as many Americans as there were in the whole Canadian unit under Brock's command. It has been persuasively argued that the Canadians fought with more commendable enthusiasm and valor than their enemies, in the early phases of the conflict, *because* they were numerically inferior and thus much more highly motivated.

Ringing in their ears must have been Henry Clay's disdainful claim: "We have the Canadas as much under our command as Great Britain has the oceans; and the way to conquer [Britain] on the ocean is to drive her from the land." William Eustis, President James Madison's Secretary of War, was even more skeptical of the Canadian military potential: "We can take Canada without soldiers," he assured his fellow war hawks. "We have only to send officers into the province and the people, disaffected towards their own government, will rally round our standard."

It was a war that would never have been fought if the ostensible causes—the maritime grievances against Great Britain—had been the true causes. There is ample evidence, which was accessible to Congress and the President at the time war was actually declared, that Britain was not only willing to conciliate but did in fact make something very like unilateral concessions before it was known in Westminster that war had been officially declared by the United States. The irony is almost too pat, but it is so nonetheless: on the maritime differences which purportedly occasioned the war, the United States won before a shot was fired. When these identical questions were raised once again at Ghent, in the autumn of 1814, during the peace negotiations, Britain had so wholly prevailed on land as well as on sea against the Americans that the concessions she had made earlier (and obviously revoked with the onset of the war) were not even obliquely touched on in the treaty that was signed on Christmas Eve.

It is not a capricious desire to revise history, as is the fashion today, or to nay-say politicians who claim that we have never lost a war, that impels one to the conclusion that the United States lost the War of 1812. Any reasonably objective standard one chooses to apply must confirm such an evaluation. The true purpose of the war was to prevent Canada from aiding the Indians in their resistance to Americans' insatiable demands for territory that had solemnly been acknowledged forever the property of the red man. As a logical corollary, the United States wished also to gain possession of Canada and Florida. Neither goal was achieved by the war. In terms of treasure expended, lives and precious trade lost, not to mention values debased to so profound a degree that they could never be restored, the war offered no offsetting gains at all. If that isn't defeat, the word and perhaps the whole language require redefinition.

The arrogant pronouncements of the war hawks can only have stiffened the already firm resolve of the Canadians to demonstrate their capacity to resist the thrusts of the Yankee imperialists—an epithet which unhappily describes precisely American foreign and military policy in the Western Hemisphere from this epoch to the very end of the nineteenth century. There was nothing particularly philosophical about the Canadians' defenses. They were protecting their birthright, and they did so with signal gusto. General Brock's stunning upset victories were demoralizing to his enemies, for they underscored the disorganized condition of American armed forces. This state was not convincingly reversed in the two years and more of conflict that remained.

Nominally under the command of General Henry Dearborn, the militias of the states from Massachusetts to Lake Erie were logistically and psychologically unprepared for the battle. As was to occur on more than one later occasion, the political desirability of the war was hotly debated. The decision to precipitate open hostilities was only narrowly carried in both the House and Senate, with a large majority of members from New York and New England (where most of the battles would be fought and most of the troops raised) strongly in opposition to it. The psychological groundwork for mutiny and near-mutiny was thus laid.

The soldiers mustered on the New York side of the Niagara were under the direct command of Brigadier General William Wadsworth. By the middle of August 1812, a couple of months after the beginning of this controversial war, they numbered five thousand men. Their period of enlistment was only six months, meaning that they could expect to be on their way home around Christmas time. The militiamen who were citizens of New York rejoiced in a further complication. Their oath as soldiers bound them not only to uphold the constitution of the United States, but that of New York State as well. A clause of that document (invoked once again, fruitlessly, in 1970) provided that no New Yorker could be compelled to wage war outside the nation's borders except as specifically stated in the Federal Constitution where the country's safety was concerned. The War of 1812 was deemed by most New York and New England politicians to be of an aggressive rather than a defensive nature. Indeed, it was thought nothing less than a stab in the back of Britain at the very moment when the former mother country (to which a great majority of Americans could trace their ancestry) was trying to bring down the ambitious Bonaparte. There was thus a tricky legal ground on which the New York militiamen could take a stand against crossing the Niagara for any military action against Canada.

Another indication of the unpopularity of the war in the American northeast is that its declaration and continuation produced pacifist rallies in New York and Boston and even as far south as Baltimore. Toward the end of the fruitless war, the

Hartford Convention of representatives from all the New England states was clearly in a mood to secede from the union; its recommendations, had they been adopted by the Congress, would have drastically curtailed the power of the President and of the federal government. Whether fortunately or not, news of the signing of the Treaty of Ghent more or less coincided with the declaration of the Hartford Convention whose purpose had, for the moment, been served. When upper Maine was occupied by the British, Bostonian Thomas Adams entered into secret negotiations with His Majesty's field commander to cede the territory to Britain and, in the event of the war's prolongation, for the British to provide funds and supplies with which the citizens might resist any American attempt to retake the land which extended eastward from the Penobscot River. What impended was civil war.

From a purely military point of view, political dissent was less dismaying than the extraordinary fact that the Canadian General Brock knew that war had been officially declared some days before the American Dearborn was informed of it—thanks, apparently, to the efficient agency of John Jacob Astor, the fur king and prototype of the new breed of American nobility that Matthew Josephson would much later call "the robber barons."

The initial action of the war in the Niagara region occurred on June 27, nine days after the President had signed the proclamation. *Commencement,* as the vessel was appropriately named, sailed out of Black Rock with a cargo of salt. Not far out into Lake Erie, she was boarded and seized by a Canadian contingent. Only the next day did the Americans learn that this was an act of declared war—not one of piracy, as they had originally claimed.

For a number of reasons, most of them political, the early months of the war saw several significant American defeats, not only at the hands of Isaac Brock, but by other Anglo-Canadian-Indian forces as well. The preponderance of troops

available for service in Canada was native—red or white; only
five thousand British regulars were in North America in June
of 1812, since Britain at this time was committed to the principal extent of her military possibilities on the peninsula of
Iberia, where the future Duke of Wellington was preparing to
drive Napoleon's armies out of Spain. United States timing for
the opening of the struggle to drive the British off the American
continent—certainly the motivation of the most bellicose—
seemed no accident. Some of our citizens have always admired
foreign despots. The welcome accorded Bonaparte's brothers
when they visited the United States after the emperor's second
downfall at Waterloo is evidence of the esteem certain of our
native "aristocrats" held for the defeated French usurper.
Moreover, we were merely following the time-honored international habit of treating the enemy of our enemy as our friend.

Niagara figured continuously and importantly through all
the thirty months of fighting. As had been the case in every

Fort George seen from Fort Niagara

conflict of the past, the spillway and its portages were regarded by both sides as of paramount strategic value. It was still a major way station on the route to the west; both British and Americans recognized the potential of the North American west. *That* was what the war was all about.

After having successfully led a numerically inferior assault force against the entrenched positions of the American General Hull at Detroit in the first weeks of August 1812, General Brock returned to Fort George on the twenty-fifth. From the opposite bank, substantial numbers of New York militamen looked on helplessly as strings of American prisoners from fallen Detroit were led down the Canadian portage to prison camps at York (Toronto), Kingston (Fort Frontenac), and Montreal. The reason for such doltish American inaction in the face of this provocation was that General Henry Dearborn, who was thought to be senescent, had improbably agreed to a temporary armistice with Canada's governor-general Sir George Prevost. Hence, a cease-fire had been declared from Maine to the Niagara without the prior approval of the United States War Department. The war was that unpopular. Dearborn's truce was formally denounced by Washington on September 9—by which time, of course, all the prisoners of war from Detroit were safely incarcerated, well out of easy American reach.

Another full month would elapse before the Niagara saw any remarkable American initiative. Just before daybreak on October 8, Captain Jesse Elliott led a mixed group of about a hundred soldiers and sailors in a few whaleboats out into the river from Black Rock, downriver a bit from Canadian Fort Erie, where two enemy vessels, *Detroit* and *Caledonia,* were riding at anchor. Quickly overcoming the sleeping crews, Elliott's raiders captured both ships. They beached *Caledonia* on the American side of the broad stream between Black Rock and the smaller village of Buffalo, at the river's opening. *Detroit,* however, was caught in the Niagara's current and drawn rapidly downward; she finally grounded herself on the rocky bank of Squaw Island, just above Grand Island. Later on, when a group of Canadians attempted to free her from the rocks, *Detroit* was demolished by American artillery fire that was directed by Lieutenant Colonel Winfield Scott, one of a handful of competent professional soldiers on the United States side of the Niagara. The enemy boarding party suffered heavy casualties. Scott later complained of the dearth of capable officers in any command he held in the course of this ugly little war, few of whom were northern Federalists and/or gentlemen. The reason was simple enough: President Madison, mindful of Federalist opposition to the war, gave commissions to Republicans (as the Jeffersonian "Democrats" were perversely called), and they, according to Winfield Scott, "consisted mostly of coarse and ignorant men."

Jesse Elliott proceeded forthwith to establish shipyards at Black Rock and at Presque Isle on Lake Erie. Vessels constructed at these two bases during the year that followed would furnish the United States with most of the fleet that gave Commodore Perry his celebrated victory off Sandusky, Ohio, in September of 1813. Elliott's intelligence and foresight were sorely wanting in much loftier American places.

An ill-starred attack against the Canadian side of the Niagara resulted in the capture of General Wadsworth and Colonel Scott, the former a less lamentable loss than the latter. A thousand other Americans were captured or lost. The principal achievement of this calamitously misled folly was the death of Isaac Brock—to whom a monument was eventually raised on the heights above Queenston. With Wadsworth gone, the command fell into the superbly inept hands of General Alexander Smyth, a Virginian with a flair for soaring rhetoric. A sample of his hortatory prose is of literary interest:

> Men of New York: The present is the hour of renown. Have you not a wish for fame? Would you not choose to be one of those who, imitating the heroes whom Montgomery led, have in spite of the season, visited the tomb of the chief

and conquered the country where he lies? Yes—You desire your share of fame. Then seize the present moment. If you do not, you will regret it; and say "the valiant have bled in vain"—the friends of my country fell and I was not there.

Advance then to our aid. I will wait for you a few days. I cannot give you the day of my departure. But come on, come in companies, half companies, pairs or singly. I will organize you for a short tour. Ride to this place, if the distance is far and send back your horses. But remember that every man who accompanies us places himself under my command, and shall submit to the salutary restraints of discipline.

We may judge Smyth's success as a recruiter by the quality of men he attracted thus to Niagara. After much dallying, he actually submitted to a vote the question of whether or not the Niagara ought to be crossed, unconsciously emulating Governor Shirley's performance at Fort Oswego, a half century before. The result of such "discipline" could have been anticipated. His officers roundly rejected the plan. Congressman Peter O. Porter, an officer serving under Smyth, was so enraged by this absurdity that his comments inspired the general to challenge him to a duel. This grotesque charade was played out on a December morning at Grand Island. Neither man was much of a shot; both missed. Smyth retired to Virginia shortly afterward.

Not until the spring of 1813 was there another attempt to seize the opposite shore of the Niagara. Under the direction of the same General Dearborn who had negotiated a cease-fire just a few seasons earlier, the Americans made a successful crossing in force, and were soon in possession of all the strongpoints of the west bank. If the victory was more apparent than real, the explanation lay in the fact that the Canadians, cleverly led, withdrew in good order, convinced that occupation of the forts was of no great and immediate importance when compared with the retention of a cohesive army. When they were prepared, they could always regain the captured forts because their supplies were more readily obtainable than those of the Americans—which must be ferried across the river.

Perry's victory on Lake Erie of September 10 seemed to herald even happier events. But when, in November, an American force attempted to capture Montreal and miserably failed, the prospect of swift British surrender faded. As winter began to set in, as it does with a will on the Niagara Frontier, the British gave evidence of interest in retaking the American-held forts. Commander of United States forces on that side of the river was General George McClure, whose instinctive response to this intelligence was to beat a retreat. This he proceeded to do, but in the process, he also gave the Canadians a taste of the kind of treatment the red men had enjoyed for two centuries.

The town of Newark, which adjoined Fort George (where McClure had his headquarters), was of no military significance at all. Yet the general gave its inhabitants two hours' notice to evacuate it on the night of December 10. As soon as the time had elapsed, he ordered Newark to be burned to the ground. Approximately four hundred residents, mostly women and children, were driven from their homes, taking with them only the possessions they could easily transport on a night of freezing cold. Eighty buildings were thus gratuitously razed. Later, when the cry of outrage was raised on both sides of the Niagara, McClure feebly explained that he had not wanted the British troops to make use of Newark for billeting. So disgusted were the general's own men that most of them returned home directly after regaining the American side of the river, in spite of the fact that they were owed three months' back pay. Nor did McClure himself wait around long for retribution. He departed, he said, to recruit more troops.

Reprisal was swift and total. The infuriated British commander Lieutenant General Sir Gordon Drummond ordered Colonel John Murray to lead a force against Fort Niagara on the night of December 18. Youngstown was overcome without the firing of a single shot. The former House of Peace was captured with comparable ease, though at the fort resistance was

Battle of Niagara, 1813

offered, with the result that the defenders suffered about eighty casualties and surrendered nearly three hundred and fifty prisoners. The British casualties numbered no more than eleven.

Nor was this the only activity of that night. A second enemy force, under the leadership of General Phineas Riall, arrived at Lewiston just as day was breaking. There his regiment of whites and Indians reciprocated for the sack of Newark—adding embellishments. Whereas the Americans at Newark had actually wounded none of the residents, the red men, fired up by drink, scalped and maimed a few hapless citizens who had failed to leave when the first alarm was sounded. Lewiston was virtually burned to the ground.

During the rest of the day of the eighteenth, Riall moved up the American side of the Niagara, burning and pillaging. A Tuscarora village on the shore was not spared as the British leveled Manchester. The troops garrisoned at Fort Schlosser, at

the south end of the Upper Rapids, offered just enough resistance to permit themselves to retreat in fair order across
Tonawanda Creek, after which they destroyed the bridge which
would give the enemy access to Black Rock.

Contented with his day's work, General Riall "borrowed"
some American boats and traversed the Niagara to Fort Chippawa. Colonel Murray's troops, however, having invested Fort
Niagara, remained there in permanence, easily supplied by
water. The sudden and savage invasion of the American side
of the river had stunned and surprised the army. In the fortnight that followed, there seemed little enough they could do
to prepare themselves for a possible resumption of the Canadian assault.

General McClure wrote on Christmas day, from the security
of Batavia, New York, to the Niagara Indian agent Erastus
Granger:

> I will send all the troops on as fast as they arrive. The
> officers commanding the regulars will not return to Buffalo
> until compelled by a positive order. I should not urge them
> unless the place is actually in danger. I could not prevail
> upon them to stay at Eleven Mile Creek nor was it safe for
> me or any that accompanied me to stay there [at Buffalo]
> or travel the road. The numerous mob that we met all cried
> out, "shoot him, damn him; shoot him." This mob is coun-
> tenanced by many of the inhabitants of Buffalo and I must
> be well convinced that they will treat me in a different way
> before I can agree to make that my headquarters.

That McClure should not have known of the imminent peril
that menaced Buffalo a full week after the Canadians had
seized Fort Niagara and sacked all the hamlets to the north of
Black Rock is inconceivable. He spoke in this same letter of
recruiting more troops and then returning for a short holiday
to his home at Bath, New York. He was more faithful to his
second promise than to his first. He never came back to the
Niagara Frontier during the war.

To replace McClure, General Amos Hall reached Buffalo the

day after Christmas and found chaos. There were no more than thirteen hundred men on hand to defend the two towns which the Canadians had so far failed to destroy. Everyone, soldier and civilian alike, was certain that the enemy would return. And return he did on the night of December 29. An eyewitness account, from the hand of the son of the Porter brothers' partner and friend James L. Barton survives:

> The citizens were compelled to flee, many half-clothed, from the murderous tomahawks of the Indians, while the pathway of their escape was lighted by the blaze of their own dwellings. In one hour's time, the hard earnings and savings of years were taken from them, and many were left nothing but their naked hands with which to provide for the wants of their families. The enemy retired to Canada after the destruction had been committed [though still retaining possession of Fort Niagara]. A very severe winter followed the destruction of Buffalo, which caused more distress to many of its people who had lost their all, and were compelled to seek shelter and food as best they could.
>
> In the spring of 1814 the people began to return, and a few plain buildings were constructed. The [American] army came into Buffalo the first week in April, and brought a large trade to the place; but, as is always the case, it was followed by a caravan of traders almost as numerous as the troops, who more than divided this trade with the citizens. Soon were to be seen shanties. . . . The village was literally one of shanties, and every thing had a lively and busy appearance.
>
> The army remained in Buffalo until the second of July, when it crossed into Canada. . . . Trade flourished. The wants of the army required large supplies, some of which the country around could furnish, and others were brought by land from Albany, and other parts of the state.

It is worth noting that Barton, whose memoir of the sack of Buffalo was published fifty years after the event, made no mention of the earlier and unprovoked assault against Newark which had precipitated the rape of the east bank, nor of the even more terrible and equally unwarranted devastation of York (Toronto). One is meant to infer, presumably, that the destruction of the American side of the Niagara was without antecedents in our own nation's conduct of the war. The fact is, moreover, that the Canadians did not return to their own side of the river after they destroyed Black Rock and Buffalo. A company of their troops occupied Fort Niagara for a very long time thereafter, as we shall have occasion to note below. Perhaps Barton was a victim of what the psychiatrists call "projection." He attributed to the enemy the faults of his own country. This is not to suggest that what the Canadians did was morally justified, but simply that the initial impulse was American, not British. In this distorted manner is national history almost invariably assembled for the consumption and edification of the general public.

A similar misunderstanding of the realities that underlay events applied to the British sack of Washington in the summer of 1814. The enemy never failed to label this gesture as an act of reprisal for the destruction of Newark and Toronto. Nevertheless, we are still soberly informing our children that the assault against the national capital was dastardly and unprovoked. Dastardly it certainly was, but it had its direct cause on the Niagara and the shores of Lake Ontario.

By the first week of 1814, the American military presence on the Niagara Frontier was apparently negligible. The most straightforward contemporary analysis of the causes of the United States' defeats is extracted from a personal report to the new Secretary of War John Armstrong (who had apologized to Sir George Prevost for the sack of Newark, calling the act "abhorrent to every American feeling") by Colonel Lewis Cass. This was composed on January 12, immediately after his complete survey of the Niagara region:

> The fall of Niagara has been owing to the most criminal negligence. The force in it was fully competent to its defense. The conduct [of the officer in charge] ought to be

strictly investigated. The force of the enemy has been greatly magnified. From the most careful examination, I am satisfied that not more than 650 [British] regulars, militia, and Indians arrived. To oppose them, we had from 2500 to 3000 militia. All except a very few of them behaved in the most cowardly manner. They fled without discharging a musket. The enemy continued on this side of the river until Saturday. All their movements betrayed symptoms of apprehension. A vast quantity of property was left in the town [of Buffalo] uninjured [*pace* Mr. Barton]. Since January 1st, they have made no movement. They continue to possess Fort Niagara.

The discrepancy between the narratives of Cass and Barton requires no underlining. Less explicable is the colonel's assertion than there were no fewer than twenty-five hundred militiamen at the several Niagara posts prior to the December 18 attack. It may be that these consisted of troops who had refused to reenlist, were waiting for their arrears in pay, or were unable to find a means of getting back to their homes. This alone would account for the lassitude of their performance during the enemy assaults. Add to it the unpopularity of the entire war among New Yorkers and New Englanders, which would produce ten months later the Hartford Convention, and one has all the elements of incipient mutiny and even civil war.

As Barton indicated, a substantial United States force did arrive at the Niagara Frontier in the spring of 1814. The Canadians were still in possession of the former House of Peace. The size of the American army here, which was commanded by General Jacob Brown (who had formerly been in charge of the shipyard at Presque Isle) left no doubt in the minds of the British and Canadian officers that a campaign of major proportions was to be anticipated. Two other generals were to participate. Peter Porter, one of the war's most persuasive advocates, had been elevated to that rank and returned to his home district to share in the glory. Winfield Scott, a brigadier general now, also made his appearance. Their joint command consisted of a motley collection of about forty-five hundred bodies, mostly militiamen, whom Scott was ordered to whip into fighting condition. This he brilliantly accomplished with a cadre of no more than a few dozen regular officers and sergeants to aid him. Having only recently been released in an exchange of prisoners, Scott meant to demonstrate that when *he* was in charge, the fate of the battle would not be determined by the incompetence of men. He believed his career to be at stake, and so it was. His disciplinary measures were rather Draconian, and his emphasis on the virtues of close-order drill seemed irrelevant to battle situations. Nevertheless, he produced what has been described as the best fighting force put together by the United States since the end of the Revolution. By early July, that little army was ready for combat.

The ensuing months witnessed the hardest-fought and bloodiest battles of the entire war. On July 3, Scott crossed the Niagara from Black Rock and quite easily took possession of Fort Erie. The next day, he marched about thirteen hundred of his troops against Fort Chippawa, one of the bastions erected by Governor John Simcoe after 1792. It was defended by a mixed force of some two thousand Canadians, Britons, and red men. After a struggle that lasted five hours, the defenders evacuated the fort, leaving behind them more than five hundred casualties. On July 5, General Brown led a second American detachment against Queenston. This was a preliminary sally to what he believed would prove the crucial phase of the Niagara campaign, an assault against Fort George, where the survivors of Chippawa had installed themselves, and the recapture of Fort Niagara, which was still in enemy hands.

Brown felt, however, that his attack against these strongly defended positions ought to be reinforced by a naval fleet. For this purpose, he sent an urgent message to Commodore Isaac Chauncey, commander of the American flotilla which was based at Fort Oswego. Chauncey's reply took a fortnight to reach General Brown. By this time, the Canadians had so significantly improved the defenses of Fort George that he considered it injudicious to remain in the undefended hamlet of Queenston. He returned his troops to the greater security of Fort Chippawa. The tone of Chauncey's dispatch, however, throws considerable and very unfortunate light on his subsequent inaction:

> That you might find the fleet somewhat of a convenience in the transportation of provisions and stores for the use of the army and an agreeable appendage to attend its marches and countermarches, I am ready to believe, but Sir, the Secretary of the Navy has honored me with a higher destiny —we intend to seek and fight the enemy's fleet. That is the great purpose of the Government in creating this fleet and I shall not be diverted in my efforts to effectuate it by *any sinister attempt to render us subordinate to or an appendage of the Army.*

Though the text of this message, as quoted variously, differs from version to version, the emphasized passage is a constant.

Battle of Queenston Heights,
July 5, 1814

Battle of Lundy's Lane, July 25, 1814

Chauncey's suggestion that there might be something "sinister" in Brown's request reminds us that interservice rivalry is as old as our nation. The commodore's evasive reply led General Brown to assume that he could expect no immediate naval assistance, and immediate assistance seemed to him the essence of his problem. The Canadians had reinvested Queenston after his withdrawal, and they were obviously preparing for an assault against Fort Chippawa. Rather than assume an abjectly defensive posture, Brown and Scott moved northward from the fort with the object of meeting the oncoming enemy on open ground.

The opposing armies encountered each other on the evening of July 25, 1814, at a crossroads called Lundy's Lane, about a half a mile west-northwest of Niagara Falls. This battle, the most savage and most costly engagement of the whole war, raged until the earliest hours of the following day. The outcome was inconclusive—which is to say that both sides claimed a victory when, in fact, both sides lost. Brown and Scott were seriously wounded, thus leaving their forces without a high officer in command. The confused Americans fell all the way back to Fort Erie. A similar fate, however, had befallen the ranking officers of the Canadian army. Consequently, though the advantage of momentum appeared to be theirs, the attackers failed to exploit it by pressing and harassing the retreating foe. Casualties of the two forces were practically identical—about eight hundred fifty for each side.

During the three weeks that followed the horrendous Battle of Lundy's Lane, Canadians and Americans alike regrouped and bound up their wounds as best they were able. Brown and Scott, hospitalized, were replaced by General George Izard, who arrived from Sacketts Harbor on the Saint Lawrence in the second week of August at the head of a substantial army— ranging in estimated size from three to six thousand.

Izard's troops had been compelled to make the journey from Irondequoit Bay to Niagara on foot—for that inlet was as far as the reluctant Isaac Chauncey would take him. The commodore feared, one surmises, a sinister plot to make the enemy a mere appendage of the army if he transported the men all the way to Four Mile Creek.

While Izard and his exhausted soldiers were making this difficult overland passage of about a hundred miles, the British commander, Sir Gordon Drummond, had been seeing to the reinforcement of his own installations. On August 15, he led an assault against Fort Erie that seemed certain of success—yet it proved a catastrophe because of the exceptional selflessness of Lieutenant Patrick McDonogh, who was in command of one of the outer bastions of Fort Erie which was overrun by the Canadian vanguard. Severely wounded in this initial action, McDonogh lay on the floor of the little redoubt as enemy troops advanced on the main fortress. He managed to crawl to a powder chest and without hesitation fired his pistol into it. The resulting explosion cost young McDonogh his life, but it also caused about three hundred enemy casualties, and so stunned the survivors that it gave Izard's garrison a chance to rally and, finally, to repel the attack. At the end of this battle, more than five hundred members of the assault force were taken prisoners. McDonogh's sacrifice had helped to save the day. His gesture was never officially recognized by the government he had so valiantly served.

During the autumn months of 1814, Izard's troops made occasional sallies out of Fort Erie and gradually forced the Canadians back down the river toward Fort George. But like General Brown, the new American commander felt it impossible to launch a successful assault against that bastion or Fort Niagara without naval support in the form of a barrage from ships standing offshore which would divert enemy artillery fire. Like Brown, Izard implored Commodore Chauncey to provide water-based firepower to help prevent the reinforcement of the two fortresses from British ships. As before, the reluctant seaman replied with conundrums that amounted to a flat refusal.

By the middle of autumn, the Canadians were notably strengthened by the arrival at Montreal of more than ten thousand veterans of Wellington's campaigns in Spain and southern France. It was absolutely vital to Izard's strategy that none of these seasoned troops be permitted to reach the Canadian-held forts at the Lake Ontario end of the Niagara River. The key to the success of this plan lay in the trembling hands of Isaac Chauncey.

American Commodore Thomas McDonough won a signal naval victory off Plattsburg, on Lake Champlain, in September. There were understandably loud huzzahs to greet this triumph—which had no bearing whatever on Izard's critical situation at Niagara. For there remained on Lake Ontario a British fleet under the command of Sir James Yeo. This contingent was operating out of Kingston (formerly Fort Frontenac) at the headwaters of the Saint Lawrence. Since Chauncey refused to help Izard, the latter hoped at the very least that the timorous commodore would attack Yeo.

However, Isaac Chauncey persistently refused to interpose

his flotilla between Kingston and Niagara, thus to thwart any possible naval reinforcement of the two Niagara forts that were under a relaxed sort of siege. Yeo, on the other hand, chanced everything to bring *his* vessels right under the guns of Forts George and Niagara, thereby aborting the slender hope that Izard's plan of reducing those remaining bastions might yet succeed.

In the face of Izard's pitiable requests that he do something, Chauncey's timidity was such that even after Yeo was known to have sailed for Niagara, he never attempted to bombard the evacuated port of Kingston. He chose instead to confine his operations to childish but safe patrols of the waters on the south shore of Lake Ontario, eastward from Fort Oswego, where he knew very well he was unlikely ever to hear a shot fired in anger by an enemy. The commodore was later criticized for his excessive "caution." This mild reprimand, however, failed to prevent him from becoming commander of the United States fleet in the Mediterranean in 1816. For he had lost no ships in all his campaigning on Lake Ontario. The fact that he had run not the slightest risk did not, on balance, work to his ultimate disadvantage.

As for poor General Izard, bereft of all hope of naval assistance, there seemed only one solution. He must evacuate the Canadian side of the Niagara before the enemy was in a position to drive him away. On November 5, he ordered the destruction of Fort Erie, and withdrew his troops to Black Rock and Buffalo, where they enjoyed a very hostile reception from their American hosts. Six weeks later, the war was officially terminated by the signing of the Treaty of Ghent—though word of this event wasn't received at the Niagara until February of the following year. As soon as he learned of the peace, Izard resigned his commission in disgust.

For practical purposes, the War of 1812 achieved nothing but a restitution of the *status quo ante*. No trade concessions were granted. Not a square foot of territory changed hands. A few military reputations were modestly enhanced; many more were dismally and properly tarnished. Political mythology has it that Andrew Jackson was eventually elected President of the United States on the strength of his successes against the Creek Indians and his victory against the British troops of Sir Edward Pakenham at New Orleans—a battle fought three weeks after the signing of the peace treaty. The fact, however, is that Jackson was a much more redoubtable politician than a general, and it was *this* ingenuity that led him to the White House. Winfield Scott, though he demonstrated good command instincts during his two brief tours at Niagara, was a much more effective commander a few decades later, when his enemies were bootless Mexicans.

The War of 1812 resulted in stalemate. The only significant outcome remotely attributable to it was the Rush-Bagot Treaty of 1816, which restricted Canadian and American naval operations on the Great Lakes, the Niagara, and the Saint Lawrence to "police patrols."

It was a shabby little war. There were a few more alarms at Niagara thereafter, as we shall have occasion to describe. However, Americans of subsequent generations sought their gore and their glory elsewhere, in the slaughter and dispossession of the Indians and the Mexicans—and, of course, in the slaughter and dispossession of one another in the Civil War. Our history is instructive, but not often very uplifting.

12
The
NIAGARA
Transfigured

Though all was not to be peace forever along the Canadian-American frontier of the Niagara River after the conclusion of the War of 1812, such few occasions of effervescence as occurred are of historical interest mainly for their power to entertain—as sideshows to the principal thrust of circumstance, the causal events which were taking place elsewhere. The permanent and durable peace established along the entire border, from the Atlantic to the Pacific, was marred in the future only by a boundary dispute which we remember today as the "Oregon Question," whose American slogan, "Fifty-four, forty, or fight," was a notable feature of the 1844 Presidential campaign. Some bellicose Yankees called for a war to secure a major section of the northwest corner of what is now the continental United States—but a compromise was reached; they found an outlet for their blood lust in scuffling with the disorganized Mexicans of Santa Ana, who were rightly deemed an easier enemy than the British and Canadians to defeat by force of arms.

The concern at Niagara from the end of the War of 1812 onward was "development," the process of rebuilding and enlarging the communities and facilities on both sides of the river which had been damaged or destroyed during that conflict. Confidence that this region would once again bask in the sunshine of trade was evidenced in a number of ways. Perhaps the most significant was the operation of the Holland Land Company.

The origins of this syndicate go back to the Revolution, when Dutch bankers had advanced important sums to the government of the rebellious American colonies. With the struggle past and the outcome favorable to the borrowers, the Amsterdam lenders naturally sought repayment. This was problematical. The British were holding large tracts of American land as ransom for Loyalist claims. There was no cash. It occurred to the bankers that land might prove a satisfactory substitute for money, but even this was rendered difficult by a New York law which prohibited aliens (especially nonresident aliens) from owning property. Laws, however, are usually exceptionable. In this case, the bankers acquired truly enormous areas of land in the Niagara region by the simplest of devices—third-party purchase. From 1792 to 1798, when the New York law against foreign possession was repealed, the bankrupt Robert Morris of New York sold to American citizens who represented the Dutch bankers almost three and a half million acres of land in the vicinity of the Niagara Frontier. It was by all measurements the most outstanding land grab of the eighteenth century, and its effects would be felt for at least fifty years thereafter.

The Holland Land Company, as it was officially known after 1798, was interested only in disposing of its huge acquisitions at a profit. Operating along lines that became classic among American developers in the century and a half to come, the company first had to discover just what it was owner of. In this interest the syndicate secured the services of Joseph Ellicott (who finished a similar but less ambitious undertaking for the United States government, completing L'Enfant's plan for the new capital of Washington). Ellicott moved to the hamlet of

Buffalo Creek and then to Batavia. In the years between 1798 and 1801, he surveyed and mapped the entire holding—which extended over most of the American side of the Niagara Frontier, excepting only the Tuscarora and Seneca reservations and the mile-wide strip of river frontage which was the property of New York State.

Asking prices as high as $3.00 per acre for uncleared land to which there was no easy access, the company began to dispose of its terrain in 1801, as soon as Ellicott had completed his charts. By the end of 1809, well over two thousand parcels had been sold. The terms, designed to attract the same sort of purchaser who is now invited to buy "retirement lots" in Florida or Arizona, seemed "easy." One deposited ten percent on the signing of the contract and repaid the balance over varying periods of years at rather substantial interest rates. Not content with enormous profits, the company arranged with certain malleable legislators to have the state of New York exempt it from all taxation until 1833, when some sense of decency caught up with the majorities of the state Assembly and Senate. To avenge this wrong, which happened to coincide with the beginnings of a financial catastrophe that shook the entire nation, the company started massive foreclosure proceedings that ruined many landowners who were just getting their farms into more or less profitable condition. By 1836, the company's agents were so unpopular that they took refuge in distant Rochester to escape the wrath of those whom they had quite lawfully but also unconscionably dispossessed. Until 1821, Joseph Ellicott remained the company's principal representative on the site. He served his principals well in that he was ruthless in his collection of monies due. He did not, in the process, fail to advance himself. Indeed, his dismissal was occasioned mainly by his having made the name of Ellicott synonymous with political control of all of western New York State.

The land acquired by the pioneers who moved westward in ever greater numbers after 1815 was just as arable as those sections along the Niagara's banks that had been placed under cultivation by Daniel Joncaire in the middle of the previous century. Moreover, as people flocked toward the spillway, it was natural that towns should thrive—though the question of which town on the American side of the river would dominate could be answered only when it was known at precisely what point the projected Erie Canal would enter the waters of Lake Erie.

While that issue was being discussed at opposite ends of the state, the restoration of Niagara villages proceeded apace. In the last months of 1817, Noah Brown saw to the laying of the keel of the first steamboat to be built for use on the Great Lakes. This ceremony was observed at Black Rock, at the shipyard created by Jesse Elliott during the recent war. This vessel, *Walk-in-the-Water,* was towed upstream to Buffalo (the town had dropped "Creek" from its name) on August 23, 1818. With twenty-nine passengers aboard, she began her maiden voyage to Cleveland and Detroit, a trip accomplished in just over forty-eight hours—a reduction by almost two-thirds of the average time required by a sailing ship. *Walk-in-the-Water* seemed certain to become a spectacular commercial success, for the lake waters were ideal for this kind of vessel. Unhappily for her owners, she burned and foundered within a couple of years of her launching. A pattern was set, however, which was to prove irreversible. The steamship was there to stay. The portage's lease on life, however, was soon to be terminated by the opening of the Erie Canal, an event that was only a few years off.

By 1821, the American traveler Philip Stansbury noted that the accommodations for an ever-increasing number of casual visitors had markedly improved since the war, and that the growth of water-powered industry, still in its infancy, had not been neglected:

> From a collection of mills and factories arranged along the American side of the [upper] rapids, denominated Grand Niagara or Manchester [Niagara Falls, New York], spreads in view the extensive bay, bounded by champaigne [sic] lands. Chippewa [sic] appears at a distance,

scattered about the mouth of the Chippewa river; Navy Island and the woody shores of the Grand Isle, lie at a distance on the left, and opposite, upon a high bushy bank, first among the roaring breakers, is Goat or Iris-Island, to the romantic walks of which, a bridge, lately rebuilt by Judge [Peter] Porter, after passing over an intermediate [Green] island, leads from the American shore. It was not without terror that I saw the violent surges beating against the slender props of this bridge, and within a stone's throw of the river leaping into the yawning gulf and involving the objects beneath the dense vapours. The small island across which the bridge passes, is called Bath-Island [now Green Island], and has upon it the toll-keeper's dwelling and a commodious bathing house. Parties, in summer, after refreshing themselves at this intermediate island, stroll among the retired groves of Iris Island, where from a precipice [Terrapin Point] of two hundred feet between the two falls, an interesting view of both sheets tumbling on the right-hand and left is obtained. There is a beautiful seclusion. While the foot-step is led by paths, among the gloomy trunks of large forest trees, one of the grandest objects of nature shows, at times, white through the bushes, and with its solemn roar, impels the mind to contemplation and awe. Adjacent, are the other little islands [the Three Sisters], with their close planted firs expanding over the banks, upon which neither man or quadruped has ever yet dared to step [there are footbridges today], and deform the rustic elegance of nature.

For the convenience of descending to the bottom of the falls, permanent stairways have been durably fixed against the sides of the precipice [the staircase is in disrepair today]. From the foot of the stairs, down the slope, steps are made of rough stones, with a rude banister for a support, leading to a ferry-boat on the shore. The Charon of the stream, as I descended, was standing at a sort of reel, with which he draws the boat out of the water, awaiting with patience the approach of adventurous passengers.

The boat in operation at this time was an oar-powered antecedent of the *Maid of the Mist*—but the last, apparently, to use Goat Island as its starting point. If tourism wasn't yet a major industry at Niagara, it was certainly well on the way. The "rustic elegance of nature" remained undisturbed during the following years, but the incursions of commerce were ever more extensive, as we can see from a report composed by a Welsh visitor, James Flint:

> The falls of Niagara are much visited by strangers, as during our short stay there we met several persons who were examining them. There is a large tavern on each side of the river, and in the *album* kept at one of these, I observed that upwards of a hundred folio pages had been written with names within five months.

From the termination of the War of 1812, the race between tourism and industry to desecrate both sides of the river, particularly beside and above the falls, was fully joined. For quite a long period, the advantage appeared to be with the innkeepers. Though visitors flocked in ever-increasing numbers to have a look at the great natural wonder of the cascade and rapids, industrialists had yet fully to appreciate the potential of the river's powerful currents as a cheap source of energy. Moreover, the importance of the two portages, so long unquestioned and unchallenged, was on the point of sudden demise.

Since 1810, as we have remarked with respect to De Witt Clinton's first visit to the Niagara Frontier, plans for the Erie Canal had been in the making. The question which would decide the destiny of two minuscule communities on the American side of the river was at which of them—Black Rock or Buffalo—the canal would reach the level of Lake Erie. Logic, as it happened, favored Buffalo, for its situation meant that the builders of the channel would have to dig two fewer feet in depth. It would be a comfort to report that logic was the decisive factor, thereby distinguishing it from most other political judgments. In the event, logic served as an excuse for a decision arrived at by more usual methods—payoffs and influence trafficking. One need not be startled by this, for what was at stake was a fairly substantial amount of possible increment;

Sailing ship under tow

whichever hamlet succeeded would, *ipso facto,* become a great city.

The triumph of Buffalo as the western terminus of the Erie Canal was not, however, achieved without genuine and commendable effort. In April 1818, some important residents of the village realized that despite its geographical advantage, Buffalo suffered from a deficiency that might blight its chances: it had no harbor, whereas Black Rock was endowed with a natural one that had been in use since the days of La Salle.

Poling a Durham boat

The Buffalonians, under the leadership of Judge Samuel Wilkeson (who had maintained law and order during the months at the end of the war when Izard's disgruntled troops had been billeted there), planned the construction of a breakwater and channel that would allow the passage of the largest vessels then making use of Black Rock's facilities. Their idea was realized in the autumn of 1820, after many difficulties. Fate—as man is often inclined to call nature—entered into the fruition of the scheme. A great storm achieved overnight what perhaps months of dredging could not have done—cutting a channel through a sandbar that separated the waters of Lake Erie from those of the man-made harbor. But it would be another two years before a vessel—designed by the same Noah Brown whose *Walk-in-the-Water* had been destroyed a year earlier—demonstrated to the satisfaction of the canal architects and planners that Buffalo's harbor was superior to that of Black Rock for the Erie Canal's western entrance.

Thus was the future of Buffalo determined. And though it would be only in our own century that Black Rock was absorbed by burgeoning Buffalo, the former's role as Niagara metropolis remained a shattered dream. In 1825, the Erie Canal was formally opened to barges. Its Niagara terminus was situated at the mouth of Tonawanda Creek. From that moment on, the American portage became obsolete, though the carriageway on the Canadian bank continued to operate for a few more years, since it served the shipping that arrived at the Niagara from Lakes Erie and Ontario—commerce bound to or from the Saint Lawrence. However, the demands placed on these limited facilities—as they were now seen to be when juxtaposed with those of the Erie Canal—would soon become so great with the increase of population west of the spillway that it was found necessary to replace them with a Canadian canal which connected Erie and Ontario. This waterway was completed in 1832; it was the ancestor of the Welland Ship Canal which would be finished a century later, year for year.

Nor were the two canals the only factors leading to the

abandonment of the two portage routes. By 1840, the Erie Canal was encountering competition for the transport of persons and goods—a railroad link from New York and Albany, with a connecting line to Albany from Boston. This was the so-called "water level" route of what became the New York Central Railroad. A second rail line to the American side of the Niagara, passing through the Alleghenies, was opened not long afterward.

This increasing accessibility to the largest of urban agglomerations made the wonders of Niagara the most popular attraction of the nation. The splendors of the lands west of the Rockies were still secrets to all but a very few of the hardiest easterners and would not become objects of pilgrimage until after the Civil War, when Americans could make the land safe for democracy by slaughtering the Indians.

The transformation of both banks of the river was rapid and, on the whole, deplorable, especially within visual range of the falls. In 1832, E. T. Coke, a young British officer, spent four days at Niagara and left us what appears to be the first recorded outcry against the land speculations which, he correctly apprehended, would soon doom the entire Niagara Frontier to the sort of spoliation that almost every major American work of nature has eventually fallen victim to.

It is worth observing, before citing Coke, that the Holland Land Company was not the sole offender. The Canadians were no less high-handed in their disdain for the integrity of contractual agreement with the red men than were the Assterdam financiers who stood behind the Holland Land Company. If they were a little more prodigal in their distribution of lands to the Indians than their American counterparts, it was not out of generosity, but because the lands they disposed of were not, at the time, deemed of great value. Eventually, the Indians of the Grand River Reservation would be pushed inexorably westward in the same fashion that those of the United States were dispossessed.

When E. T. Coke came to the Niagara in 1832, Buffalo was

on its way to becoming a thriving city. The American towns
of Manchester (Niagara Falls), Black Rock, Lewiston, and
Youngstown were enjoying varying degrees of prosperity. Since
the Erie Canal route was the main focus of shipping commerce,
the banks of the Niagara below Tonawanda Creek were for the
most part left to the tourists and those who exploited them.
The single important exception to this rule was water-powered
industry, which was proliferating on both sides of the river
above the falls. With icy fury, Coke looked into the Niagara's
future and was right:

> The company of speculators intend erecting grist-mills,
> storehouses, saw-mills, and all other kinds of unornamental
> buildings [in the process of founding what would eventually
> be the town of Niagara Falls, Ontario], entertaining the most
> sanguine hopes of living to see a very populous city. The die
> then is cast, and the beautiful scenery about the Falls is
> doomed to be destroyed. Year after year will it become less
> and less attractive. Even at this time they were surveying
> and allotting, and the proprietors were planning one front
> of their houses upon the Falls, the other upon Lundy's
> Lane, and meditating the levelling of some rock, so as to
> form a pretty little flower garden. It would not surprise me
> to hear, before many years have elapsed, that a suspension
> bridge has been thrown across the grand Horse-shoe to Goat
> Island, so that the good people of Clifton [Niagara Falls,
> Ontario] may be better enabled to watch the pyramidical
> [sic] bubbles of air rising from the foot of the cataract. 'Tis
> a pity that such ground was not reserved as sacred in per-
> petuum; that the great forest trees were not allowed to
> luxuriate in all the wild and savage beauty about a spot
> where the works of man will ever appear paltry, and can
> never be in accordance. For my own part, most sincerely do
> I congratulate myself upon having viewed the scene before
> such profanation takes place. The small manufacturing town
> of Manchester (what a romantic name and what associa-
> tions!), upon the American Bank, at present detracts nothing
> from the charm of the place, the neat white-washed houses
> being interspersed with trees and gardens; but when once

the red and yellow painted stores, with their green Venetian blinds, tin roofs, and huge smoking chimneys arise, farewell to a great portion of the attraction Niagara now possesses.

A ferry-boat, half a mile below the Canadian Fall, crosses to Manchester, landing the passengers within fifty yards of the American one, . . . The prosperity of this village has been much retarded by two causes, one from its liability to destruction, being a frontier settlement; and the other—by no means uncommon to the United States,—the extravagant price demanded by an individual, the great proprietor [The Porter-Barton Company], for a grant of the water privileges allowed by the Rapids. Two or three hundred yards from the bank above the Ferry, at the entrance to the village, a wooden bridge has been thrown over the Rapids to [Green Island] on which there is a paper mill, and connected with Goat Island, which is of considerable extent, and divides the two falls. Truly the men who were employed in the erection of this bridge must have been in full possession of Horace's *aes triplex,* for a more perilous situation could scarcely be imagined. A slip of a workman's foot would precipitate him into the Rapids, whence he would pass with the rapidity of lightning over the Falls. It was constructed at the expense of General Porter, an American officer of distinction, during the late war, and appears strongly and firmly situated. The piers

Peter Porter's
footbridge

are loose stones, confined together by a wooden frame or box, and a floor of planks twelve feet in width. There was one erected previously at the upper end of the island, and out of the power of the rapids, but it was continually subject to injury from the drift-ice, whereas in its present situation the Rapids render the ice harmless, by breaking it before it arrives so low as the bridge.

The prognosis for Peter Porter's footbridge from Manchester to the islands near the American bank was not nearly so bright as the otherwise clairvoyant Coke imagined. Whether it was pack ice or the stormy rapids that eventually undermined its piers, it collapsed not very long after he had considered its method of construction. His prophecy of a suspension bridge, however, was uncanny—though he situated it inaccurately. Less than a quarter of a century later, the first of many bridges would span the whole Niagara River, and a few years after that, the great John Roebling would here totally revolutionize the art of the suspension bridge.

Charles Joseph Latrobe, evidently no close kin of the master architect, visited Niagara the year after Coke had come here, and his report leaves no doubt that "progress" was being made at a heady rate:

How is it now? The forest has everywhere yielded to the axe. Hotels, with their snug shubberies, outhouses, gardens, and paltry establishments, stare you in the face; museums, mills, staircases, tools, and grog-shops, all the petty trickery [of English resorts], greet the eye of the traveller. Bridges are thrown across from island to island; and Goat Island is reached without adventure. A scheming company on the Canadian side have planned a "City of the Falls," to be filled with snug cottages, symmetrically arranged, to let for the season; and, in fine, you write to your friend in Quebec, giving him rendezvous at Niagara for a certain hour, start yourself from Richmond, in Virginia, for the point proposed, with a moral certainty of meeting at the very day and hour specified, by taking advantage of the improvements of the age, and the well-arranged mode of conveyance by steamers,

railroads, canals, and coaches. In short, Niagara . . . is now
. . . hackneyed . . . and, all things considered, the observation an unimaginative "Eastern man" is said to have made,
addressing a young lady-tourist, who was gazing breathlessly
for the first time at the scene, was not so out of keeping with
it. "Isn't it nice, Miss?" Yes, all is nice, that that active little
biped man has done or is doing.

What is particularly surprising about Latrobe's description
is that it almost exactly resembles the Niagara of our own
day—wanting only the more lurid towers and lighting of the
Canadian shore and the appalling squalor of the American side
of the Upper Niagara to fill out his scene. The factories and
their attendant slums had yet to materialize. Public transport,
on the other hand, was obviously a great deal better organized
and far more reliable than it is now. "That active little biped
man" had more work to do.

The clergy got into the act in this same year of 1833, with a
visit to Niagara of two British Congregationalists, Andrew
Reed and James Matheson, whose letters to their parishioners
back in the mother country were composed in the first person
singular, presumably to give them urgency as well as intimacy:

> "I am sorry . . . that I cannot say much for the taste
> either of the visitors or inhabitants of this spot. The visitors
> seemed to regard the Falls as an object of curiosity than
> otherwise, and when they had satisfied their curiosity (which
> in most cases was very quickly done), and could report
> that they had seen them, the duty was discharged. Such
> persons drove in on the morning, explored for a couple of
> hours, dined, and hurried away. Or, if they stayed, they had
> had enough of Niagara, and they made an excursion to see
> the burning [sulfur] springs [on the Canadian side, above
> Chippawa]. . . .
> With the residents I am half disposed to be angry. On the
> American side they have got up a shabby town, and called
> it Manchester. Manchester and the Falls of Niagara! A pro-
> position has been made to buy Goat Island and turn it into
> a botanical garden, to improve the scenery—and such

scenery! On the Canadian side, a money-seeking party have bought up 400 acres, with the hope of erecting "The City of the Falls;" and still worse, close on the Table Rock, some party has been busy in erecting a mill dam! The universal voice ought to interfere, and prevent them. Niagara does not belong to them; Niagara does not belong to Canada or America. Such spots should be deemed the property of civilized mankind; and nothing should be allowed to weaken their efficacy on the tastes, the morals, and the enjoyments of all men.

The point was amply made, then, early in the fourth decade of the nineteenth cenutry: industrial and residential and touristic developers were visiting a wholly new sort of havoc on the region. Niagara had taken the road, within twenty years of the end of the War of 1812, that it was to follow ever after. The outcries of perceptive visitors (some of whom sound, for all the world, like David Brower) were scarcely heeded by the resident and absentee exploiters of the area, or by those who were to settle here in the years to come. They frantically developed the shores of the river from the falls to Lake Erie— sparing only, and imperfectly, the stretch of the Niagara gorge to Lewiston and Queenston; and this only because the cliff-side was notoriously unstable.

Indeed, we must presume that the voices raised weren't even heard at Niagara. To the degree that protests appeared in print, it seems probable they were unknown here. Whatever else it was, Niagara's shores were not exactly a center of culture where books and periodicals (excepting local newspapers) were often or seriously perused. It remained only for technology to add its special form of depredation to a scene whose general outlines were already so clearly and so distressingly delineated—and so firmly established.

Yet, before the spell cast by the falls and the surrounding countryside that remained unblemished by man was completely dispelled, their wonders were to prompt some illustrious writers to indite words that, for one reason or another, merit recollection. Mrs. Harriet Beecher Stowe, whom Abraham Lincoln is supposed to have described as the nice little lady who brought us the Civil War, visited Niagara for the first time in 1834, and was moved to contemplations of a magnificent death—like that, perhaps, of the apocryphal Indian maiden that local guides were pleased to tell her about: "I felt as if I could have *gone over* with the waters; it would be so beautiful a death; there would be no fear in it. I felt the rock tremble under me with a sort of joy. I was so maddened that I could have gone, too, if it had gone."

Nathaniel Hawthorne came to Niagara in the same year and has left us a brilliant memoir:

> Never did a pilgrim approach Niagara with deeper enthusiasm than mine. I had lingered away from it, and wandered to other scenes, because my treasury of anticipated enjoyments, comprising all the wonders of the world, had nothing else so magnificent, and I was loath to exchange the pleasures of hope for those of memory so soon. At length the day came. The stage-coach, with a Frenchman and myself on the back seat, had already left Lewiston, and in less than an hour would set us down in Manchester. I began to listen for the roar of the cataract, and trembled with a sensation like dread, as the moment drew nigh, when its voice of ages must roll, for the first time, on my ear. The French gentleman stretched himself from the window, and expressed loud admiration, while, by a sudden impulse, I threw myself back and closed my eyes. When the scene shut in, I was glad to think that for me the whole burst of Niagara was yet in futurity. We rolled on, and entered the village of Manchester, bordering on the falls.
>
> I am quite ashamed of myself here. Not that I ran, like a madman to the falls, and plunged into the thickest of the spray,—never stopping to breathe, till breathing was impossible: not that I committed this, or any other suitable extravagance. On the contrary, I alighted with perfect decency and composure, and gave my cloak to the black waiter, pointed out my luggage, and inquired, not the nearest way

to the cataract, but about the dinner-hour. The interval was
spent in arranging my dress. Within the last fifteen minutes,
my mind had grown strangely numbed, and my spirits apa-
thetic, with a slight depression, not decided enough to be
termed madness. My enthusiasm was in a deathlike slumber.
Without aspiring to immortality, as he did, I could have
imitated that English traveler, who turned back from the
point where he first heard the thunder of Niagara, after crossing the ocean to behold it. Many a western trader, by the by,
has performed a similar act of heroism with more heroic
simplicity, deeming it no such wonderful feat to dine at the
hotel and resume his route to Buffalo or Lewiston, while the
cataract was roaring unseen.

Such has often been my apathy, when objects, long
sought, and earnestly desired, were placed within my reach.
After dinner—at which an unwonted and perverse epicur-
ism detained me longer than usual—I lighted a cigar and
paced the piazza, minutely attentive to the aspect and business of a very ordinary village. Finally, with reluctant step
and the feeling of an intruder, I walked towards Goat Island.
At the toll-house, there were further excuses for delaying the
inevitable moment. My signature was required in a huge
ledger, containing similar records innumerable, many of
which I read. The skin of a great sturgeon, and other fishes,
beasts, and reptiles; a collection of minerals, such as lie in
heaps near the falls; some Indian mocassins, and other
trifles, made of deer-skin and embroidered with beads; several newspapers from Montreal, New York, and Boston,—all
attracted me in turn. Out of a number of twisted sticks, the
manufacture of a Tuscarora Indian, I selected one of curled
maple, curiously convoluted, and adorned with the carved
images of a snake and a fish. Using this as my pilgrim's staff,
I crossed the bridge. Above and below me were the rapids,
a river of tempestuous snow, with here and there a dark
rock amid its whiteness, resisting all the physical fury, as any
cold spirit did the moral influences of the scene. On reaching
Goat Island, . . . I chose the right-hand path, and followed
it to the edge of the American cascade. There, while the
falling sheet was yet invisible, I saw the vapor that never
vanishes, and the Eternal Rainbow of Niagara.

It was an afternoon of glorious sunshine, without a cloud, save those of the cataracts. I gained an insulated rock, and beheld the broad sheet of brilliant and unbroken foam, not shooting in a curved line from the top of the precipice, but falling headlong down from height to depth. A narrow stream [the Bridal Veil Falls] diverged from the main branch, and hurried over the crag by a channel of its own, leaving a little pine-clad island and a streak of precipice between itself and the larger sheet. Below arose the mist, on which was painted a dazzling sunbow with two concentric shadows,—one, almost as perfect as the original brightness; and the other, drawn faintly round the broken edge of the cloud.

Still I had not half seen Niagara. Following the verge of the island, the path lead [sic] me to the Horseshoe, where the real, broad St. Lawrence [sic—he was technically correct], rushing along on a level with its banks, pours its whole breadth over a concave line of precipice, and then pursues its course between lofty crags towards Ontario. A sort of bridge [the first to extend from Terrapin Point], two or three feet wide, stretches out along the edge of the descending sheet, and hangs upon the rising mist, as if that were the foundation of the frail structure. Here I stationed myself in the blast of the wind, which the rushing river bore along with it. The bridge was tremulous beneath me, and marked the tremor of the solid earth. I looked along the whitening rapids, and endeavored to distinguish a mass of water far above the falls, to follow it to their verge, and go down with it, in fancy, to the abyss of clouds and storm. Casting my eyes across the river, and [sic] every side, I took in the whole scene at a glance, and tried to comprehend it in one vast idea. After an hour spent thus, I left the bridge, and, by a staircase, descended to the base of the precipice [to the foot of Goat Island]. From that point, my path lay over slippery stones, and among great fragments of the [fallen] cliff, to the edge of the cataract, where the wind at once enveloped me in spray, and perhaps dashed the rainbow round me. Were my long desires fulfilled? And had I seen Niagara?

Oh that I had never heard of Niagara till I beheld it!

Blessed were the wanderers of old, who heard its deep roar, sounding through the woods, as the summons to an unknown wonder, and approached its awful brink, in all the freshness of native feeling. Had its own mysterious voice been the first to warn me of its existence, then, indeed, I might have knelt down and worshipped. But I had come thither, haunted with a vision of foam and fury, and dizzy cliffs, and an ocean tumbling down out of the sky,—a scene, in short, which nature had too much good taste and calm simplicity to realize. My mind had struggled to adapt these false conceptions to the reality, and finding the effort vain, a wretched sense of disappointment weighed me down. I climbed the precipice, and threw myself on the earth, feeling that I was unworthy to look at the Great Falls, and careless about beholding them again . . .

All that night, as there has been and will be for ages past and to come, a rushing sound was heard, as if a great tempest was sweeping through the air. It mingled with my dreams, and made them full of storm and whirlwind. Whenever I awoke, and heard this dread sound in the air, and the windows rattling as with a mighty blast, I could not rest again, till looking forth, I saw how bright the stars were, and that every leaf in the garden was motionless. Never was a summer night more calm to the eye, nor a gale of autumn louder to the ear. The rushing sound proceeds from the rapids, and the rattling of the casement is but an effect of the vibration of the whole house, shaken by the jar of the cataract. The noise of the rapids draws attention from the true voice of Niagara, which is a dull, muffled thunder, resounding between the cliffs. I spent a wakeful hour at midnight, in distinguishing its reverberations, and rejoiced to find that my former awe and enthusiasm were reviving.

Gradually, and after much contemplation, I came to know, by my own feelings, that Niagara is indeed a wonder of the world, and not the less wonderful, because time and thought must be employed in comprehending it. Casting aside all preconceived notions, and preparations to be dire-struck or delighted, the beholder must stand beside it in the simplicity of his heart, suffering the mighty scene to work its own

impression. Night after night, I dreamed of it, and was glad-
dened every morning by the consciousness of a growing
capacity to enjoy it. Yet I will not pretend to the all-absorb-
ing enthusiasm of some more fortunate spectators, nor deny
that very trifling causes would draw my eyes and thoughts
from the cataract.

The last day that I was to spend at Niagara, . . . I sat upon
the Table Rock. This celebrated station did not now, as of
old, project fifty feet beyond the line of the precipice, but
was shattered by the fall of an immense fragment, which
lay distant on the shore below. Still, on the utmost verge of
the rock, with my feet hanging over it, I felt as if suspended
in the open air. Never before had my mind been in such
perfect unison with the scene. There were intervals, when
I was conscious of nothing but the great river, rolling calmly
into the abyss, rather descending than precipitating itself,
and acquiring ten-fold majesty from its unhurried motion. It
came like the march of Destiny. It was not taken by surprise,
but seemed to have anticipated, in all its course through the
broad lakes, that it must pour their collected waters down
this height. The perfect foam of the river, after its descent,
and the ever-varying shapes of mist, rising up, to become
clouds in the sky, would be the very picture of confusion,
were it merely transient, like the rage of a tempest. But
when the beholder has stood awhile, and perceives no lull in
the storm, and considers that the vapor and foam are as
everlasting as the rocks which produce them, all this turmoil
assumes a sort of calmness. It soothes, while it awes the
mind.

Leaning over the cliff, I saw the guide conducting two
adventurers behind the falls. It was pleasant, from that high
seat in the sunshine, to observe them struggling against the
eternal storms of the lower regions, with heads bent down,
now faltering, now pressing forward, and finally swallowed
up in their victory. After their disappearance, a blast rushed
out with an old hat, which had been swept from one of their
heads. The rock, to which they were directing their unseen
course, is marked, at a fearful distance on the exterior of the
sheet, by a jet of foam. The attempt to reach it appears both

poetical and perilous on the exterior of the sheet, but may be accomplished without much more difficulty or hazard, than in stemming a violent northeaster. In a few moments, forth came the children of the mist. Dripping and breathless, they crept along the base of the cliff, ascended to the guide's cottage, and received, I presume, a certificate of their achievement, and three verses of sublime poetry on the back.

My contemplations were often interrupted by strangers who came down from Forsyth's [Hotel, at Clifton—Niagara Falls, Ontario] to take their first view of the falls. A short, ruddy, middle-aged gentleman, from Old England, peeped over the rock, and evinced his approbation by a broad grin. His spouse, a very robust lady, afforded a sweet example of maternal solicitude, being so intent on the safety of her little boy that she did not even glance at Niagara. As for the child, he gave himself wholly to the enjoyment of a stick of candy. Another traveler, a native American, and no rare character among us, produced a volume of Captain Hull's tour [a popular guidebook], and labored earnestly to adjust Niagara to the captain's description, departing, at last, without one new idea or sensation of his own. The next comer was provided, not with a printed book, but with a blank sheet of foolscap, from top to bottom of which, by means of an ever-pointed pencil, the cataract was made to thunder. In a little talk, which we had together, he awarded his approbation to the general view, but censured the position of Goat Island, observing that it should have been farther to the right, so as to widen the American falls, and contract those of the Horseshoe. Next appeared two traders of Michigan, who declared, that, upon the whole, the sight was worth looking at; there certainly was an immense water-power here; but that, after all, they would go twice as far to see the noble stone-works of Lockport, where the Grand [Erie] Canal is locked down a descent of sixty feet. They were succeeded by a young fellow, in a homespun cotton dress, with a staff in his hand, and a pack over his shoulders. He advanced to the edge of the rock, where his attention, at first wavering among the different components of the scene, finally became fixed in the angle of the Horseshoe falls, which is, indeed, the central point of interest. His whole soul seemed to go forth and be transported thither, till the staff slipped from his relaxed grasp, and falling down—down—down—struck upon the fragment of the Table Rock [in the abyss at the base of the falls].

In this manner I spent some hours, watching the varied impression, made by the cataract, on those who disturbed me, and returning to unwearied contemplation, when left alone. At length my time came to depart. There is a grassy footpath, through the woods, along the summit of the bank, to a point whence a causeway, hewn in the side of the precipice, goes winding down to the Ferry, about a half a mile below the Table Rock. The sun was near setting, when I emerged from the shadows of the trees, and began the descent. The indirectness of my downward road continually changed the point of view, and showed me, in rich and repeated succession, now, the whitening rapids and majestic leap of the main river, which appeared more deeply massive as the light departed; now, the lovelier picture, yet still sublime, of Goat Island, with its rocks and grove, and the lesser falls, tumbling over the right bank of the St. Lawrence, like a tributary stream; now, the long vista of the river, as it eddied and whirled between the cliffs, to pass through Ontario toward the sea, and everywhere to be wondered at, for this one unrivalled scene. The golden sunshine tinged the sheets of the American cascade, and painted on its heaving spray the broken semicircle of a rainbow, heaven's own beauty crowning earth's sublimity. My steps were slow, and I paused long at every turn of the descent, as one lingers and pauses who discerns a brighter and brightening excellence in what he must soon behold no more. The solitude of the old wilderness now reigned over the whole vicinity of the falls. My enjoyment became the more rapturous, because no poet shared it, nor wretch devoid of poetry profaned it; but the spot so famous through the world was all my own!

Although countless other writers of renown and hordes of poets, ranging in degree of competence from great genius to blandest indifference, would come to Niagara to behold its glories after Nathaniel Hawthorne paid his visit in 1834, none has ever left us with a portrait comparable to his, one that conveys at once all its aspects and the intensity of its impact upon a sensibility that made him the worldliest of America's unworldly authors—or perhaps the most unworldly of our worldly ones.

Before any other visitor of transcendent consequence paid a call at the Niagara and departed, according to the increasingly fashionable custom, the region became briefly but rather headily involved in William Lyon Mackenzie's abortive but colorful attempt to wrest control of the Canadian government from the Crown of Westminster.

13

Boom—
Bust—
Bang

From the opening of the Erie Canal in 1825, Buffalo's growth was rapid and mostly unattractive. Its waterfront sprawled from the mouth of Tonawanda Creek south to the ever-enlarging harbor near Buffalo Creek. The Holland Land Company was increasingly impatient to realize vast profits from its holdings of undeveloped acreage that extended as far south as Lake Chautauqua. The period of boom was clearly at hand, particularly on the American side of the Niagara. Youngstown, Lewiston, Manchester, Black Rock were all to enjoy a kind of spin-off prosperity either from the canal traffic or the tourist traffic, though the latter appeared still to favor the Canadian shore, because of the better views.

Yet were there more reverses to be endured. Late in the spring of 1832, an epidemic of cholera traveled up the Saint Lawrence, reaching the Niagara Frontier initially in July. Though tourists continued to come to pay homage to the falls, as we have had evidence of from the recollections they recorded, permanent settlers were conspicuously more cautious during the two-year period when the wasting disease held the numerous Niagara communities in its remorseless and frightening grasp. This was an altogether new variety of testing time.

Among the heroic few who willingly risked their health and quite possibly their lives to nurse the afflicted was Lydia Harper, of Buffalo—the town that was by far the hardest hit by the epidemic because it was the most populous of Niagara communities and by far the most squalid. In a description composed about 1874, Lewis F. Allen offers us an archetypally sanctimonious example of complacent Victorian-American prose in which he extols her service to humanity during the cholera days. This extract deserves a modest corner in the museum of American literature, for it reads like a laundered passage out of a salacious book of the last century:

> Lydia Harper was a fallen woman. Whether she became so by the wiles of seduction, or by her own volition, was unknown to the people of Buffalo. She had lived in Rochester time past, as it was said, but her home for some years had been in Buffalo. Her personal appearance was decent; of middling size, well-formed, bright eyes, good complexion, modest in carriage and dress, as she passed the streets, healthy in look, with intelligent, expressive features, she would appear to the stranger a respectable woman. Her age was perhaps thirty. But she was not what she should have been, and her home was among the wayside localities of the abandoned of her sex. To the public, as she appeared among them, her conduct was correct, and only to those who consorted with her kind was her vocation familiar. Yet rumor told various acts of kindness and charity at her hands, and the name of Lydia Harper was not always accompanied with approbrium [sic], or censure. She knew enough of the world to understand her own position, never sought to conceal it, nor did she thrust her presence in unwelcome places. So she passed, unobtrusive to society, and apparently content with the lot her own fallen nature had chosen.
>
> When the cholera, in 1834, had broken out, and attendants on the sick were much needed, this woman offered her ser-

vices as a nurse in places where they were appropriate, simply for such labors as she could render without regard for her social recognition. She asked no pay. She was ready to work, she could work, and she did work with a readiness, a facility, an aptitude of which many better women were incapable; and she entered houses whose inmates were respectable, and where her efforts were gratefully appreciated. She could do everything required of a female nurse, prepare food and drinks, give medicines, bathe the sick, smooth their pillows, and minister all those gentle attentions so grateful to the stricken and afflicted, and with a decorum and fidelity admirable in their manner. And she did all these throughout the cholera season. Was not that woman a heroine—a *true* woman indeed—in all the virtues of a repentant Magdalen? Let charity excuse her frailties, while gratitude applauds her kindly efforts to relieve the miseries of her race. It was not "putting on" of hers for the occasion, but a genuine philanthropy, innate in her being, which broke out at the cry of distress, ceasing only when the occasion for its action had passed. Lydia lived some years afterward in her vocation as before, and died some years since in this city [Buffalo]. In what part of the common burying ground her remains were deposited no one perhaps now knows, for no tombstone tells the tale of her good deed or records the story of her frailties. Let this simple narrative perpetuate the one, and oblivion blot out the other.

A complaint that is lodged against chroniclers of the life on various portions of the American frontier may be phrased succinctly thus: all one hears about, where women are concerned, are whores. Undoubtedly, the National Organization of Women or Women's Liberation will undertake yet another revisionist historical movement whose thrust will be to disclose what is already patent: women were sorely put upon in those pioneer days. They were compelled to suffer all the hardships of their men and to endure the additional and even more desperate menace of childbirth. Maternal and infant mortality rates on the frontier were staggering. One has only to glance at the tombstones of early American cemeteries to note how frequently men took three and even four wives—having worn out their predecessors with work and/or killed them with childbearing. The difficulty of the woman's role, so far as the teller of this tangled tale is involved, lies in the fact that at Niagara, the women did what they did everywhere on the outland farms of America. They were born, were married, were subordinate to husbands (whom they may, all the same, have governed), and died. It is a true pity, and pity it is that it's true. The exceptions are usually lies. One example is that of the "legendary" Indian maiden going over the falls in a canoe every spring. Another is of Laura Secord, a resident of Clifton, who is supposed to have alerted the Canadians of the impending American assault against Fort Chippawa. Unhappily, in the latter instance, the chronology doesn't test out. So Laura Secord, whatever else she might have done for her country, didn't act as Paul Revere is supposed to have done—and didn't.

The cholera epidemic had run its full, fearful course before the end of 1834. The stage at last seemed set for the inflation of the Niagara bubble, and indeed it inflated itself at a fantastic rate during the following two years and a bit—to be burst prematurely by the Great Panic of 1837—a financial crisis which was produced by the struggle for fiduciary power between President Andrew Jackson (just retired from office) and the United States Bank. This battle, which may be reasonably compared to the longer-lasting but even more fateful struggle to maintain civilian control of the military establishment, had its immediate consequence in the form of a calamitous inflation and an overextension of credit which, when the sudden boom collapsed, resulted in an unprecedented number of local bank failures and attendant bankruptcies—not the least numerous of which were the work of the Holland Land Company, whose ire was aroused by the New York legislature's refusal to favor it with a continuing tax exemption. With land on which it had foreclosed, the company—which had already reaped prodigious profits from its millions of acres—was prepared to sit back and wait for the next wave of westward expansion that was inevitable. The foreclosed land was cleared, and therefore many times more valuable than it had been when originally sold.

As if to divert the populations on both sides of the Niagara from their more pressing economic woes, William Lyon Mackenzie burst into Buffalo at the end of 1837 with the militia and constabulary of Upper Canada hot on his trail. There was a poetic turn to his appearance here, for he had begun his campaign against the tyrannical indifference of absentee British government, just across the Niagara, at Queenston, thirteen years before. There he had issued the first editions of *The Colonial Advocate,* an extremely headstrong periodical of political opinion which represented his initial strides on the hitherto tranquil stage of Canada's domestic affairs.

Mackenzie's ill-conceived and worse-starred little "Patriots' Revolt" had centered about a somewhat romantic scheme to kidnap Upper Canada's lieutenant governor in Toronto and to establish a provisional government of republican style—resembling that of the United States. It was to be a regime which would not be dependent on the whims of Westminster. This *coup d'état* had had its immediate inspiration in a sharp and completely unexpected reverse at the provincial election polls in 1836. The reformers, naturally including Mackenzie, had been almost totally evicted from the Upper Canada parliament where they had previously enjoyed a reasonable majority. Mackenzie's mob, assembled appropriately at a spot called Gallows Hill in Toronto, tried and miserably failed to create the anticipated general uprising among the provincial citizens. He and his most intimate disciples had made haste for refuge on the American side of the Niagara, for the Canadian officials lost no time in placing a good price on his head.

In December of 1837, Buffalo had more than its share of discontented farmers driven off their land by foreclosure and of roustabouts made unemployed by the bank panic and its resultant financial crash. Mackenzie had little difficulty in rally-

ing a fair number of desperadoes to join him in his new and
even more chimerical campaign to take possession of Canadian-
owned Navy Island and there to set up a sort of government
in exile. The "Committee of Fifteen" over which Mackenzie
presided consisted of refugees who had followed him from
Toronto. Within days of his arrival in Buffalo, nearly a hundred
Canadians had joyously affiliated themselves with Mackenzie's
rather splendid little folly. On December 15, this little band,
with its American hangers-on, encountered slight resistance in
taking over the modest Canadian garrison on Navy Island. The
leader at once proclaimed himself to be the chief of a provisional government. He called for volunteers to augment his
ranks.

During the next fortnight, as the ice began gradually to
accumulate on the calmer reaches of the Upper Niagara, Mackenzie's men frantically dug themselves in on Navy Island,
awaiting arms and reinforcements, and wondering when the
Upper Canada militiamen would begin their efforts to dislodge
them. On the morning of the twenty-ninth, the battered old
lake steamer *Caroline* broke her way sluggishly through the
thickening crust of ice as she made her way downriver from
Black Rock to Schlosser Landing, three miles below Navy Island on the American side. There she was to take on supplies
and additional volunteers, most of them United States citizens.

So numerous were the new adherents to a certainly lost
cause that *Caroline* remained at the pier all through the daylight hours as they boarded. Not a single official American hand
was raised to prevent this patent violation of United States
neutrality agreements with the government of Canada, an
oversight made the more scandalous because it was well known
that most of the weapons and ammunition being loaded aboard
the dilapidated ship had been stolen a few days earlier from
the army's arsenal at Buffalo.

In the early winter's nightfall, twenty-five men and quantities of materiel were still standing on the pier. The vessel's

Navy Island

master Captain Gilman Appleby thought it most ill advised
to attempt the upriver voyage before dawn. The volunteers remained aboard after depositing the remainder of the precious
cargo in the holds. By the morning's first light, *Caroline* would
be on her way to Navy Island—or so Captain Appleby and
his complement of fanatics and drunkards imagined.

The day's extraordinary activities at Schlosser Landing had
certainly not gone unobserved from the opposite shore. At
Fort Chippawa, the commander of the Upper Canada militia,
Colonel Allen McNab, had been following the operations with
keenest interest through his spyglass. His original plan had
been to intercept *Caroline* the moment her bow entered Canadian waters—approximately at the center of the Niagara's path,
before she was able to unload her men and supplies on Navy
Island. But when he realized that the steamer was going to
lie at Schlosser Landing's wharf through the night, he rapidly

altered his thinking, and at ten that evening he dispatched seven whaleboats, under the leadership of Captain Allen Drew, to board *Caroline* and overcome her crew. It was first-rate military tactics, but dreadful diplomacy.

Two of the Canadian assault craft missed the narrow channel between Grand and Navy Islands, were caught by the powerful main current of the Niagara as they drifted toward the Upper Rapids, and were nearly carried over the falls. The remaining five boats, however, negotiated the passage satisfactorily and drew over to the east bank of the river, allowing the stream to bring them in total silence down to Schlosser Landing. These hardy commandos were aboard *Caroline* just as the solitary watch saw them and was able to utter a single cry of alarm. One pistol shot finished him. The crew and the hundred-odd Patriot volunteers who were enjoying a slumber of exhaustion below decks were roused, intimidated, and quietly herded off the ship.

Captain Drew ordered *Caroline*'s dormant boilers to be stoked. As soon as she had built up sufficient steam to produce motion, he headed her out into the river, trailing the five whaleboats astern. While Drew steered the heavily laden craft downstream toward the main current, his men set fires at several strategic points. As she approached the Upper Rapids, Drew lashed *Caroline*'s helm and joined his men for an escape in the little boats they had been towing. They rowed desperately against the ever-hastening current to gain the Canadian shore, their mission brilliantly accomplished.

Caroline, by now a raft of flame and explosion, hurtled her way down the deadly rapids on the Canadian side of Goat Island, brushing frequently against its rocky flanks. She finally impaled herself on a prominent upcropping of stone less than a hundred yards from the brink of the Horseshoe Falls. There she consumed herself in fire and powder blasts for the rest of the long December night.

On the morning of the thirtieth, there was a loud and not altogether understandable cry of outrage on the American side of the Niagara. It was one thing for William Lyon Mackenzie to avail himself of New York's hospitality for the purpose of plotting an uprising against the government of Upper Canada; it was quite another for an official Canadian raiding party to violate American territorial integrity and property rights by seizing and demolishing *Caroline,* a vessel under United States registry, and to kill a crew member who was an American national. The fact that Mackenzie's party had looted the Buffalo arsenal and that *Caroline* had been operating in broad daylight on a venture that was in itself a violation of the law was not to be taken into account. Legality, like beauty, reposes in the eye of the beholder. Something had to be done, but there was no one at Buffalo or at Fort Niagara with the authority necessary to take whatever action was deemed suitable.

A message to President Martin Van Buren required five full days to reach him at Washington. He instantly convened his cabinet and after its meeting was adjourned he ordered General Winfield Scott, that old Niagara hand, to proceed forthwith to the scene of this terrible atrocity against American property. Scott was accorded full discretionary powers to take whatever action he considered necessary to protect American interests and to redeem American honor. The general passed through Albany on his way, gathering up Governor William Marcy (whose principal distinction would be that a mountain was to bear his family name). The notion appears to have been that Marcy would give Scott moral support. He badly needed it. The pair arrived at Buffalo on January 12, 1838— to do just what, they knew not.

By this time, the incident had been blown by publicity into a very considerable *cause célèbre*—at least as far as Canadian and American journalists were concerned. Papers in both countries were calling for war to avenge reciprocal wounds to national pride. Indeed, there was war already, of a sort. Colonel McNab's artillery was exchanging blasts with the handful of fieldpieces on Navy Island. There was even a smattering of musket fire between Mackenzie's lunatics and the militia-

Barcelona

men at Fort Chippawa—though this was mainly of a ceremonial nature, since the distance between the two posts made
musketry not much more hazardous to life than pea-shooting.

Scott uttered an order that no United States vessel of any
description be leased, lent, sold, or otherwise placed at the
disposal of Mackenzie's rebels. This gesture was, both he and
Governor Marcy agreed, and rightly, strictly a domestic Canadian affair which was, after all, being resolved entirely on
Canadian soil.

Someone, however, wasn't paying very strict attention to the
general's edict. For on the night of January 14, an American
vessel ferried most of Mackenzie's volunteers—the ones who
had been evicted from *Caroline* a fortnight earlier—from some
secret point on the east bank of the Niagara to Grand Island.
Since Grand Island was American soil, a foxy lawyer argued,
the act was not a very clear violation of Scott's order. These
volunteers were joined the next day by Mackenzie and his
original band, after McNab's militiamen attacked Navy Island
and repossessed it in the name of Canada. The opposing forces
began to exchange fire across the two thousand feet of water

that separated Grand and Navy islands. The war was once again an international business.

Both Scott and McNab now faced an identical and equally embarrassing difficulty—how to end the fighting without the sort of intervention that would expand it into an idiotic but full-scale war which neither the United States nor Canada desired—but which an important number of "patriots" on both sides were eagerly, even feverishly, clamoring for. Scott determined that the solution to his dilemma lay in arresting Mackenzie and his supporters for making improper use of American territory. He informed McNab that for this purpose he was sending the steamer *Barcelona* to Grand Island. The rebels would be subdued, if they offered resistance, and returned to Black Rock for trial.

Because he offered no reply to the communication from the American general, and because he ordered three armed patrol boats to ply the Niagara between Forts Erie and Chippawa, many New Yorkers who spent all their free time watching from their side of the river imagined (some wishfully) that Colonel McNab meant to treat Scott's gesture as an act of hostility rather than a well-meant attempt to resolve their mutual problem; they believed that the Canadian picket ships had instructions to sink *Barcelona* if she entered Canadian waters.

Fortunately, such baleful interpretations proved utterly groundless. When *Barcelona* reached Grand Island on January 16, she landed a platoon of American soldiers who encountered no resistance at all on the part of the Patriots. They appeared willing to renounce a scheme that had been doomed from its inception. Nor did the American ship meet with any Canadian interference as she made her way back to Black Rock.

The rebels were surprisingly meek as they set foot once again on American soil. With the exception of Mackenzie himself, all were immediately released. The hapless leader was transferred to Rochester, seat of the nearest federal district court, where he was indicted for violating United States neutrality laws. His trial was postponed until June of 1839, at which time he was convicted of the offense and sentenced to eighteen months' imprisonment. He actually served less than a year. Though Mackenzie lived until 1861, and though he was eventually allowed to return to Canada under the terms of a general amnesty, and though he once again embroiled himself in his country's political life, the storm had gone out of this petrel. Yet because he was on the side of history, Mackenzie's name survives.

The Niagara would have to wait almost thirty years before once again, and for the very last time, it was to be the scene of such martial excitement. In the interim, it remained a frontier that was very closely watched by anxious military figures of both nations—in spite of the fact (as we shall see) that the region had become the most visited of eastern North American wonders of nature for the tourists of the world, and so remains today.

The reason for this concern was that the more tranquil passages of the river, above and below the falls and rapids, served as one of the principal routes of egress for the celebrated and extremely controversial Underground Railway. It has been estimated that between 1820 and 1860, something like seventy-five thousand runaway slaves found permanent refuge in Canada by way of crossings of the Niagara. It was at nearby Lockport, on his return from Queenston, that the Reverend Josiah Henson recounted to Harriet Beecher Stowe his harrowing experiences as shepherd to no less than six hundred escaped blacks whom he had deposited safely on the Canadian shore of the river. The inscription on Henson's gravestone proudly identifies him as the original for Mrs. Stowe's Uncle Tom. The description, at the time of his death, was thought complimentary.

Today, the disparity between the appearance of the American and Canadian sides of the river distinctly favors the latter. It was apparently so from a relatively early date. A year before William Lyon Mackenzie staged his last stand on Grand

Island, Mrs. A. B. M. Jameson wrote at some length about her
visit to Niagara, and took particular notice of the "City of the
Falls," the Canadian real estate development to which initial
reference had been made by writers who came to the region
a couple of years earlier:

> Perhaps even for my sake you may now and then look
> upon a map of Canada, and there . . . you will find not a
> few towns and cities laid down by name which you might in
> vain look for within the precincts of the province [of Upper
> Canada], seeing that they are non-extant, as yet, at least,
> though surely *to be,* some time or other, somewhere or other,
> when this fair country shall have fair play, and its fair quota
> of population. But from this anticipation I would willingly
> except a certain CITY OF THE FALLS which I have seen
> marked on so many maps, and mentioned in so many books,
> as already laid out and commenced, that I had no doubt of
> its existence till I came here for the first time last winter. But
> here it is not—*Grazie a Dio!* nor likely to be, as far as I
> can judge, for a century to come. Were a city to rise here,
> it would necessarily become a manufacturing place, because
> of the "water power and privileges," below and above the
> cataract. Fancy, if you can, a range of cotton factories, iron
> foundries, grist mills, saw mills, where now the mighty waters
> rush along in glee and liberty—where the maple and pine
> woods now bend and wave along the heights. Surely they
> have done enough already with their wooden hotels, mu-
> seums, and curiosity stalls: neither in such a case were red
> brick tenements, gas-lights, and smoke chimneys, the worst
> abominations to be feared. There would be moral pollution
> brought into this majestic scene, far more degrading; more
> than all those rushing waters, with their "thirteen millions of
> tons per minute," would wash away.

As early as 1836, we can see that a sort of pattern of development was establishing itself. Industry was confined largely to
the American side of the Niagara, upriver of the falls, while
tourism was primarily the concern of the Canadians. As Mrs.
Jameson observed, touristic enterprises at Niagara were not

very tastefully exploited even in her day. They rarely are, anywhere. But in the main, the most tawdry tourist traps were confined from the onset of the region's extraordinary popularity to the area in the immediate vicinity of the falls—happily still the case today. The remaining portions of the Canadian side, upriver and down, were free of the major desecration that is the blight of the river from Niagara Falls, New York, to Buffalo.

The falls were an irresistible magnet. Captain Frederick Marryat, who came here in 1839, three years after having given the world *Mr. Midshipman Easy*, but well before producing his masterpiece *The Children of the New Forest*, had one of the oddest inspirations about Niagara that was ever to be recorded:

> I wished myself a magician, that I might transport the falls to Italy, and pour their whole volume of waters into the crater of Mount Vesuvius; witness the terrible conflict between the contending elements, and create the largest steam-boiler that ever entered into the imagination of man.

In June of 1848, the greatest American poet of his century paid his first visit to the region and recorded the occasion, to wit: "Got in the cars and went to Niagara; went under the falls—saw the whirlpool and all the other sights." Thirty-two years later, the same Walt Whitman returned and showed himself to be somewhat more impressed:

> For really seizing a great picture or book, or piece of music, or architecture, or grand scenery—or perhaps for the first time even the common sunshine, or landscape, or maybe even the mystery of identity, most curious mystery of all—there comes some lucky five minutes of a man's life, set amid a fortuitous concurrence of circumstances, and bringing in a brief flash the culmination of years of reading and travel and thought. The present case about two o'clock this afternoon gave me Niagara, its superb severity of action and color and majestic grouping, in one short, indescribable show. We

were very slowly crossing the Suspension bridge—not a full stop anywhere, but next to it—the day clear, sunny, still—and I out on the platform. The falls were in plain view about a mile off, but very distinct, and no roar—hardly a murmur. The river tumbling green and white, far below me; the dark high banks, the plentiful umbrage, many bronze cedars, in shadow; and tempering and arching all the immense materiality, a clear sky overhead, with a few white clouds, limpid, spiritual. Brief, and as quiet as brief, that picture—a remembrance always afterwards.

As a rule, he preferred persons to places. It is all the more gratifying that he was able to find at Niagara something of its primeval wonder—for the place must have been, by 1880 when the foregoing note was composed, all but totally obscured by persons and the most sordid of their works.

Many other major literary figures had been drawn to the Niagara before Walt Whitman's second visit and as many followed it. None added substantially to our understanding of the Frontier by what they wrote about it. The reason is not difficult to ascertain: there was just so much that could be said, so much emotion that could be invoked. The prose and verse that were dedicated to the falls and gorge and surrounding countryside became repetitious. After reading most of the words on the subject, one falls victim to a surfeit of awe.

Not quite the same condition applies to the artists who called at Niagara and left a record of what they saw and how it affected them. The first surviving image of the Niagara, indeed, was drawn by an artist who never made the visit. He was the illustrator of Father Hennepin's *Nouvelle Découverte*, his account of his adventures in the New World in the company of the great La Salle. The limner, in this instance, based his engraving on Hennepin's description and it is not totally destitute of accuracy. It would serve for nearly a century as the model for all subsequent delineations of the falls—these too made by engravers who had never made the journey to the site.

Amateur painters in their thousands placed their easels or

drawing pads on Table Rock before it tumbled altogether
into the pool below the Horseshoe Falls. And a few profes-
sionals devoted some time to the Niagara scene. Since art,
even more than literature, defies objective criticism, it is difficult to make categorical statements about the varying quality
of the work produced without offering the initial *caveat* that
they are the subjective observations of a deeply committed devotee of art—but an amateur, in the literal sense, nonetheless.
That is, I am not a painter, but I know what I like.

The art evoked by visits to Niagara falls into two general
categories—accurate views of the sort that we now obtain
through the intercession of the camera, and impressions inspired by the site. The former are self-explanatory. The latter
may be much more fanciful.

Of the painters who came to the Frontier before most of it
had been covered over by people and their multifarious mani-
festations—hotels, houses, places of amusement, factories,
power plants, highways—the first whose reputation has survived (or been revived) was John Vanderlyn, a landscape
painter of some distinction who traveled to Italy to improve
his technique and also studied with the renowned portraitist
Gilbert Stuart. This native of Kingston, New York, came to
Niagara about 1800 and created a remarkably Italianate
rendering of the falls.

A little more than a half-century later, Frederic E. Church,
another artist to have connections with the banks of the Hudson River (he died in a miraculous house he built on the
heights overlooking that great American fiord), came to Niagara in 1857, when he was about thirty. His visit was undoubtedly inspired by his principal teacher, the remarkable
Thomas Cole, one of the founders of what is now called the
Hudson River School of artists. Cole had painted Niagara in
1830.

The man who surveyed and laid out the plots for the Holland Land Company, Andrew Ellicott, made extremely faithful line drawings and engravings of many of the points of

interest on the river. The English landscapist William Henry Bartlett added the Niagara to his repertory of American things seen which he eventually published in 1840. Another Englishman, William James Bennett, who eventually settled at Nyack on the Hudson, came to Niagara in 1831, contributing his paintings and drawings of the wonders there to his *oeuvre,* which was chiefly landscape and cityscape.

If I have appeared to pass rather quickly over the achievements of a large and generally skilled group of artists, it is because their efforts—so far as Niagara is concerned—seem minor when compared with the little and apparently unique picture made of the falls by Edward Hicks, the Pennsylvania Quaker quietist primitive, whose view of life was so frequently rendered in a series of paintings depicting what he called the "Peaceable Kingdom," in which the lamb lay down beside the lion in the best of all possible worlds. No less than a hundred examples of this subject are now extant. His intensely religious orientation is evident in all his surviving pictures, which are endowed with a gentle simplicity, a naïveté, that would find a single parallel in the work of Henri Rousseau, who certainly never saw a Hicks picture. Hicks is believed to have visited Niagara in 1819, though his painting of the falls is thought to have been painted in 1830. Faithful to his custom of inscribing his frames with quotations he considered suitable to the matter he depicted, Hicks cited couplets from "The Forester," a poem by Alexander Wilson, on the borders of his picture of the cataract. Here, indeed, is the Niagara beatified.

14

Across the
RIVER,
One Way or
Another

The Niagara had for so long constituted so formidable a physical barrier as well as an international Frontier demarcation that when William Hamilton Merritt, the Canadian who had conceived the first Welland Canal which, after 1832, linked Lakes Ontario and Erie, proposed a bridge across the narrowest portion of the Whirlpool Rapids gorge, the idea was immediately dismissed as impracticable and (if practicable) undesirable. Yet by 1846, Merritt had succeeded in persuading the governments of Canada and the United States to permit the creation of two private joint stock companies which would collectively undertake the financing and operation of the structure he so rashly proposed.

Late in the following year, the Philadelphia architect Charles Ellett was awarded a contract to design and build the first of the many bridges that would eventually span the Niagara River. It was to occupy a site where the high, sheer cliffs of the Whirlpool gorge were about eight hundred feet apart. The initial difficulty, to pass the first line from one side of the roaring rapids to the other, was overcome by the staging

Ellett's kite-flying contest, 1847

of a kite-flying contest. The lad who first caused his kite to land on the opposite bank would receive a prize of five or ten dollars (there is disagreement among chroniclers over the amount). The honor went to an American boy, Homan Walsh. With his kite string serving as the first strand, larger and heavier lines were drawn across the river, to be followed ultimately by iron cables.

As bridges went, Ellett's confection was fairly primitive, clearly intended more as a novelty for the tourists and as a convenience for local residents than as a route for the growing commercial traffic drawn by canal and rail lines to Buffalo on the New York side and to Fort Erie in Canada. Over stout wooden pylons at opposite ends, Ellett passed heavy iron wires that were almost twelve hundred feet in length. On these tightened cables was suspended a carriageway eight feet wide. Construction was not without its moments of drama and trauma. A sudden squall threatened the entire fabrication in the late spring of 1848:

The unfinished structure was torn and wafted backwards and forwards like a broken web of a spider and four helpless human beings, two hundred feet from shore, supported by two tiny strands of wire, were in constant expectation of a headlong plunge into the raging waters far below. Oh, who can tell those men's thoughts just then? But, the tiny threads which held them to existence proved strong enough to outlast the gale.

At the beginning of August 1848, the first Niagara Suspension Bridge, its main span seven hundred and sixty-two feet long, with an oak-planked surface riding two hundred and twenty feet above the turbulent Whirlpool gorge, was opened for business. And business was very good—so good, in fact, that it was soon evident that Ellett's bridge could not possibly accommodate the volume or weight of the carts, carriages, and wagons that were seeking to make use of it.

Five years after it was put into operation, there appeared at

Roebling's suspension bridge,
completed in 1855

Niagara a German-born engineer, John Roebling, who had previously designed and built a number of suspension bridges spanning narrower water courses than this one and intended to bear comparatively light loads. But Roebling was convinced that the basic principle of his method of bridge construction could be readily adapted to the kind of burden demanded by potential users at Niagara. His secret reposed in the technique he had invented for the manufacture and winding of steel cable. A bridge could sustain almost any amount of vertical or horizontal stress, he maintained, for which its pylons were sufficiently strong and rigid and its flexible cables sufficiently large. To carry the great loads of fully laden trains which now had to be emptied at railheads on either side of the Niagara, Roebling proposed a suspension bridge of two levels, the lower one for horse-drawn vehicles and pedestrians, the upper deck for train traffic. "They" said it couldn't be done. And it is as much a tribute to Roebling's persuasiveness as a salesman as to his engineering genius that he succeeded in procuring a contract and the required capital that allowed him to demonstrate that it could indeed be done.

Like Ellett's bridge, Roebling's underwent some extremely harrowing moments in the course of its completion. When some scaffolding collapsed in October of 1854, two workers were hurled to their ultimate reward in the moiling waters of the rapids. Two others survived this mishap because of the courage of a colleague, William Ellis, who risked his own life to rescue them. But construction continued. On March 8, 1855, the steam engine *London*, weighing twenty-three tons, crossed John Roebling's bridge at a speed of eight miles per hour, causing his splendidly handsome span to sag less than four inches at its very center. There could be no doubt that the brilliant engineer's conviction had been more than adequately justified by the reality.

Photographs of Roebling's first major suspension bridge disclose it to have borne a surprisingly close resemblance to his

masterpiece of a quarter of a century later the Brooklyn
Bridge, a work of masonry and steel of very considered elegance and functional beauty. His Niagara bridge was to serve
without repair or alteration for more than twenty years.
Beginning in 1877, however, the stresses imposed by constant
loads that were much in excess of those for which it had been
designed necessitated its gradual and total reconstruction. In
the process, the bridge lost all its weblike lightness of appearance. Nevertheless, Niagara had a distinction of which
it could quite properly be proud. It had accorded John
Roebling the opportunity to build the first truly magnificent
suspension bridge in the world.

Five years after its completion, the bridge was given the
indubitable honor of supporting the weight of His Royal Highness, Albert Edward, Prince of Wales. "Bertie" was on a state
visit to Canada, the first made by an heir presumptive to the
British New World, a tour whose rigid formality was briefly
interrupted by a stay at Niagara—which must have been something of a relief to a youth of nineteen. Roebling's engineering
marvel was said to have been a source of inspiration to the
prince, whose travels in North America were recorded for pos-
terity by Nicholas A. Woods, reporter for *The Times* of London.

This correspondent offered one of the earliest and most
vivid accounts of yet another Niagara phenomenon, Jean-
François Gravelet—whose name has come down in Niagara
and international legend as "The Great Blondin." To Blondin
belongs the distinction of being the first and most successful
of the numerous daredevils attracted to Niagara, the author
of the perpetual summer circus that the river and falls were
to feature forever afterward.

Blondin had offered Niagara's first "spectacular" the year
before, in 1859. Most who followed his example were pallid
and often simply foolhardy imitators. Nicholas Woods re-
counts an especially exciting moment in Blondin's career, one
that was, moreover, to shape the rest of the great aerialist's
future as an "artiste."

. . . His Royal Highness saw M. Blondin execute his most terrific feat—that of crossing the Rapids on a tight rope with a man on his back. To leave the study of these eternal cataracts to witness the feats of any rope-dancer, however skilful, is very much like shutting your prayer-books to go and witness a pantomime. Nevertheless, among the Americans Blondin is a great favourite, and many of them actually carry their admiration of his feats so far as to say that unless you see "Blondin walk" you don't see Niagara. Without being too analytical in searching after motives, I verily believe that at least one-half of the crowds that go to see Blondin go in the firm expectation that as he must fall and be lost some day or other, they may have the good fortune to be there when he does so miss his footing, and witness the whole catastrophe from the best point of view. One thing, however, is certain, that if you do go to see Blondin, when he once begins his feats you can never take your eyes off him (unless you shut them from a very sickness of terror), till he is safe back again on land. The place where his rope was stretched was about a quarter of a mile below the [Roebling] Suspension Bridge, over the Rapids, and about two miles below the Falls. To do Blondin justice, his skill is so great that he would as soon stretch his rope along the edge of the Falls themselves as not, but at this place there is no point on either side to which he could secure it. All the waters of Niagara, however, could not make his fate more certain and inevitable than it would be if he fell from the place where his rope was then fixed.

It was stretched between two of the steepest cliffs over the Rapids, about 230 feet from where the waters boil and roar and plunge on in massive waves at the rate of some twenty [in fact, nearer thirty] miles an hour. To see him venture out on this tiny cord and turn summersaults [sic] in the centre, standing on his head, or sitting down holding by his hands, revolving backwards over the rope like a Catherine wheel, is bad enough for nervous people; but on this Saturday, after keeping every one's hair on end thus for twenty minutes, he prepared to carry a man across on his back. The mere physical exertion of carrying any one nearly a distance

Blondin crossing the
Niagara, 1860

of half a mile is no slight feat, but when the space has to be
traversed on a half-tight rope higher than the Monument
[in London], from the sea of boiling rapids beneath, where
one false movement, the tremour of a single nerve, a moment's gust of wind, or temporary faintness, would hurry
both to an instant and dreadful death, the attempt is so
full of sickening terror that not many can bring themselves
to witness it [countless thousands did, and repeatedly], and
those who do, remain cold, trembling, and silent till the
dreadful venture is safely passed. Blondin took the whole
thing coolly enough. His Royal Highness was urgent with
him not to attempt it, but he replied that there was far less
real danger in the feat than appeared to lookers-on, that he

was quite used to it and felt quite at ease, and that as he had everywhere announced his intention of performing it before relinquishing his attempts for the season, he felt bound to go on. He accordingly divested himself of his Indian chief's head-dress and bead-work coat, and put two strong straps crosswise over his broad muscular shoulders, each strap fitted with a flat wide iron hook, to rest on his hips, for in those his adventurous companion was to place his legs. Mr. Calcourt [Woods erred; see below] was the man to be carried, and this person, in addition to his own coolness and confidence in Blondin, had a sufficient knowledge of rope-walking to enable him to stand on it alone whenever Blondin wanted rest. The preparations were soon made. Blondin took a very long and rather heavy balance pole. Calcourt divested himself of his boots, and put on a pair of ordinary slippers, the soles of which were well chalked. Blondin then stood steadily, and Calcourt, grasping him round the neck, gently and slowly hoisted first one leg into the hook and then the other, and allowing his limbs to swing as relaxed as possible, the venture commenced. Of course, with a rope nearly half-a-mile long no power could draw it straight across such a gulf. It therefore sloped rapidly down at both sides from the edges of the cliffs on which it was secured. This made the attempt look doubly fearful, for it seemed impossible, as Blondin went down the steep incline of the cord with slow, cautious, trembling feet, with body carefully thrown back to keep his balance as he almost felt his way, that he could avoid slipping, and being dashed to fragments on the rocks far down beneath. At last, however, he passed it [?], though very slowly, and in about five minutes more gained the centre of the rope and stopped, when Calcourt, gently raising his legs from the hooks, slid down and stood upon the cord while Blondin rested. Getting upon his back again was a terrible business. Twice Calcourt missed raising his legs to the hooks, and Blondin oscillated violently under the efforts made on his back. This unintentional awkwardness, which no doubt arose from nervousness, I was afterwards informed, led to a fierce altercation between the voyageurs [sic], and Blondin swore,

if Calcourt was not more careful, or more fortunate on his
third attempt, he would leave him on the rope to get back
as best he could. Awed by this threat, Calcourt was more
careful, or more fortunate on his third attempt, and the
dreadful walk was resumed. Three more such stoppages for
rest were made [other annalists say that there were as many
as five more]. During one, when almost in the centre of the
rope, there was a violent gust of wind, which fluttered Calcourt's coat tails about as if it would blow them away,
and made both men sway on the little cord till the spectators
were almost sick with fear and anxiety. The whole passage
occupied about a quarter of an hour.

Blondin then performed the still more dangerous task of
returning along the rope *on stilts* about three feet high, and
this he did quickly and with apparent ease.

Niagarans had first heard the name of Blondin in June of
1859, but it was no novelty to Americans already addicted to
the spectacles that were being offered them by P. T. Barnum.
During the previous four years, as leading member of the
French aerial acrobatic troupe called the Ravels, Blondin had
toured most of the domesticated regions of North America.
But it was at Niagara that he achieved his apotheosis, at the
comparatively advanced age (for acrobats) of thirty-five. On
his arrival at Manchester, New York (Niagara Falls), he announced to the skeptical press his intention of crossing the
gorge on a rope during the afternoon of June 30. According
to one account, the reporters who heard this boast were so
dubious that they failed even to notify their editors. Another
has it that although the local papers recorded Blondin's vow,
their readers refused to credit this highly improbable statement and, consequently, failed to turn up in significant numbers to observe the event.

At five p.m. of that day [June 30, 1859] that was to mark
a new era in Niagara history, Blondin walked out on the
American side with the sun glaring in his eyes and using a
balancing pole, reputed by numerous newspapers of that

era to be from 35 to 45 feet in length. In the middle of the river, the Maid of the Mist sailed under him and waited. He dropped a cord and picked up a bottle of wine, drew it up and drank it. Then he proceeded to the Canadian shore, where he was wined, dined, and feted. His crossing time had been fifteen minutes. He then calmly announced that he would return to the American side in less time than any of them [sic] could cross by bridge. With the sun behind him, he returned in seven minutes.

From that first sensational round trip, Blondin's career at the Niagara went from strength to strength, attracting greater and greater numbers of spectators for each performance, all of whom clamored for ever more daring feats. The intrepid Frenchman rarely disappointed his admirers. He made the crossing blindfolded; he rode over the swaying rope on a bicycle; he pushed a rather gorgeous wheelbarrow from one side of the river to the other. One particularly engaging stunt involved the transportation of a small coal stove to the center of the rope; there he paused, prepared a full meal, and lowered it by cord to the crew of the *Maid of the Mist* which attended him below. He made at least one crossing with both his hands and his legs shackled.

The crossing with a man on his back which was described by Nicholas Woods occurred in September of 1860. The first such effort, however, made little more than a year earlier, is the subject still of lively controversy. The name of the passenger whom Blondin carried across on the occasion of the Prince of Wales's visit to Niagara was apparently Romain Mouton, an assistant. The first to make that hair-raising journey on Blondin's back, in 1859, was Harry Colcord, the Frenchman's Chicago-born manager. The combination of Mouton's French nationality and Colcord's cognomen probably led to Woods' confusion.

Announcement of this initial endeavor attracted crowds to the viewing area two days before it was scheduled to take place. Reporters who covered the event for newspapers all over the northeast suggest that gamblers, betting against Blondin's success, sought to improve their position by sabotaging the guylines that helped to steady the walking-rope. The loosening or severing of these laterally affixed wires increased manifold the precariousness of a passage that was not, in any case, exactly as simple as taking a dog for a stroll. One journalist records that Harry Colcord was not at all eager to participate in this experiment. Obviously, his skepticism was misplaced.

Having conquered the Niagara in every conceivable way, Blondin was induced by the bedazzled young Prince of Wales to come to London to perform in the Crystal Palace. The crowds drawn by his spectacular aerial acrobatics in that fantasy of ironwork and glass are said to have made the Crystal Palace a paying proposition until it was razed by flames. Blondin's final public appearance, however, took place in Dublin in 1896. He died peacefully at his home in Ealing, near London, a year afterward, at the age of seventy-one. Never again, after 1860, did he perform at the Niagara—but the fashion he established and the standard he set continued to draw emulators for more than a century.

Three days after Blondin carried Romain Mouton over the Whirlpool gorge in 1860, Enrico Farini, a Canadian aerialist (who rightly presumed that an Italian pseudonym would serve him better in the eyes of the great unwashed who flocked to see him), appeared on the scene. A performer of comparable aplomb, he was much more of a clown than Blondin (who took his work very seriously). Farini advertised that at four in the afternoon of September 5, 1860, he would

> . . . introduce himself in his Wonderful and Laughable Character of BIDDY O'FLAHERTY THE IRISH WASHERWOMAN, by carrying out upon his cable a new PATENT WASHING MACHINE! Standing over Six feet high and weighing nearly 100 pounds, when he will Draw up Water from the River AND DO HIS OWN WASHING Hanging his clothes out to dry upon his Guys, where he can leave them out all night without fear of having them stolen. If any one doubts their being washed, they can go out and examine them.

Farini's derring-do could not be entirely obscured by his attempts to tickle his audience's risibilities. But in August of 1864, his sense of humor failed him completely. Having already done just about everything it was humanly possible for him to do while standing or walking or running on a length of rope, he elected to wade about on the brink of the American Falls on stilts, stalking back and forth within less than a hundred yards of the appalling precipice. The crowds gathered on the shores of Manchester and Goat Island were delighted with this audacious stunt. Then, quite unexpectedly, something went hilariously but terribly wrong. The dangerous farce was abruptly transmuted into farcical danger. One of Farini's stilts slipped into a narrow crevice of the torrent's bottom. He was lodged firmly and, much worse from his point of view, ludicrously. Only after several hours of effort and delay could a rope be attached to him so that he might drag himself most ignominiously to safety. It was Enrico Farini's finale at Niagara.

In the course of the next fifteen years many other men braved the currents of the river as they crossed the chasm on ropes or cables. But in 1876, Signorina Maria Spelterina, a genuine Italian acrobat this time, struck a sharp blow for equality of women with men. Not only did this shapely young lady accomplish almost everything that Blondin and Farini and their male imitators had done (save only for carrying another human over the rapids), but she did it with baskets attached to her feet. She terminated one spectacular performance at Niagara by traversing the rope backward from one side of the river to the other. Because of her beauty and her sex, Signorina Spelterina was at least as great an attraction as the immortal Blondin.

These exercises on a cable were simply curtain raisers, the first exploitations of the Niagara's temptations for the publicity-seeking daredevil. Before other modes of defying death, many of them unsuccessful, were devised, the American Civil War erupted. And for a time, there was a marked degree of tension along the thirty-five miles of the Niagara border.

The *Trent* affair, which involved the removal from the

British vessel *Trent*, on the high seas at the time, of two Confederate diplomats, John Slidell and James Murray Mason, produced the only overt international incident to exacerbate British-American relations—but such was not the case between the United States and Canada. Canadians, though certainly long hostile to the principle and practice of slavery, were not for that reason sympathetic with the Union cause—for the Union had never demonstrated any particular friendliness toward Canada. If this great British colony to the north gave refuge to runaway slaves in their thousands, so too did it prove hospitable to escaped Confederate prisoners of war and, altogether unofficially of course, for Confederate secret agents.

During the last months of 1861, United States fortifications along the Niagara were significantly strengthened with guns and men. And even after Slidell and Mason had been released from custody, following strong and prolonged British protest, at the beginning of the following year, Canadian admiration for the Confederate cause persisted—in spite of the slavery issue, which sophisticated foreigners (and not a few Unionists) perceived to be an emotional red herring. This particular fact of political life was obscured for most Americans a year later, when they heard of the Emancipation Proclamation—but failed to read its text with any care. President Lincoln had not, by this edict, freed *all* the slaves, but merely those who resided in southern territory still under the control of enemies of the Union. Slaves in the border states and in certain parishes of Louisiana were specifically left in bondage. The gesture which was to give the martyred Lincoln the name of the "Great Emancipator" was shamelessly political and selective, designed to split the Confederacy by allowing southerners to infer that if they only caused their states to rejoin the Union, they might retain their "peculiar institution." As such, therefore, the Emancipation Proclamation accomplished nothing concrete—though it undoubtedly gave northerners a feeling of complacency. It emancipated no one. It would require three amendments to the Constitution and the passage of more than a century before "emancipation" had any real meaning—and it would be for the blacks to emancipate themselves.

In July 1864, there was a modest flurry of excitement at Niagara when James Murray Mason, who had proceeded directly to Britain following his release from American custody at Boston, returned to North America. After a brief stopover at Quebec, Mason hastened to Clifton (Niagara Falls, Ontario) for the purpose of making personal contact with the celebrated and very influential journalist-editor Horace Greeley. Greeley had long advocated an immediate termination of the Civil War on almost any terms. Mason, instructed by Jefferson Davis, the Confederacy's President, proposed that the secessionist states be accorded diplomatic recognition by the Union as a separate political entity, with frontiers that would generally follow the southern banks of the Potomac and the Ohio rivers. The New Yorker lost no time in passing these suggestions on to the President in Washington. Lincoln, who knew by this time that the Union had been preserved and that southern acceptance of this reality was only a question of time and the incomprehensible human need to satisfy "honor," was in no frame of mind to negotiate any sort of compromise. Victory was at hand.

The British government and its administration in colonial Canada had managed with great difficulty to maintain a policy of relaxed neutrality throughout the long conflict that sundered the United States. Unofficially, however, many individual Canadians aided and abetted agents of the Confederacy in a variety of ways. As the Civil War entered its conclusive year, there were several related incidents on Lake Erie which could not possibly have occurred without the complying negligence of Canadian naval patrols.

In September 1864, a dozen Confederates hijacked the American steamer *Philo Parsons* off Sandusky, Ohio, near the scene of Perry's famous victory of 1813. They ordered her master to sail for Johnson Island, a Union prison camp which housed thirty-five hundred Confederate officers. The installation was protected by a few antiquated cannons and a single ironclad ship *Michigan,* the only one of its kind then plying the Great Lakes. On the voyage toward Johnson Island, *Philo Parsons* intercepted *Island Queen,* another steam side-wheeler, and took possession of her as well, in the name of the Confederacy. These apparently inconsequential acts of piracy were actually parts of a rather astonishing and nearly successful conspiracy.

The plan was to overcome the crew of *Michigan,* a ship of the United States Navy. This vessel's powerful guns were to be turned against the defenses of Johnson Island. After subduing the island garrison, the Confederate prisoners there, invaluable to an army that was desperately lacking in trained officers, would be released and returned to service. To effect this daring operation, the assistance of Miss Annie Davis, keeper of a Sandusky brothel which was much frequented by the crew of *Michigan,* was enlisted—for a considerable price. Annie's girls, one of whom proved to be a Pinkerton agent in the employ of the Union, were to board the ironclad, as was their custom, and then to drug the crew by polluting a bowl of punch.

On the afternoon of September 19, Annie Davis and her gallant young Confederate escort, the Virginian John Yates Beall, took her "young ladies" to visit with *Michigan's* company. While Mr. Beall allowed himself to be taken on an apparently innocent tour of the ship, Annie was preparing the dollop of chloral hydrate to introduce into the punch. Beall carefully noted the positions of *Philo Parsons* and *Island Queen,* moored at a distance from *Michigan* of about a thousand yards. All was in readiness for the culminating moments of the plot—or so it seemed.

However, in the interim, the lady Pinkerton had informed *Michigan's* captain of the scheme that was afoot. The instant Beall reappeared in the wardroom for what was to be the dramatic denouement, *Michigan's* master struck him on the head. Other officers arrested Annie Davis and her girls. Minutes afterward, *Michigan* fired warning shots across the bows

of *Island Queen* and *Philo Parsons* and commanded their
pirate crews to surrender or see the vessels blasted out of the
water. The great and brilliant conspiracy was in ashes.

During the following months, there were scattered raids
across the Saint Lawrence against the crops and farmhouses of
northern Maine, Vermont, and New Hampshire. These were
excessively annoying to the victims. Some Unionists, confident
now of eventual victory over the Confederacy, seriously advocated war against Canada in reprisal for having offered refuge
and comfort to enemy marauders. It seemed to the more ag-
gressively land-hungry northerners the ideal time to try to
annex the immense tracts of the British colony—thus to place
all of continental North America (except for Central American
and Alaskan antipodes) under the genial aegis of Washington.
How impressed President Lincoln was by such proposals may
be measured by the sharpness with which he turned them
aside. He recognized that most of the Unionists were heartily
sick of the war they were still waging and that the recon-
stitution of the South's economy and the settlement of the
West—which was still to be stolen wholesale from the Indians
—would provide ample outlets for remaining American energies. The United States didn't need another war just then.

Within a year of the Civil War's termination, the Niagara
Frontier witnessed its very last episode of international vio-
lence. This occurrence, for once, had its origins neither in the
United States nor in Canada, but in Ireland. Since Hibernia's
doleful little history has no place in this narrative (and since,
if it did, there would be room for nothing else), it must suffice
to remark that in the seventh decade of the last century there
developed in Ireland yet another movement intended to detach the British yoke. This movement called itself the Irish
Republican Brotherhood, whose members were better known
as the Fenians.

No one can accurately estimate how many Irish immigrants
there were in the United States and Canada as of 1866. They
could certainly be numbered in the several millions, for their

ranks had been enormously augmented from the middle of the century onward as a result of the calamitous Irish famine of that period. Concern with the outcome of the American Civil War had prevented Irish-Americans from taking a very active personal interest in the Fenian rising that impended in the land of their birth. John O'Neill, a former Union infantry officer, began not very secretly to organize a force of his fellow Irish sympathizers at Buffalo—by now second in size only to New York among the state's cities. This was the nucleus of the force that would take part in the "Fenian Invasion" of Canada.

About fifteen hundred Irish-American Fenians, most of them Union veterans like their leader, took possession of the abandoned Canadian redoubt of Fort Erie and the village that now adjoined it. This occurred in the late spring of 1866. Their announced intention was to march the thirty-odd miles westward to the Welland Canal, to blow up one of its locks, and then to hold a section of the Canadian area of the Niagara Frontier as ransom for Ireland's release from British "occupation." The Irish Republican Brotherhood in the motherland had never conceived a plan so audacious nor so obviously madcap.

Even more extraordinary (unless one recalls official American reaction to Mackenzie's exploits of 1837 and 1838) was the failure of the United States government to intervene in the face of so palpable a violation of neutrality agreements. There were street gatherings in several American communities on the banks of the Niagara. Shamrock pennants and banners demanding "Freedom for Ireland" were prominently displayed. There was, more significantly, an accumulation of arms and ammunition that clearly portended more than an early celebration of the Fourth of July.

There are historians who remain convinced that while official American policy deplored John O'Neill's folly, not a few legislators (of the same stripe as those who had earlier supported the War of 1812 and the Mexican War and more recently a war against Canada) hoped that he would manage,

against all the conclusive evidence, to bring it off—or hoped at
the very least that his action would result in the defection of
Upper Canada to the American Union—a possibility that
seemed enhanced by the fact that an important majority of
the residents of that province had emigrated from the United
States. It is interesting to observe the persistence of the American conviction that beneath every foreigner's skin there beats
the heart of a secret American. As we shall note, the Fenian
exploit had a quite different outcome.

On the night of May 31, 1866, canal barges and tugs assembled along the wharves of Black Rock and Buffalo. In the
earliest hours of the next morning, they began to cross the
relatively calm Niagara waters to Fort Erie, which they occupied without encountering a bit of armed resistance. O'Neill
had expected none. Indeed, he had been promised additional
volunteers and large quantities of supplies from Canadian
sympathizers of Irish extraction. Neither appeared. The commander then ordered his irregular little army to forage for
food among the residents of Fort Erie—something his troops
did with the same kind of rough enthusiasm they were supposed
to have demonstrated in the communities of the American South
which they had invested. They took all the food they could
find and, as well, all the whiskey, horses, and vehicles. According to some reports, they took not a few pretty Canadian girls
and women, too.

Instead of the anticipated reinforcements, O'Neill soon found
himself confronted by about eight hundred ill-organized but
zealous Canadian militiamen who were extremely annoyed that
their farmlands and villages should figure in a struggle that had
nothing at all to do with them. O'Neill's immediate reaction
was to avoid direct conflict. He moved his men off in the
direction of the Welland Canal, determined to destroy one of
its locks as a symbolic gesture. The Canadians attacked and
were easily rebuffed, but O'Neill suddenly began to think as a
soldier, not merely as an Irish fanatic. He appreciated that a
second and more competently directed effort would soon be

mounted against him. A wise and compassionate officer, John O'Neill abruptly changed his mind, ordering his now-straggling collection of less than seven hundred to return to the Niagara and make their way back across the river in individual groups, as best they could.

Several hundred of them, including their romantic leader, were immediately placed under arrest by American authorities. However, all of them were soon released without ever being indicted for their offense against United States neutrality acts. Not a single trial resulted from O'Neill's fantastic conspiracy. Moreover, the United States government refused to assume responsibility for the depredations the Fenians, American citizens all, had visited on the Canadians. There would be no reparations, though numbers of Canadian militiamen had been killed or wounded by American nationals who had assembled and armed themselves in broad daylight on American soil. The Fenian Invasion was a Canadian Bay of Pigs—with the difference that the United States held itself blameless in the incident and could not be brought to book for its indifference in the face of such provocation.

John O'Neill and his thickheaded hoodlums accomplished nothing whatever for Mother Ireland. But they *were* instrumental, unwittingly, in bringing to a swift conclusion a debate on the status of Canada that had begun, on the banks of the Niagara, a half-century before by William Lyon Mackenzie. Within a year of the abortive Fenian Invasion, citizens of New Brunswick and Nova Scotia opted to join those of Lower and Upper Canada in a petition to the Crown at Westminster for the establishment of all Canada as an independent, federated Dominion of Queen Victoria's invincible British Empire.

15

Over the FALLS, Down the Rapids

What of nature man finds himself unable to destroy he often does his conscientious best to despoil. From the period after the end of the War of 1812, when Niagara had first begun to attract tourists by the thousands, the river's terrible ferocity appeared to invite lurid spectacles. The proprietors of the growing number of hotels and rooming houses on both sides of the falls felt the need to create "happenings." William Forsyth and John Brown, both Canadian hoteliers, and Parkhurst Whitney, owner of the Eagle Hotel in Manchester, New York, undertook in 1827 the first and, in its bizarre way, perhaps the most monstrous spectacle of all the countless efforts offered at Niagara.

A broadside which was distributed throughout western New York and Upper Canada during the month of August admirably conveys the flavor and spirit of the event that was projected:

> The Pirate, MICHIGAN, with a cargo of ferocious animals, will pass the great rapids and falls of NIAGARA, 8th September, 1827, at 6 o'clock.

The first passage of a vessel of the largest class which sails on Erie and the Upper Lakes, through the Great Rapids, and over the stupendous precipice of Niagara Falls, it is proposed to effect, on the 8th of September next.

The *Michigan* has long braved the billows of Erie, with success, as a merchant vessel; but having been *condemned* by her owners as unfit to sail long proudly *"above;"* her present proprietors, together with several publick spirited friends, have appointed her to convey a cargo of Living Animals of the Forests, which surround the Upper Lakes, through the white tossing, and the deep rolling rapids of the Niagara, and down its great precipice, into the basin *"below."*

The greatest exertions are being made to procure Animals of the most ferocious kind, such as Panthers, Wild Cats, and Wolves; but in lieu of some of these, which it may be impossible to obtain, a few vicious or worthless dogs, such as may possess considerable strength and activity, and perhaps a few of the toughest of the Lesser Animals will be added to, and compose, the cargo.

Capt. *James Rough*, of Black Rock, the oldest navigator of the Upper Lakes, has generously volunteered his services to manage this enterprise, in which he will be seconded by Mr. *Levi Allen*, mate of the steamboat *Niagara*—the publick may rest assured that they will select none but capable assistants. The manager will proceed seasonably with experiments, to ascertain the most practicable and eligible point, from which to detach the *Michigan* for the Rapids.

It is intended to have the *Michigan* fitted up in the style in which she is to make her splendid but perilous descent, at *Black Rock*, where she now lies. She will be dressed as a *Pirate;* besides her *Menagerie* of Wild Animals, and probably some tame ones, it is proposed to place *a Crew* (in effigy) at proper stations on board. The Animals will be caged or otherwise secured on board the *"condemned vessel,"* on the morning of the 7th [of September], at the Ferry [from Black Rock to Fort Erie], where the curious can examine her with her *"cargo"* during the day, at a trifling expense. On the morning of the 8th, the *Michigan* will be towed from her position at *Black Rock,* to the foot of Navy Island, by the Steamboat Chippewa [sic], from whence she will be conducted by her manager to her last moorings. Passage can be obtained in the *Michigan* from *Black Rock* to *Navy Island,* at *half a dollar* each.

Should the vessel take her course through the *deepest of the Rapids,* it is confidently believed, that she will reach the *Horse Shoe,* unbroken; if so, she will perform her voyage, *to the water of the Gulf beneath,* which is of great depth and buoyancy, entire; *but what her fate may be, the* trial *will decide.* Should the Animals be young and hardy, and *possessed of great muscular power, and joining their fate* with that of the Vessel, remain on board until she reaches the water below, there is a great possibility that many of them, will *have performed the terrible jaunt, unhurt!*

Such as may survive, and be retaken, will be sent to the Museums at New York and Montreal, and some perhaps to London.

It may be proper to observe, that several Steamboats are expected to be in readiness at *Buffalo,* together with numerous Coaches, for the conveyance of Passengers down, on the morning of the 8th. Coaches will leave Buffalo, at 2 o'clock, on the afternoon of the 7th, for the Falls on both sides of the River, for the convenience of those who may be desirous of securing accommodations at the Falls on the 8th, Ample means of conveyance to Visitors, will be provided at *Tonawanda,* at *Lockport,* at *Lewiston,* at *Queenston,* and at *Fort George,* to either side.

As no probable estimate can now be made of the numbers which the proposed exhibition may bring together; great disappointments regarding the extent of our accommodations may possibly be anticipated by some; in respect of which, we beg leave to assure our respective friends and the publick in general, that, in addition to our own [Brown's, Forsyth's, and the Eagle Hotel], which are large, (and will on the occasion be furnished to their utmost limits,) there are other Publick Houses, besides many private ones at which comfortable entertainment can be had, for all who may visit the Falls on the present Occasion—an occasion which will for its novelty and the remarkable spectacle it will present, be unequalled in the annals of *invernal* [sic] navigation.

Truth in advertising was not a prerequisite in 1827. Though the entrepreneurs may well have done their best to populate the rotting schooner with "ferocious Animals," the most alarming examples they succeeded in laying their hands on were a bison and two bears. To this company they added a pair of raccoons, a dog, and a goose. Nevertheless, the desperate voyage did take place on the appointed afternoon. It was witnessed by a throng variously estimated from fifteen to thirty thousand souls—an absolutely enormous gathering even at the lower calculation, given the difficulties of transport at the time and the relatively small number of residents in the immediate vicinity.

When *Michigan* entered the Upper Rapids, she was almost immediately holed by some shallow rocks. However, she progressed swiftly toward the edge of the Horseshoe Fall. The bears, the only creatures on board that had been neither caged nor lashed in place, leaped from the vessel and managed to swim to safety. The other beasts that had been consigned to the doomed vessel were not so fortunate, for they perished in the drop and hence failed to find their way (unless they were stuffed—which is not so unlikely) to the "museums" of Montreal or New York or London. *Michigan* did indeed go over the falls, with her decks flooded, at which juncture she was probably drawing something like twenty feet of water—a fact that gives some notion of the depth of the river as it reached the edge of the precipice in the days before the Niagara Hydro system went into operation. Everyone, we have to imagine, was delighted with this dreadful spectacle. It is therefore all the more surprising that it should prove an enterprise that was never repeated—although, as we have already seen, the warship *Caroline* was aimed in the same direction a decade later—but in a rather different interest.

One of those who came to the Niagara's banks to see the

demise of *Michigan* was Sam Patch, originator of all the more personal "stunts" that were to be a feature of summers at the falls. Studying the vast crowd assembled for the event, he conceived a sudden passion to gain fame and fortune by performing a remarkable individual feat at the site. He secured the backing of some local hotel men for the construction of a platform about a hundred feet high, which was erected just below the American falls. From its top, he made several spectacular dives into the tumultuous river. He soon became a great favorite and did indeed make quite a bit of money in the process. Though Sam Patch was never injured in any of his adventures at Niagara, he was killed soon afterward when he attempted a similar plunge into the pool at the foot of Genesee Falls.

The massive attendance attracted by this kind of display soon lured quantities of hucksters to Niagara, most of them very casual in their concern for the more rudimentary ethical principles. The "petrified spray" that was, in scientific fact, a calcitic limestone formation known as calcite, spar, or surfstone, was collected assiduously from the water and rocks below the falls and marketed with such zeal that domestic supplies were very rapidly exhausted. Artifacts purportedly fabricated from native "spray" were actually made of material imported to the Niagara Frontier from distant Derbyshire, in England—the product similar in texture and appearance to the matter that nature no longer provided in sufficient quantity at the base of the falls. "Indian handcrafts" were, more often than not, turned out in shamelessly great batches in local sweatshops, mainly by hapless Irish immigrants. Cabdrivers shilled for hoteliers, brothel-keepers, and the proprietors of souvenir shops—the most colorful of which was Captain Webb's Indian Bazaar, which stood near Table Rock, on the Canadian side.

After 1846, the *Maid of the Mist*, first of the steam-powered craft successfully to negotiate the gulf below Niagara Falls, made commonplace the spectacular voyage along the vaporous fringes of the two cascades. The process of cheapening the whole experience of visiting this marvel of nature, once begun, was irresistible and self-accelerating. It has yet to be arrested—though its progress may now have been contained simply because it has descended to a nadir it seems difficult to get lower than.

A second ship, a rival *Maid of the Mist,* was constructed in 1856. She was commanded by Captain Joel E. Robinson. From the beginning of her career of competition with the original vessel, the second craft was plagued by financial difficulties—not the least of which was brought on by the outbreak of the American Civil War, a circumstance that produced a sudden and drastic reduction in the flow of tourists to Niagara. In the spring of 1861, when it was obvious that the newer of the side-wheelers was not soon to be a commercial success below the falls, her owners, besieged by their American creditors, offered the intrepid master a bounty of $500 for an attempt to bring her safely down the two sets of rapids to Queenston, on the Canadian side. The mortgage-holders rightly appreciated

Maid of the Mist in the Whirlpool, 1861

the negligible resale value of a property locked forever in the Niagara pool; foreclosure there would have been the emptiest of gestures. But merely to contemplate the voyage from the foot of the falls to Queenston, by any means of surface conveyance, was exceptionally daunting—except, apparently, to Captain Joel Robinson, who must have kept his eye firmly on the bonus of $500.

Orrin E. Dunlap, an indefatigable chronicler of eccentric occurrences at Niagara, described the horrendous trip forty-one years afterwards for readers of *Cosmopolitan*:

The steamer "Maid of the Mist" was then [in 1861] heavily mortgaged, and Captain Robinson reckoned he wasn't going to have her tied up, if running her to a Canadian port could avert it. Accordingly, on the afternoon of June 6th, with only his two associates MacIntyre and Jones aboard, Robinson gave the signal to go ahead, but to the surprise of those who saw the boat the bow was directed right toward the rapids instead of toward the falls. Under full steam the little steamer sped down the river and dashed into the waves [of the Whirlpool Rapids]. She plunged through the rolling white-caps with a rush, but lost her smokestack as the huge waves swept her deck. The voyage was fierce but short, and in a few minutes the boat was in the whirlpool. She answered to her rudder, and turning her nose out of the outlet, Robinson soon had her speeding [through the Lower Rapids] toward the peaceful waters five miles below. Practically uninjured, the boat landed at Queenston, and Robinson was a hero.

Hero though he must certainly have been proclaimed by all who knew of his remarkable achievement, and $500 more prosperous, Captain Joel Robinson was by way of being a broken man at the conclusion of this improbable and hazardous trip down the two most treacherous and steep rapids in eastern North America. It is recorded, therefore, that this master riverine navigator never again ventured out into the waters of the Niagara. One may readily comprehend the reason for his diffidence. Perhaps the most audacious stunt ever attempted on the rapids, this final river voyage of the *Maid of the Mist* on the raging waters of her birth wasn't a stunt at all. Robinson had seen the face of death and, unlike Captain Ahab, found it extremely unattractive. As we shall have occasion to describe, the face of death was evidently not very alarming to those who later dared the falls and rapids. It may even have possessed a hypnotic allure; it wasn't that they were tempting death, but rather that they were tempted *by* it.

A desire for celebrity and its attendant improvement in their financial circumstances drew fools, inventors, and the full complement of charlatans to dare the terrible stretches of the Lower Niagara in a number of peculiar conveyances. On July 11, 1886, Carlisle Graham, a barrelmaker transplanted from England to Philadelphia, made the first run down the Whirlpool Rapids. His craft was a barrel of his own manufacture, into which he placed himself after donning a water-resistant canvas sack. Once the barrel's lid was sealed, Graham grasped special handles inside and waited with impatience for his cylindrical vehicle to be lowered into the mainstream of the river between the falls and the Whirlpool Rapids. The barrel revolved incessantly for the half hour of his perilous journey, a phenomenon that made Graham wretchedly ill; but he survived this attempt and even lived through a second—this one with his head protruding. Between his initial assault on the rapids and his second, George Hazlett and William Potts made the trip together in a barrel. In the autumn of that same year of 1886, Hazlett had another go at it, this time in the company of Miss Sadie Allen—who thus became the first woman to go down the rapids in a barrel.

To stand at the water's level beside any stretch of the Whirlpool Rapids is to invite a sort of vertigo. The effect is rather like that created by a perpetually incoming tide on a perpetually enraged sea. But only "rather," for there is nothing really comparable to the invincibly majestic fury of these rolling, churning whitecaps which surmount a relentless flow of ominously dark green water. To contemplate an attempt to swim from one end of these savage rapids to the other is not merely to consider flirting with death, but actively to solicit it—and with a moral certainty that it will come.

Captain Matthew Webb, who had already swum the English Channel, arrived at the Niagara in the early months of the summer of 1883 with the loudly anounced intention that he would conquer the Whirlpool Rapids without benefit of any kind of protection at all. Orrin E. Dunlap takes up the narrative:

> It was generally believed that when Webb reached Niagara and viewed the rapids, he would reconsider his determination. But he did not lose confidence, and on July 24, 1883, he entered a small boat, with Jack McCloy at the oars, and started down the river. When yet several hundred feet from the rapids, he leaped from the boat, and with nothing on but a pair of red trunks, swam with all his skill in the foaming waters. Thousands were on the cliff-tops and bridges. As Webb passed under the suspension-bridge, he swam with much grace and beauty. Right into the crested waves he was hurled as the force of his own strong strokes and the current sent him forward. He was seen to pass a few of the swells, and then he was sucked under by a mighty wave. Four days later his lifeless body was picked up seven miles down the river, and to-day it rests in a grave in Oakwood Cemetery. Webb's mistake was in failing to recognize that even if he could have battled with the swirling currents, the air-charged waters of the gorge lacked the buoyancy necessary to support him.

Webb's fatal adventure failed to deter James Scott, a Lewiston fisherman who had grown up on the banks of the Niagara and who thought himself, quite mistakenly, its master. *His* attempt suffered an identical outcome. Three years after Webb's calamitous assault on the Whirlpool Rapids, William

Kendall, a Boston constable, did make the terrible journey in safety—but he took the precaution of wearing a lifejacket. And in 1901, the same Carlisle Graham who had twice descended the dreadful stretch of the river in a barrel, swam the somewhat less treacherous Lower Rapids and survived.

In October of the same year, the first human to attempt to go over the Horseshoe Falls in a barrel was successful. (No one ever intentionally ventured a trip over the American Falls because of the jagged line of massive rocks upon which the water tumbles.) The New York saloonkeeper Steve Brodie, who boasted that he had survived a leap into the East River from the center of John Roebling's Brooklyn Bridge, claimed to have gone over the Canadian Falls in 1889, wearing nothing more protective than a padded rubber suit. However, contemporary scholars of Niagara madness dismiss Brodie's assertion as hubris without substantiation.

The honor of 1901 belongs to a woman, Mrs. Anna Edson Taylor, a schoolmistress from Bay City, Michigan, who was a dignified forty-three when she risked all to improve her desperate financial plight. Willis E. Beese has composed an amiable account of this remarkable "first" in Niagara's gaudy history:

> Daredevil though she was, Mrs. Taylor refused to pose for pictures garbed in the costume she had prepared for the trip. "It would be unbecoming a woman of my refinement and my years to parade before a holiday crowd in an abbreviated skirt," she explained.
>
> On Grass Island [which flanks Goat Island on the Canadian side], starting place of the voyage, Mrs. Taylor shooed her male assistants to the far end of the island while she donned the abbreviated dress, which, incidentally, extended well below her knees, and got safely inside her barrel before recalling the men. They tightened up her harness, pumped into her make-shift air supply "enough gas to last her a week," and set her adrift.
>
> Because of the 100-pound anvil in its bottom, her cask floated in an upright position. After lurching through the

upper rapids, the barrel tipped slightly forward on the brink of the Horseshoe Falls and disappeared into the spray. Seventeen minutes later it was stranded on a reef just off the Canadian shore. The watery gap was quickly bridged with poles and planks, but to free the imprisoned woman, attendants had to saw off the top of her heavy oak barrel.

Although thoroughly soaked and slightly cut on the jaw, Mrs. Taylor was not otherwise badly injured, and after a half hour of delirium, seemed quite herself again. But, alas, the "Queen of the Mist" did not escape that dreadful fate which had driven her to this reckless deed. Robbed of the proceeds of her desperate adventure and of her barrel as well, she died in the poorhouse twenty years later.

After Anna Taylor's bold step forward for mankind, many males emulated her feat—some successfully, others fatally. Going over the falls and down the rapids became a fashion, like eating goldfish or burning draft cards. The only interest, aside from that ghoulish curiosity that also attracts crowds to bullfights, prizefights, and automobile races, lay in the method any particular "artiste" chose for the attempt.

A combination of extremely aggressive press-agentry and the fact that millions of people came to Niagara every year, regardless of what spectacular stunt was being promoted, kept these boring iterations in the news. Anything that happened at Niagara made good copy because the dateline was so well known. Incidentally, no one knows why or when the tradition of honeymooning at Niagara Falls began or why it should persist. The most plausible surmise is that prior to the Civil War, when the site was first a major pilgrimage for visitors of *every* kind, it seemed an ideal place for embarrassed newlyweds to lose themselves among great quantities of souls who were not only total strangers to them, but to one another as well, a crowd of individuals—a lonely crowd.

The ultimate adventure to occur at Niagara was totally inadvertent, yet it eclipsed every stunt performed there—even Captain Joel Robinson's descent of the rapids in *Maid of the*

Mist. What would be called the miracle of Niagara took place on July 9, 1960, a classic midsummer's day, at the very height of the tourist season.

The cast selected for this drama were two children and a young man—Deanne and Roger Woodward, recently moved to Niagara Falls, and Jim Honeycutt, who worked with the children's father at the New York State Power Authority. Jim owned a frail little aluminum outboard motorboat with whose proper operation on the river he was imperfectly familiar. He offered to take the Woodward children for an outing on the upper Niagara, an invitation which their father readily accepted, with the stipulation that both wear lifejackets—just as a precaution. There were apparently only two of these devices on board.

As they set out, some five miles upstream from the falls, Roger dutifully donned his lifejacket. Deanne declined. Jim didn't insist. The girl placed herself at the bow. The boy sat near Jim at the stern. They headed downriver, a journey that was safe only above the Ontario Hydro Control Dam, a structure which, in 1960, spanned about a third of the river from the Canadian shore, little more than a mile above the precipice of the Horseshoe Falls. Apart from serving to tranquilize the turbulent waters of the Upper Rapids, the dam is also symbolic. A craft which passes below it is beyond ordinary salvation. It may have the good fortune to be holed and consequently to founder, but a safe landing is out of the question. Honeycutt, however, was conscious of no such hazard as his little boat swept beyond the dam.

Only moments later, when he was able to discern the figures of tourists on the west bank of Goat Island did the master of this doomed vessel suddenly appreciate that he and his two passengers were in direst peril. By this time, they were perhaps a half-mile above the edge of the Horseshoe. Deanne, who could see the spray rising high above the gulf at the base of the falls, was also aware of the impending danger. She put on her lifejacket. Only her younger brother failed to comprehend the magnitude of their predicament.

Honeycutt made a sharp right turn and tried to take the boat to Goat Island, but they were now in the moiling waters of the rapids where the current's speed approached twenty-five miles per hour. The shear pin of the motor broke, probably as the propeller struck one of the countless rocks just beneath the surface. The directionless boat broached almost at once, hurling its three passengers into the treacherous water. Roger and Jim were drawn out toward the center of the raging stream. Deanne was caught beneath the craft, and when she freed herself, she found nothing on the boat to which she could securely cling. She made for the shore of Goat Island, thrashing badly in her panic and being carried all the while toward the precipice.

Her only hope of rescue was to come close enough to the edge of Terrapin Point to be lifted from the water by a concerned tourist. There were literally hundreds to choose from, yet only one came forward, John R. Hayes, a black truck driver and auxiliary policeman from New Jersey, who climbed over the iron-pipe railing. He managed to grasp one of Deanne's hands and arrest her downward progress at the last possible moment. But he was unable to draw her toward the concrete retaining wall. He called for help and, for a moment (for reasons one hesitates to consider), it seemed that no one would heed his cry. When Hayes thought he could no longer keep his grip on the girl, John Quattrochi, another man from New Jersey, rushed to his side and secured Deanne's free hand. Together, the men brought her safely ashore. When she had caught her breath, all the child could murmur was the name of her brother, whom she had last glimpsed passing toward the middle of the rapids on his way over the falls.

While the two men and a sudden host of well-wishers were comforting Deanne Woodward on Goat Island, Roger was flailing his arms wildly and calling for help—at the foot of the Horseshoe Fall. Niagara theorists conjecture that it was a combination of sheer chance and Roger's buoyancy (he weighed only fifty-five pounds and he was wearing a lifejacket) that enabled him to become the first identifiable human safely to negotiate that most perilous of journeys without the aid of a complicated contraption.

The orange lifejacket bobbing about in the slowly circling waters of the steaming pool beneath the Horseshoe Falls attracted the notice of Captain Clifford Keech, master of a *Maid of the Mist*. He maneuvered his large craft cleverly, bringing her alongside the frantic ten-year-old. Deckhands lifted him aboard. He was taken to a hospital on the Canadian side while his sister, consoled by the knowledge of his survival, was under observation in a New York State hospital. Neither child was seriously injured. A ream of journalists posed each of them silly questions: "What did you feel? How does it feel to be alive?" Roger replied succinctly, "I could feel I was falling. I was holding on to Jim but I had to let him go. Then I was falling. . . ."

After two nights in hospital, the Woodward children were released. Two days later, the lifeless body of Jim Honeycutt was found on the bank of the Lower Niagara. All other experiences at this site seem uninteresting when compared with the long accident that befell him and the Woodward children.

Roger Woodward is the only human known to have survived a tumble over the falls with no more protection than a life jacket. It was and almost surely will remain the ultimate Niagara adventure.

16
Power
to the
People

In the years that followed the opening of the Erie Canal, the folklore of New York State was enriched by the addition of a number of songs rendered, usually in a state of inebriation, by the boatmen who congregated at Buffalo after their long haul from the Hudson. There they met the sailors who manned the ships that plied the Great Lakes—the latter regarding the former as essentially landlubbers, "navvies," as the canal navigators of England were called. These unkind allusions produced brawls in which the proud lakesmen often came out losers simply because their inferiority happened to be numerical.

For perhaps a century, Buffalo was the largest more or less domesticated community between Philadelphia and Chicago—and until the railways assumed an importance that was capital, it would be the biggest town of the American "west." The canal was solely responsible for this growth, and the transients it drew to Buffalo were not remarkable for the culture they carried. The harbor area alone sheltered more than ninety saloons after 1880, and women far less noble than the Lydia Harper who succored those stricken with cholera in 1834 patrolled the extensive dock sides with impunity. The next year, an English visitor, Thomas Woodcock, found the Canal Street section a "corrupt place, with its denizens in a melancholy state morally."

Worse was to come, because Buffalo got bigger and looser and more dangerous to the innocent. The most celebrated brothel-keeper of her era was Mother Carey, who dispensed whiskey in her saloon, entertainment in her dance hall, solace in her boardinghouse, and apparently operated one of the earliest American send-out prostitution services, dispatching "chicks" to the barges and ships so that men who stood watch could do so lying down as well.

If the complaint be lodged again that this narrative more often chronicles the activities of whores than of "good" women, I must respond by saying that it was a very long time before "good" women in the Niagara region did anything so conspicuous as the whores. Moreover, there wasn't much in the Buffalo and Niagara region of the mid-nineteenth century to attract "good" women. There were few good men, for example. The city gave the country one of its least memorable presidents, Millard Fillmore—whose accomplishments were mainly decorative. In 1870, the sheriff of Erie County was Grover Cleveland, who attempted to deal with the prostitution problem—there were more than five hundred single women living in Buffalo's tenderloin, all of them self-described as innocent seamstresses and laundresses and followers of like crafts. Cleveland found things easier as governor of the state, and was much more successful in reducing venality in the federal bureaucracy, during his two terms as President of the United States, than in coping with the whores of Buffalo. It was not, one must understand, that the city fathers of Buffalo were attempting to suppress the oldest profession. They meant simply to restrict the practitioners to an area where their importunities would not offend the effete snobs who prospered from other aspects of the canal and lake trade, and from burgeoning Niagara-powered industries.

When the Pan-American Exposition of 1901 signaled Buffalo's arrival as a city of world renown, to be visited by no less a figure than William McKinley—a president whose memory is still revered in certain upstate New York quarters, where the only serious complaint is that he ended the Spanish-American War—the whores of Buffalo were suddenly aware of an influx of fresh flesh from the city of New York. A civil war, which could properly be described only by Henry Fielding or Tobias Smollett, ensued. Smoldering rivalries were fanned into flames one night—before the President's arrival. Heated words led to impetuous deeds. The horse-drawn patrol wagons from nearby police stations made no fewer than thirty-two trips, each one filled to capacity with infuriated visitors from New York who, the next day, were ordered to return to their own turf. The whores of Buffalo were protected from further incursions on what must have been a bonanza traffic.

President McKinley's visit to Buffalo was "nonpolitical," though the phrase had not yet been coined and could never apply to anything any president did. The occasion was, as we've noted, the Pan-American Exposition of 1901—the first such orgy of civic self-righteousness to be illuminated by alternating-current electricity. About *that,* more will be said in a bit. The President, basking in the knowledge that he would be able to do what Mark Hanna told him to do until March 4, 1905, was not a universally popular figure. It would be too strong to say he was the plaything of the robber barons, who had come into their own after the Civil War, but he was certainly amenable to their blandishments and hospitable to their plans for economic plunder. This view had, as a necessary concomitant, an extension which had found expression in the Spanish-American War with its attendant atrocities, especially in the Philippines, where natives saw no particular virtues in the substitution of American for Spanish rule and who were slaughtered for their desire to determine their own form of government.

In the summer following his second inauguration, McKinley and a large party made a tour of the United States which was to culminate with a visit to Buffalo's exposition, a setting that served, on the evening of September 5, as the setting for a speech on foreign and tariff policies. The next day, the President attended a reception in the largest of the exposition's buildings for the usual round of handshaking. Leon Czolgosz, a young man who professed to be an anarchist and who gave it as his opinion that all heads of state ought to be assassinated, put two pistol shots into the Chief Executive's person from close range. One of the bullets penetrated McKinley's abdomen. After what was ostensibly a successful operation, the President survived eight days, then abruptly succumbed. Czolgosz never expressed remorse for his act, for which he paid with his own life.

The assassination of McKinley probably had a more demoralizing effect on Buffalo than on the rest of the country. Always feeling itself something of a frontier town, the Dodge City of the East, it responded to this calamity in much the same way that Dallas would later react to the assassination of President Kennedy. There was an orgy of tears, followed by the erection of a public monument. Although he was the third president to die by the gun in thirty-six years, no great cry was raised against the general possession of firearms. Indeed, McKinley's successor Teddy Roosevelt was a devotee of the gun—the hero of San Juan Hill and a famous big game hunter.

Though it remains the second city of New York State, Buffalo today is remarkable for not very much; it suffers from all the ills common to major urban agglomerations—pollution, ghetto slums, depopulation, and unimaginative government. It has a splendid university which is viewed with suspicion by the "right people" who have moved to fashionable suburbs. It has a fine museum of arts, the Albright Knox Art Gallery, remarkable for the juxtaposition of architectural styles and for a peerless collection of contemporary paintings and sculpture. It has an industrial sprawl and pall that envelop the whole east bank of the Niagara River from Lake Erie to Niagara Falls and gives the visitor who views them from the opposite shore an impression of bleakest desuetude. For practical purposes, there is nothing to distinguish the city of Niagara Falls from Buffalo —except its proximity to the falls themselves, a property which is "protected" against further human depredation but is unable to undo, as of this writing, the spoliations of the recent industrial past. It also provides the only really ugly view available from the New York side of the river—that of Niagara Falls, Ontario, which is a large amusement park, studded with hideous towers against which the only defense is to go to their tops; from those points they are less obtrusive.

Downriver from Niagara Falls, New York, the prospects are much happier. The villages of Lewiston and Youngstown have managed to keep their charm because, perhaps, they do not afford breathtaking vistas. There is protected park land on either side of these communities, and one can still get some slightest impression of what this magnificent, brief river once was. In Canada, as we shall note, they order these things differently.

An act of the New York State legislature, passed in February of 1848, authorized "the promotion of corporations for manufacturing, mining, mechanical, or chemical purposes." It was in the nature of the site that Niagara should sooner or later be recognized as one of the most important sources of energy in North America; it was inevitable that the exploitation of that energy would prove greedy almost beyond credulity. Just how avaricious the process would become, and how rapidly, and what a price the American side of the river above the falls would have to pay, no one in the middle of the last century could have ventured to imagine.

Almost a decade elapsed between the enactment of the law permitting the development and creation of the Niagara Falls Water Power Company, in the spring of 1857. In the intervening years, the descendants of the Porter brothers, who had established a modest gristmill on the Upper Rapids, began to dispose of their substantial riparian holdings to eastern speculators who, in turn, hoped to sell these off in plots to proprietors of industries requiring large quantities of cheap energy.

Out of this initial transfer of land grew the Niagara Falls Canal Company, whose purpose was to construct a conduit that would make use of the drop of three hundred and twenty-five feet that the river's level managed from old Fort Schlosser to the foot of the Lower Rapids to turn industrial wheels that would operate belt-driven machinery. Electricity was not yet in the picture. The purely physical difficulties of building this great tunnel were worsened by labor problems. The firm went bankrupt on the eve of the Civil War. Its successor had the advantage of newly invented dynamite to facilitate the displacement of great quantities of rock. But not before 1877 was the tunnel completed and the first customer, a flour mill, drawing waterpower from the complex system of sluiceways and wheels and belts. But that time, with a total investment of more than $1,500,000, the second company was unable any longer to stand off its creditors. The assets were auctioned that year to a Buffalo industrialist, Joseph Schoellkopf, for little more than $71,000.

It was Schoellkopf and his associates who were to determine the future course of industrial, commercial, political, and social development of the American bank of the Niagara. Five years after he had taken possession of the auctioned properties, Schoellkopf was selling hydraulic energy to seven factories below the falls and, in addition, he had constructed a small electrical generator—the first to make use of the Niagara's enormous potential. But Schoellkopf, a pioneer industrialist whose name would be remembered by a great power plant that was crushed by a Niagara rock slide in 1956, had a major problem. He could generate electrical power—but no one as yet knew quite what to use it for.

In the same year that Schoellkopf had taken over the defunct canal company, Carl Wilhelm Siemens, a German-born English-man who had revolutionized steel production and was an authority on electricity, told members of the Iron and Steel Institute of London:

> The amount of water passing over [Niagara Falls] has been estimated at one hundred millions of tons per hour, and its perpendicular drop may be taken at 150 feet, with-out counting the rapids, making a total of 300 feet between lake and lake. But the force represented by the principal fall alone amounts to 16,800,000 horse-power, an amount which if it had to be produced by steam, would necessitate an expenditure of not less than 266,000,000 tons of coal per annum. . . . In other words, all the coal raised throughout the world would barely suffice to produce the amount of power that continually runs to waste at this one great fall. It would not be difficult, indeed to realize a large proportion of the power so wasted, by means of turbines and water wheel erected on the shore of the deep river below the Falls, supply them from races cut along the edge. But it would be impossible to utilize the power on the spot, the district being devoid of mineral wealth, or other natural induce-ments for the establishment of factories. In order to render available the force of falling water at this and hundreds of other places similarly situated, we must devise a practicable means of transporting the power. . . . Time will probably reveal to us effectual means of carrying power to great dis-tances, but I cannot refrain from alluding to one which is in my opinion, worthy of consideration, namely, the elec-trical conductor. Suppose water power to be employed to give motion to a dynamo electrical machine, a very power-ful electrical current will be the result, which may be carried to a great distance, through a large metallic conductor, and then be made to impart motion to electro-magnetic engines, to ignite the carbon points of electric [arc] lamps, or to effect the separation of metals [particularly the isolation of aluminum from bauxite] from their combinations. A copper rod 3 inches in diameter would be capable of transmitting 1,000 horse-power a distance of say thirty miles, an amount

sufficient to supply one-quarter of a million candle power which would suffice to illuminate a moderately sized town.

Siemens merits citation not only because he was one of the first engineering wizards to recognize the immense industrial potential of the Niagara's fall, but also for his uncanny prophecy of the method by which Niagara-generated power could be transmitted. Another engineer, Benjamin Rhodes, also foresaw in 1877 the economical transmission of electricity to points as remote as one hundred fifty miles from its source. Both prophets, however, failed to resolve the fundamental difficulty: direct current, like great wine, doesn't travel well; it loses a lot in the process of displacement.

In 1877, there was formed a company with a most ominous name: the Niagara Falls Hydraulic Tunnel Power and Sewer Company. It was the first time anyone had linked waterpower and sewage in the same line of type. Two years later, Elias A. Long, who wrote frequently and enthusiastically about the industrial prospects of the Niagara region, gave the apparent lie to Siemens's prediction that industry couldn't flourish on the banks of the river:

> Let but the 1) vastness and 2) cheapness of power, couple with the 3) limitless raw materials of the lakes regions, attainable here at 4) a saving of millions of dollars yearly on freight, and then the 5) cheap distribution [by lake, canal, and rail] to the world's markets be considered, and who can fail to be startled by the aggregate advantages presented by the Niagara.

Plainly, Long wasn't at all startled. He didn't even terminate his rhetorical question with a question mark.

The development of electricity as a cheap source of industrially usable energy still suffered from the inhibition of inefficient means of transmission. The enormous possibilities of Niagara could, therefore, only be exploited at or very near Niagara Falls. Charles Brush, inventor of the carbon arc light, came here around 1880 to make use of Schoellkopf's generator to power his brilliant lamps. But for the time being, it seemed like just another sideshow spectacle—a headline grabber to be classified with Blondin's ropewalking or Anna Taylor's descent of the cascade in a barrel, a stunt that had no practical application beyond a very restricted geographical perimeter. Brush installed sixteen of his arc lights at Niagara, the first of their kind in permanent use anywhere—another Niagara first that seemed to mean not very much.

But the essential problem remained unresolved. Direct current couldn't be economically transmitted even as far as Buffalo, only twenty miles away. Officials of the Niagara Falls Tunnel Power and Sewer Company, despairing of their increasing investment in races and conduits, offered a prize of $100,000 to anyone who offered a practicable solution to the riddle. However, with construction well advanced on what was called the "Evershed Plan"—a year-round, ice-proof tunnel system, two and a half miles in length, that would eventually drive thirty-eight turbines—the original company gave way to a receiver-successor, the Niagara Falls Power Company. Its chief designer and consultant was the brilliant Philadelphia engineer Coleman Sellers. Sellers's major accomplishment here was to produce a generating plant of improbable immensity (in terms of the late nineteenth-century demands for electricity).

While Sellers concentrated on the completion of the power facilities, a commission was formed in London under the auspicious direction of Sir William Thomson (later Lord Kelvin—whose inventions eventually ended visits from the iceman). The commission was to continue the search for an economical means of conveying electrical current over long distances. It was not, however, in Europe that the solution would be found, but in East Orange, New Jersey.

The provider of the vital answer was a European, Nikola Tesla, a Croatian by birth. His experiments with alternating current provided the clue to the resolution of the problem. His transformers and turbine generators were contracted for at the end of 1895. A year later, a transmission line from

Niagara Falls to Buffalo was put formally into operation. Buffalo was the first city in the world to be illuminated by alternating current. The age of hydroelectric power had finally dawned. Not a major mountain river in the world would ever be completely safe again.

Even before the acceptance of the Tesla system by the developers of power on the American side of Niagara, the Canadians (with financial backing from Americans) were moving in a similar direction. But there was, from the very inception, an important difference between the operations of the two generating companies—one that had been dictated by the differing policies of the governments of the respective states.

Shortly after the first of Charles Brush's arc lights was used to illuminate the falls in 1881, the Province of Ontario government, led by Sir Oliver Mowat, sought passage of a piece of legislation called the Rivers and Streams Bill. Its objective was simple enough—not to throw the baby out with the bath water; to allow the use of the Niagara's stupendous force without unduly desecrating the natural beauty of the river's banks. Only after three years of struggle against industrial resistance and public indifference did Mowat finally succeed in securing the bill's approval by the Privy Council at Ottawa. A year after that, in 1885, the Parliament of Ontario uttered the Niagara Falls Park Act, one of the first and surely most important pieces of environmental protection laws enacted in North America during the nineteenth century.

The effects of that legislation are to be found today on the Canadian banks of the Niagara. On the one hand, it was possible for the power company to exploit the river's potentialities; on the other, it was not possible for plunderers to line the stream's shores with factories to spew various forms of waste into the air and water. Save for the already existing towns on the west bank—Fort Erie, Niagara Falls, Queenston, and Niagara-on-the-Lake—the entire Canadian side was incorporated as Queen Victoria Park, a tract that is now under the administration of the Niagara Falls Park Commission.

Park lands, with discreetly deployed housing, adorn the remainder of the shore and immediately adjacent terrain. The only major intrusion on the woods and greenswards is the towering monument to Isaac Brock, hero of the War of 1812, which is believed by some to be decorative and which is certainly more praiseworthy than the clusters of industrial chimneys that mark the upriver portions of the American bank.

The state of New York reacted to the problem of Niagara with the same kind of protective impulse that had motivated Sir Oliver Mowat, and at practically the same time. By an act of 1885, the state acquired ownership of Goat Island and the islets that flanked it, together with the river frontage that lines the Upper Rapids. This was, however, only a start—though a reading of the speeches that commemorated the dedication of the State Reservation would easily give one the impression of a total victory. All that had been protected against industrial and commercial spoliation was but a minor fraction of what merited protection.

Future generations would see a few additions made to the reservation at various points along the New York shore, but these appear negligible when juxtaposed—as they must inevitably be by the most casual visitor today—with the farsighted and comprehensive action taken in 1885 by the Province of Ontario. Add to the initial niggardliness of New York State's original purchase the later solution of the motor traffic problem—the construction of a superhighway following the river's flow from the outskirts of Buffalo all the way to Lewiston—and one immediately perceives that the difference in outlook toward the environment between Canada and the United States was and remains very nearly absolute.

For all that the Canadians were profoundly eager to preserve *their* Niagara's slightly sullied rustic wonder, they didn't neglect the river as a natural and national resource, and their record in its development is not an example of flawless high-mindedness. The first scenic railway, powered by current developed from the Niagara's controlled flow, was a Canadian creation. It ran from Queenston to Chippawa, and only ceased operations permanently in 1932, after protracted and ultimately luckless struggle against its main hazard, rockfalls. In 1905, the Ontario Power Company harnessed the force of the Horseshoe Falls to drive a plant that was far more productive than its counterpart on the New York side.

For a considerable period of time, the Niagara's fall was capable of generating a lot more electricity than there was demand for. The power companies did their enterprising best to close that gap, with such resounding success that by 1950 it was evident that the gradually increased facilities would soon be inadequate for the gigantic postwar augmentation of electrical consumption. Action was taken by Ontario Hydro and the New York State Power Authority—the latter under the chairmanship of Robert Moses. Moses, it should be recalled, had a reputation in New York City as the Parks Commissioner who had made it possible to drive from the suburbs to the center of the city more rapidly and more reliably than one could make the journey by rail; he was the man who, almost single-handedly, had doomed commuter railroads in the United States.

Two enormous generating stations, at Queenston and Lewiston, resulted from this concerted international effort at last to use the descent of the Niagara as efficiently as possible. Together, they comprise the largest water-powered electrical generating facilities in the world. The Lewiston plant, named for Moses, is by way of being what is gleefully described as "an engineering wonder." Its appearance, architecturally, is remarkable for its austerity—representing a commendable attempt to harmonize with the striated walls of the Niagara gorge into which it is built. The two stations supply about twenty-five percent of all the power utilized in Ontario and New York State. This fact, like so many statistics about Niagara, may be staggering—but from ecologists and humbler amateurs of the wilds, it tends to evince a cosmic yawn of boredom.

For what has all this additional power really accomplished?

Ironically, it has almost certainly saved the Horseshoe Falls from catastrophic erosion. The foils described earlier in the account of Roger Woodward's extraordinary escape, that now extend almost two-thirds of the way across the river from the Canadian side, do serve their purpose of diffusing the flow of water over that precipice. Moreover, the power companies' insatiable greed for Niagara water has also slowed the pace of natural erosion to which both the Horseshoe and Rainbow Falls are subject. It is one of the more notable examples of industry coming to the rescue of nature.

The tourist interests and those of the generating plants have achieved what appears to be a more or less satisfactory compromise. At peak visiting seasons, especially in the summer months, approximately half the river's flow is permitted to pass over the falls. The rest of the water is diverted to power production through enormous tunnels passing deep beneath the cities on either side. At night, and in winter, the amount of water going over the falls is reduced to about one-quarter.

For a number of months in 1969, the American Falls were turned off completely, by the erection of an earth-and-rock cofferdam spanning the river between New York and Goat Island, so that Army Engineers might study the river bottom at the edge of the precipice to determine the causes for major rock falls and erosion—doubtless, in this process, finding the narrow cracks into one of which Enrico Farini's stilts had lodged themselves more than a century earlier. Early in 1971, Canadian authorities reluctantly disclosed that despite all their efforts, erosion seriously threatened the Horseshoe Falls as well. In neither instance does there appear an immediate solution to the problem.

On the American side of Niagara, from Niagara Falls to Buffalo, New York, man has failed to be very generous in his dealings with nature. Where hitherto the river was lined with factories that utilized cheap electricity to fabricate such a wide variety of comestibles and industrial products as nutritionless breakfast cereals and abrasive carborundum (giving the re-

Niagara Falls, May 1969

gions, as by-products, a particularly noxious and persistent variety of effluents), there is now the Robert Moses Expressway—four appropriately landscaped lanes of concrete that offer the cautious fifty-mile-per-hour motorist a few fleeting glimpses of the Niagara to the west and, to the east, an uninterrupted impression of industrial horror.

Nor is it merely the land and the air that are being corrupted. One single factory at Niagara was discovered to be contributing twenty-three pounds of mercury per day to the river—this in the autumn of 1970. In fairness, one must concede that though this quantity of poison is great, it is negligible when placed alongside the other lethal compounds that are dumped, every minute around the clock, into the waters of the Upper Lakes.

A study of Lake Erie's bottom in this same season of 1970 disclosed that there is a layer of industrial sludge approximately eighteen inches in average thickness coating the lake's floor, from one end to the other. The lake is believed to have aged fifteen thousand years in the past two decades—in terms of the decrease, to the point of virtual elimination, of its supplies of oxygen. As we observed at the beginning of this volume, Lake Erie is America's Dead Sea. This means, among other things, that all the waters of the Upper Lakes are killed by the time they reached Niagara. It is extremely unlikely that Lake Erie can be resuscitated during the lifetime of anyone born in this century. What is only a little less unlikely is that a conscientious effort will be made to revive it at all.

To stand on the footbridge traversing the river from Niagara Falls, New York, to Goat Island and to peer down at the shallow rapids is to invite tears. The water here is no more than a foot deep in most spots. It is not very watery. That is to say, it is not transparent; it is milky, translucent. Despite the swiftness of the current, algae cling to the many rocks and appear to flourish—a positive sign that the waters of the Great Lakes, all eighty-seven thousand square miles of them, are deleterious to fish . . . and to man.

Yet it would be erroneous to conclude on a note of total depression, to suggest that because so much is wrong at Niagara, everything is wrong. There is much of great interest here. History can be recalled in the fine restorations accomplished at Forts Erie, George, and Niagara—the ancient House of Peace. An elevator ride to the top of one of the four or five exceptionally hideous observation towers on the Ontario side of the falls will afford really breathtaking views, especially at night, when the cascade is illuminated and all else (including the other towers) remains in obscurity. A helicopter ride over the river's more spectacular stretches gives one some faint notion of what it must have been like in its pristine state.

The Niagara Frontier has certainly suffered more than its normal share of every sort of humiliation that ingenious man has known how to bring to it—the industrial and electrical revolutions, war and pillage, land speculation, and nine million

sightseers per annum. But for all that, Niagara has survived.
And there is something rather stupendous in that simple fact.
For all that man—the same white European who has strewn
all the world's lands and waters and air with his refuse and is
now polluting outer space and even the moon with his exotic
garbage—has done to deprave this noble and awesome
stretch of milky water, there it still flows, relentless and won-
derfully proud—like a mortally wounded beast that refuses to
die. Without survival, there is no relevance.

Bibliography
and
Index

Selected Bibliography

In addition to the specific volumes listed below, the reader with a passionate interest in the social, economic, and political history of the Niagara Frontier should betake himself to a library endowed with a full run of the journals of the Buffalo Historical Society—now the Buffalo and Erie County Historical Society. It was from these annals that I extracted the Barton chronicle of the sack of Buffalo in 1813 and the account of Lydia Harper's ministrations to the victims of cholera. There is no run of publications comparable to these for the Canadian side of the river—or the Canadian side of the narrative.

Albright-Knox Art Gallery *Three Centuries of Niagara Falls*, Buffalo, 1964

John B. Brebner *The Explorers of North America*, New York, 1955

Dee Brown *Bury My Heart at Wounded Knee*, New York, 1971

Mrs. Richard Crowley *Echoes from Niagara*, Buffalo, 1890

Charles M. Dow *Anthology and Bibliography of Niagara Falls*, Albany, 1921. With few exceptions, long and short quotations have been extracted from this invaluable work

W. J. Eccles *Canada Under Louis XIV, 1663–1701*, Toronto, 1964

S. Lane Faison, Jr. *Art Tours and Detours in New York State*, New York, 1964

James T. Flexner *Mohawk Baronet: Sir William Johnson of New York*, New York, 1959

G. C. Forrester *The Falls of Niagara*, New York, 1928

A. W. Grabau *Guide to the Geology and Palaeontology of Niagara Falls and Vicinity*, [Bulletin of the New York State Museum, number 45/9] Albany, 1901

Lloyd Graham *Niagara Country*, New York, 1949

Edwin C. Guillet *Early Life in Upper Canada*, Toronto, 1933

Horatio Hale, editor *The Iroquois Book of Rites*, Toronto, 1963

Nathaniel Hawthorne *Passages from the American Notebooks,* Boston, 1862

George W. Holly *The Falls of Niagara,* New York, 1883

William J. Holt, editor *Niagara Falls, Canada,* Niagara Falls, Ontario, 1967

Robert West Howard *Thundergate,* New York, 1968

Diamond Jenness *The Indians of Canada,* Ottawa, 1955

Charles M. Johnston, editor *Valley of the Six Nations,* Toronto, 1964

Agnes Halsey Jones *Hudson River School,* Geneseo, New York, 1968

Edna Kenyon, editor *The Jesuit Relations,* New York, 1954

William Kirby *Annals of Niagara,* Toronto, 1927

James C. Morden *Historic Niagara Falls,* Niagara Falls, Ontario, 1932

John W. Orr *Pictorial Guide to the Falls of Niagara,* Buffalo, 1842

Francis Parkman *Discovery of the Great West,* Boston, 1869
  The Jesuits in North America, Boston, 1885

Horatio A. Parsons *The Book of Niagara Falls,* New York, 1838

William A. Ritchie *The Archaeology of New York State,* New York, 1965

Sigmund Samuel *The Seven Years' War in Canada,* Toronto, 1934

J. W. W. Spencer *The Falls of Niagara,* Ottawa, 1907

Francis St. G. Spendlove *The Face of Early Canada,* Toronto, 1958

Theodora Vinal *Niagara Portage,* Buffalo, 1949

Walt Whitman *Specimen Days and Collects,* New York, 1882

Edmund Wilson *Apologies to the Iroquois,* New York, 1959

Clark Wissler *Indians of the United States,* New York, 1966

Index

279

ACKNOWLEDGMENTS A series as venerable and durable as "The Rivers of America" has so many progenitors that, in a sense, one scarcely knows whom to acknowledge.

Carl Carmer, present editor of the series, is the great literary figure to whom I gratefully bow for his role as guide and counselor. Betty and Carl Carmer received me more than once at Octagon House with cordiality, refreshments, and gentle questions in lieu of harsh instruction.

However, I would never have met Carl had it not been for the intercession of his friends and mine, Agnes and Louis Jones of Cooperstown, New York, to whom this volume is dedicated. Moreover, to the entire staff of the New York State Historical Association, of which Lou Jones is director and in whose precincts I did most of the research, I am also in considerable debt.

To Mr. Constantine and the Department of Iconography of the Buffalo and Erie County Historical Society I am grateful for the illustrations that furnish this book.

To Jean Crawford, associate editor of the series, I am in debt for some sharpish reminders that there has always been more than one gender and for her pertinent queries of fact and emphasis.

Finally, I would not forgive myself for failing to express very important gratitude to Pace Barnes, senior editor of Holt, Rinehart and Winston, who has seen me through this book and seen this book through its various stages of production—and, in the process, become a friend.

D. B.

Redding, Connecticut
October 1971